SWAG

Southern Women Aging Gracefully

by Melinda Rainey Thompson

John F. Blair, Publisher
Winston-Salem, North Carolina

The paper in this book meets the guidelines
for permanence and durability of the Committee on
Production Guidelines for Book Longevity
of the Council on Library Resources.

Cover Art
Springtime by J D Adams, Invogueart

Library of Congress Cataloging-in-Publication Data

Thompson, Melinda Rainey, 1963-
Swag : Southern women aging gracefully / by Melinda Rainey
Thompson.
p.   cm.
Includes bibliographical references.
ISBN-13: 978-0-89587-329-3 (alk. paper)
ISBN-10: 0-89587-329-X
1. Women—Southern States. 2. Middle-aged women—Southern
States. 3. Women—Southern States—Humor. I. Title.
HQ1438.S63T46   2006
305.244′20975—dc22   2006018036

Design by Angela Taylor Harwood

This book is dedicated to all the Southern women who have enriched my life: grandmother, mother, sister, aunts, Vivian, Tricia, Florrye, Laura, and especially Phyllis. And to my favorite future SWAG, Lily.

Contents

Preface   *ix*

Southern Vanity

Aging Gracefully   3
What to Wear   9
How You Know You Have a Best Friend   13
Red Lipstick   14
In Search of the Fountain of Youth   16
Pocketbooks   20
Never a Good Idea   22
The Swimsuit Dilemma   24
My First Gym Experience   29

Outside the Screen Door

Stealing Magnolia   37
Southern Women and Their Trees   39
Summer Whine   43
Some Things I Love About Summer   48
Gardening at Our House   49
Rules Children Garden By   52
Falling Leaves   53
The Hydrangea   55
Spring Planting   58
The Squirrel Wars   62

The Family Gallery

Family Novels 69
The Family Reunion 73
Questions to Avoid Asking at the Family Reunion 77
Hands 78
The Family Gallery 80
SWAG Translations 84
The Porch Swing 85
Within These Walls 88

Southern Women and Southern Men

A Love Story 95
In Love in a Movie 96
Surefire Ways to a SWAG's Heart 102
The One Thing 104
Sleeping With a Snoring Man 106
Things Southern Women Find Suspicious 110
Dr. Stone and Wife 112
Things a Southern Woman Could Live Without 115
Are You a Kappa Kappa Gamma? 116
You Know You're a Bossy Woman If... 118

A Full Nest

Watching Caterpillars 121
Sounds of Children 123
Things Not To Say To a New Mother 127
The Pear Tree 128
Your Mama Was Right When She Said 130
A Point of View 131
Sick Children 133
Reasons Children Wake Their Parents
in the Middle of the Night 138
The Real Value of Money 139
Mama Drivers 141

Letter to My Son's Kindergarten Teacher   144
New Car Woes   146
Something to Tell You   151

The Church Halls

Waiting in the Church Halls   159
Things SWAGs Should Never Wear in Church   163
The Child Behind Me   164
SWAG Rules for Children in Church   167
The Wedding Director   168
Southern Wedding No-Nos   173
Southern Women and Cemeteries   174
Rules for Burying a SWAG   179
Thank-you Notes   180

SWAG Specialties

Gifted Flower Arrangers   187
Women Who Sew and Women Who Do Not   190
Southern Women and Monogramming   194
Things a SWAG Might Monogram   199
Glue-gun Adventures   200
A SWAG's Checklist for Obsessive Behavior   203
The Ultimate Paint Chip   204
A SWAG Business Glossary   208

World of Work

The Big Red Cleaning Machine   211
Ten Good Reasons to Clean House   215
The Coffin   216
Things You Should Never Do
Without Professional Help   221
Computer Trouble   222
Things Not to Say to the Workmen   226
The Workmen are Coming!   227

6:00 PM *Conversation: The Homemaker
and the Husband*   232

Did You Have Enough to Eat?

Did You Have Enough to Eat?   237
For the Love of Tomatoes   239
The Gumbo Mystique   243
Shrimp Po' Boys   245
Ode to Sweet Tea   249
*Things Parents Actually Say to Their Children
in Restaurants*   252

Surviving the Holidays

Crowded Calendars   257
Candy Etiquette   261
The Halloween Costume   265
Thanksgiving Table Tips   268
Holiday Temptations   270
Thanksgiving Vows for Southern Women   273
Christmas Photo Cards   274
What to Get a SWAG for Christmas   280
A Christmas Tree Adventure   281
New Year's Eve   285
A SWAG's New Year's Resolutions   288

Southern Eccentrics and Eccentricities

Southern Eccentrics   293
The Pity-Party Box   295
Southern Women and Theme Parties   298
Party Conversations Unveiled   302
Y'all Come See Us   303
What That SWAG Really Means   305
Out-of-towners   306
Standing in Line at the Piggly Wiggly   308

Author Information   310

Preface

In August of 1999, the first issue of *The SWAG Letter* came off the press. SWAG stands for *Southern Women Aging Gracefully*, and I am a living, breathing example of one. This monthly letter began as a lark, but it soon grew into a small business with thousands of yearly subscribers across the country. In this volume, I have collected the favorite essays of *SWAG* subscribers everywhere and added new, unseen material.

I have found great joy in writing about the everyday aspects of Southern women's lives, and I consider it a privilege to give a new-millennium voice to the everyday experiences that reflect our common heritage. A tradition of good manners, regional eccentricities, and generations of demanding Southern matriarchs make for a rich writing well. I have come to rejoice in our unique brand of humor that is the product of heat, oppression, and sheer perseverance.

This humor is the peculiar product of our culture, geography, and perspective. Fortunately, Southern humor translates well to others living outside the region. I have been surprised to learn how many women—and men—are attracted to, or somehow feel connected to, Southern humor. I am astonished by the laundry basket full of letters from people I have never met who tell me, "I feel like you are writing about my life!"

I find it remarkable how similar women's lives are, especially when the superficial details make us appear so dissimilar to the world. The important things in life, of course, are not of this world, and women feel the same worldwide about the things that really matter. We all care about our families, our friends and neighbors, our countries, and our spirituality. We are friends, mothers, sisters, wives, and daughters. I think about all the women who read these words as if we share a common voice because, in many ways, we do. Although I never cease to be amazed by the depths that we humans can sink to, I am also awed by the heights to which we are equally capable of aspiring. In a time when the burden of being a Southern woman sometimes seems a heavy load, I have found Southern women to be an optimistic group, overall.

The Southern woman's everyday life is often viewed as too mundane to merit attention, but there is no greater adventure than regular life being lived full speed ahead. When I die, if I could pick my own epitaph, it would be that my life was an example of an ordinary life that had been well-lived. As the old saying goes, "This ain't no dress rehearsal, darlin'!" I believe it, and I aim to live and write about it!

I invite you into these pages to squander a little time. It is, after all, the ultimate luxury. Join me in celebrating the humor to be found in all our delightfully ordinary lives full of joy and wonder. I am proud to be a woman of the South, and I am aging as gracefully as I can without any outright sweating.

Aging Gracefully

Before I turned forty, I was much more philosophical when contemplating the negative side effects of aging. In lofty tones, I was quick to point out aging's entirely natural and predictable effects upon the human body, and I laughed condescendingly at women who went to drastic, painful, and often humiliating ends to stave off the inevitable flab, sag, and wrinkles. "How vain! How silly!" I would sniff snootily.

I still believe all that—in theory. The problem is that the theoretical effects of my own physical aging process as viewed by my under-forty brain, sitting squarely on top of thighs still vaguely reminiscent of my girlish figure, were just that—entirely hypothetical. The harsh reality of all those *hypothetical* aging horrors you read about in women's magazines is that they look much, much worse on me than other people.

Occasionally, I discover new evidence of aging that appalls me—age spots that look like a medieval monk's illustration of the plague, for instance. Other aspects of aging are surprisingly painful to experience—joints that creak when I get up from the prayer bench, despite my self-righteous, three-times-a-week workouts. Finally, I have been downright embarrassed by some of my aging body parts—neck wrinkles that get in my way when fastening jewelry, just to give you one horrifying example.

I have determined that aging issues are more vexing than the worst bad-hair day. Sometimes my aging body can actually be nauseating (the discovery of a new fat roll, for example). I have observed that while aging statistics may be accurate in a technical sense, they do not tell the whole story. You need pictures of yourself at twenty-five and forty-five side by side on the refrigerator to tell the whole truth about aging at a glance. I'm here to tell you that the ravages of time are *not* photogenic.

Turning forty was fun: a great party, kind of festive, a milestone, the advent of a decade where I anticipated being completely comfortable in my own skin, self-confident personally and professionally. I felt at peace with the world, ready to do my part to make the world a better place, yet realistic and able to compromise beautifully.

It was about a year after I blew out forty candles on that chocolate layer cake that things really began to fall apart. The aging process no longer seems *quaint* to me. I now believe that only those women viewing aging from a pre-forty decade can continue to see a bed-and-breakfast body written all over a seedy-roadside-motel body that is fast turning into a flophouse.

I am no longer amused by the ever-increasing strands of gray hair, the "yes, ma'am" from the bag boy at the supermarket with whom I could swear I went to high school. I have arrived at a point in my personal aging process where no one will ever again mistake me for a woman under forty—even if I lose twenty pounds, promise a cosmetic surgeon my first grandchild, and only allow public viewing of select parts of my body by candlelight.

I thought I was ready for old age, the accompanying matronly respect, the abandonment of control-top stockings and other uncomfortable clothing items (since nobody would ever be looking at my body again except to examine for hip fractures, etc.), but I was wrong! In the end, when I came face-to-face with my aging body, I discovered a fundamental truth about myself that does not show me in a flattering light—literally or metaphorically. I am sad to report the real truth is that aging really hurts my feelings.

What's worse is that I don't really know what I want to do about it. I'm torn between the philosophy of, on the one hand, accepting, as gracefully as possible, the inevitable slash-and-burn effects of aging on my body, which would require big, swishy skirts, European comfort shoes, and maybe forgoing hair spray and gel so my curly hair would fly in all directions. On the other hand, I could put up a last-ditch, fight-to-the-death battle for every cell, which would be time-consuming, expensive, and might get in the way of a whole lot of other fun things I like to do with my friends.

The question of whether or not to color my hair is a conundrum all by itself. The whole business is pricey, exhausting, and ripe with potential for public humiliation. For the first time in my life, I envy my blonde friends who can get highlights without risking an allover-color disaster like I experienced in my one previous hair-coloring foray. (There's no need to go into that here. It was *bad*. Trust me.)

Personally, I find naturally graying, salt-and-pepper hair attractive, and I love the silver-white gray hair that some women get. Sadly, it took about six seconds for my hairdresser of umpteen years to rain on my silver-white-hair parade; he said only about one percent of women live long enough to enjoy that silver-fox look. Of course, he lies if I ask him to do something to my hair that he's not in the mood to do, so I might have to get a second opinion on that.

If I start coloring my hair, then I'm locked into it like a carnival ride that's too scary to ride and too dangerous to jump off. I just know that hair coloring requires a lot of salon time (I can't stand the salon chitchat or the blaring music for long), sun avoidance (not bloody likely), and maintenance time (did I mention that I have three children?)—all things for which I have never before shown much patience or aptitude. Of course, I could color my own hair at home, but once when I tried to paint my own kitchen, I muffed the job so badly that I had to call in professionals to fix it, and they had trouble finding my crown molding.

If I have my hair colored professionally and then fail to keep regular appointments, I'm afraid I'll look like one of those women in the grocery store who has hair that changes color every few inches—a state of affairs that I find so distracting in conversations that I sometimes lose my train of thought. "Does this woman not know her hair is five different colors?" I wonder. "Does she not care? Did she color it that way on purpose? If so, why? Did someone tell her she looks good like that? Did she actually pay someone to tie-dye her hair?" I find such mysteries distracting. Inevitably, I miss some appropriate responses in our conversation, and even if I manage a few "um-hmns" in our exchange, I fear that my friend may notice that my eyes, independent of my better judgment and good manners, wander freely to view every hair on her head in intimate detail.

(By the way, have you noticed how many Russian women dye their hair that hideous shade of red? I am puzzled by this. Is the old-fashioned henna rinse that Lucille Ball used the only shade available over there or what? These women are beautiful, but their hair color is jarring. Maybe it's some cultural response to aging in their society. If so, then, well, I feel their pain.)

My hair doesn't seem to have aged politely. It isn't just gray; it has white streaks that look like the plastic strips in cheerleader pompoms sprouting out of the crown of my head like cotton tentacles from a dirty mop. I look like someone cracked an "aging" egg on the top of my head and watched it slide down over my ears. The ends of my hair seem not to have grayed so much as to have simply faded to a muddy-brown color you'll never find on a paint chip because no one would ever choose to paint anything that color. The color reminds me of boat bottoms that have been sitting in stagnant water all winter.

It makes me furious to admit that I have spent the better part of a morning writing about hair color. All my life I've prided myself on not being one of those vain women who doesn't realize what is important in life. It was a lot easier to be cavalier about vanity when I was young. Now I've discovered that even if I'm not one extreme or the other—a go with the flow, grow my own vegetables, move to a commune, natural woman, or a woman who runs screaming to the closest plastic surgeon at the appearance of every new wrinkle—I *still* find myself wrestling with some fundamental aging issues, and, honestly, I'm not proud of that fact.

Bottom line: I want to be healthy, exercise, eat well (with the occasional splurge since life without chocolate is not worth living), and while I don't want to show my tummy to anyone without a medical degree ever again, I want to make the most of what's left. For me, this means that I will probably never tuck in another shirt. I'm okay with that. I'm not willing to welcome potential pain or surgical risk for vanity's sake, but I'll try any new topical makeup a snake-oil salesman wants to dream up as long as it's legal and doesn't gross me out too much. (Do you remember sheep's placenta face creams?)

It infuriates me that men rarely face these soul-searching aging questions. Ask any reasonable person in the nearest parking deck (for a scientific sample): Would you rather be a fat woman or a fat man? They'll all agree: Much easier to be a fat man. The same holds true for aging. Men are expected to look old when they *are* old. Women are expected to look young forever. I guess there is some evening out in the end, however, since women tend to outlive those old, ugly men.

The uncertainty of whether to dye one's hair back to its original youthful color, or to a slightly lighter shade (the current trend), or to highlight certain colors (which I'm told by paid professionals are already there in the hair somewhere), or not to dye it at all, is just a bit player on the aging stage. It's the whole process that I find so overwhelming. Is it only Southern women who are reared to think of themselves as somehow eternally youthful in appearance until we finally rebel and turn into formidable grande dames who no longer care what anyone thinks about us—women who scare the bloomers off every young woman in our social circle? Is it, in the end, such a relief to shed any expectation of physical attractiveness that makes our matriarchs such intimidating personages?

If these forceful women have somehow achieved a measure of enviable inner peace about their bodies, faces, and hair colors, then I say more power to them, but I suspect they have unresolved aging issues just like the rest of us. Have you ever gotten in the way of an old Southern woman's standing weekly beauty parlor appointment? They *never* miss their appointments for a weekly wash and helmet-head styling, and interrupting that beauty ritual is more than your life is worth. Better to schedule your wedding date around a standing hair appointment. I know for a fact that some of those women have scheduled open-heart surgery around a weekly wash and set.

Maybe the desire to be youthful and attractive to others is the result of innate genetic programming. Maybe it's all part of the attract-a-mate-and-preserve-the-species animal behavior that we shouldn't fight because it's our biological destiny.

I sure hate to think about the kind of person I'm going to attract in another decade or so. If I live long enough, I'll be bottom fishing at the deep, dark end of the gene pool, and I can't even imagine what kinds of monsters lurk there.

What to Wear

The question, "What shall I wear today?" is no simple query. The infinite variety of ever-changing variables involved in determining what to wear for every social occasion, as well as the run-of-the-mill errand running of life, has reduced otherwise sane, mature women to frantic dives under the bedcovers in order to avoid the what-to-put-on-for-the-day drama.

There is no mathematical formula that allows women to plug in all the "if that, then this" variables of function, comfort, attractiveness, and appropriateness to satisfy the maddening debates between form verses function, beauty versus comfort, attitude versus age, and a hundred other wardrobe options that must be considered before a woman can commit to one outfit for the entire length and breadth of a calendar day.

In addition, once one choice has been made, the consequences of that choice ripple out in all directions and must be fully contemplated from every angle. For example, can you live with the circulation to your lower extremities being cut off if your control-top stockings make you look fifteen pounds lighter? Life's a trade-off. Clothing selections have risks (sometimes of life and limb) and benefits, advantages and disadvantages.

If, for example, you choose to wear your most attractive

evening dress to tonight's party (which you are sorely tempted to do because you are convinced you look stunning in it), then you will not be able to wear it next weekend when you meet your husband's high-school sweetheart because some of the same people may be on the guest list. In addition, while the cocktail dress is perfect for the after-work reception, you fear that you may appear to be propositioning business clients at your 10:00 AM meeting—and the jacket and scarf really aren't going to adequately disguise the cocktail-party nature of the outfit.

Perhaps the biggest problem women face is the age-old clash between comfort and vanity. I am, unabashedly, a comfort advocate, and I'm afraid it shows abysmally. I am of that breed of women who believe we should all be issued overalls at birth. Is there any more comfortable garment on earth? Unfortunately, I can't think of very many activities in which I participate that overalls are an acceptable clothing choice for grownups. I was one of those women who sincerely considered writing every shoemaker on the European continent to thank them for all the trendy, new, European comfort shoes. Hallelujah!

While we are talking about shoes, is there any better example of just how far down the path of destruction a woman's vanity will lead her? Just look at the damage to women's feet that is caused by wearing high heels. I'm telling you that you could film a cautionary documentary showing a typical fifty-something-year-old woman getting a pedicure and scare some teenage girls into wearing sneakers every day for the rest of their lives.

I knew at an early age that stuffing my feet into pointy-toed shoes while teetering around on thin, shaky heels was a ridiculous idea. Besides, I never learned to walk in heels without turning my ankles. I'm amazed that anyone does. The sight of one of those high-heeled women wandering around museum displays deploring the sad plight of Asian women in the days of bound feet seems incredibly ironic to me. I put all that American bunion deformity right up there with African necks elongated by stacks of permanent necklaces and lips stretched out to the size of dinner plates. That degree of vanity is not for me.

Another unpleasant aspect of daily clothing choices is the painful reminder that many of us are no longer living in our salad days. While the halter top with the beaded sunflower might actually be cute on a hundred-pound fourteen-year-old, it would certainly lose some of its allure on a size twelve with sagging ankles and baggy arms. One must observe certain clothing-selection discretion with age. Unfortunately, for many of us, our mental image of ourselves is not always an accurate reflection of the physical reality.

The most common clothing hazard for all women is the occasional failure to observe well-established and clearly delineated clothing categories. For example, you probably have a favorite T-shirt and sweatpants that are too comfortable to throw away. While this outfit might be a perfectly acceptable clothing choice if you are painting your shutters, you shouldn't wear it if you can be seen by cars passing on the street. More importantly, you shouldn't go to the grocery store in this outfit to pick up a gallon of milk even if you tell every person you meet, "I am just a mess, but I'm just going to run into the grocery store for one minute!" We all know the punishment for such behavior. In the grocery store, you will undoubtedly run into your first college beau, whom you haven't seen for thirty years, who will then tell every mutual friend who crosses his path that you have turned into a bag lady.

If men could comprehend all the factors that must be weighed (in more ways than one) in the getting-dressed campaign, I am sure they would be more understanding. Because this process can be lengthy, I keep a supply of chocolate truffles in my closet (in the pockets of my winter coat) for decision-making emergencies.

Like most women, I have at least three sizes of clothing in my closet. In a nutshell, I have: clothes that fit, clothes that are too small, and clothes that are *really* too small. I don't know what the statute of limitations is on blue jeans that I haven't been able to get more than one leg inside in years. The problem is that if I give them away, isn't that just giving in to a closet of fat clothes? Once I surrender to that mind set, won't I then be in danger of buying even bigger fat clothes? You see how treacherous and far-reaching a simple daily clothing choice can be.

I have a selection of clothing that my children refer to as my *Ripley's Believe It or Not* clothes. They flip through my wedding-party outfits and other prehistoric garments, hold them up, and mutter, "Can you believe Mom was ever this size?"

Every woman I know also has a few items in her closet that are fashion disasters. I have more than a few. Last summer, I bought the most beautiful silk sari—really, it's a work of art. However, there just isn't that much call in my social life here in Birmingham, Alabama, for an authentic Indian sari. I look outrageous, slightly culturally insensitive, and silly.

Most of us also have a wish-I-had-the-nerve list. At the very top of my list is a long, black, velvet opera cape. I'd be willing to sit through an entire opera—in German—to get to wear one of those capes. I just know that if I wore that cape, some handsome stranger would feel moved to offer me a red rose and ask me to try on a glass slipper. (Of course, after three children, my foot wouldn't fit into it anymore.) My three-year-old daughter also yearns for a velvet cape and glass slippers. There are just some dreams women never give up.

For Southern women, there are additional closet minefields. Some of us display abnormal attachments to offbeat items. I love my aforementioned overalls and am also irrationally fond of a gardening hat and a fringed shawl. Because we cannot bear to ever part with these favorites, we become the strange little old ladies in short stories who smell as odd as we look, like old moth balls and Evening in Paris perfume all mixed up together. My real fear is that in senility, I may actually appear in public in all three favorites—a sort of greatest-hits parade featuring a Southern woman in overalls, flowered gardening hat, and Italian fringed shawl.

If you are still in possession of all your faculties, and you see me in the front yard in all my finery, please change my clothes before you take me to the loony bin. Also, I have a never-before-worn nightgown in the top drawer of my dresser that I've been saving in case I need to look presentable for visiting day at the asylum.

How You Know You Have a Best Friend

You'd rather have a fight with your
husband than with her.

She is as excited about your new wallpaper as you are.

She picks lint off your clothes like you are
part of a troop of female gibbons.

She will baby-sit your children for you—day or
night—even if they're horrible, and everybody knows it.

She will detest or love your husband with you,
depending on your mood.

She understands that you need to talk through the same
problem ten times before you make a decision.

If you don't talk to her at least once a day,
you feel like you've missed something.

You will go with her to do something or see someone
you hate just because you love her.

You can't imagine life without her—or your mother.

She will bring you chocolate even
when you're on a diet.

She is supportive of you even when she
knows you are wrong.

You can tell what she is thinking by her body language,
even if she is across the room.

You can envision yourself cheerfully slugging her
husband if he cheats on her.

You don't feel you've enjoyed a party completely until you've
dissected it with her over the telephone the next day.

If she ever goes to prison, you'll bring her brownies.

Red Lipstick

I wear red lipstick. All the time. No matter what. I do this on purpose, regardless of fashion. It's a cultural thing and probably not too polite of you to notice or comment upon.

And I'm not alone. Many Southern women wear blood-red lipstick. In general, we also wear too much makeup. There's no doubt about it. We are the only women in the country who can't exercise without "putting our face on."

We don't worry about having on clean underwear in the event of a car accident. Who looks at underwear? But if there is going to be a gut-wrenching picture of us dead on the highway in the newspaper, we'd prefer to be in full makeup.

We are under no illusions that red lipstick is a natural look. This is no misguided attempt to regain our youthful Snow White appeal. We would just prefer not to look like the old crone who gave her the apple.

We can be progressive. We have other shades of lipstick. We've tried the more natural look that the Clinique lady practically vaults over the counter to share with every red-lipsticked, aging Southern belle she spots. I just know we are on some sort of most-wanted beauty makeover list somewhere up North. What I would like to know is what is so hot about the no-makeup babes up North? Besides, I've cut down on the eyeliner, mascara, the colorful eye shadows—all the fun stuff. Nothing in my makeup bag has any more color in it than the gravel in my driveway. The red lipstick is all I have left.

Nothing says summer to me more than a fresh manicure and pedicure in a bright-red shade that perfectly matches my lipstick. There is something deeply satisfying to the Southern woman's soul about anything that matches; don't you think?

I have a friend who has repeatedly warned her girlfriends that we all need to have a small makeup bag handy with specific instructions in the event of our unexpected demise. She will never forget seeing her mother laid out in the funeral home in a lovely, pink suit with pink lipstick to match when her mother never wore anything except the same shade of Estée Lauder red her whole life. I have put this friend in charge of my own personal funereal lipstick arrangements.

My grandmother always wore red lipstick, and when I visited her in the nursing home, one of the things that upset me most was seeing her without lipstick. I always dolled her up before I left.

I have another friend whose mother-in-law says one of the ways you know you are getting senile is when you are missing an article of clothing after you dress for dinner, or you don't know what your hair looks like in the back. I am sure this woman remembers to apply lipstick.

Red lipstick is more than makeup to Southern women. It is more like battle armor. When you get up to face the day, if your makeup is just right, you can face almost anything the Southern men in your life can dish out.

I have to admit that I have been known to cheat a little. My standard beachwear is dark glasses and no makeup except the red lipstick. In a pinch, this will do if you don't have to be admired too close up. This also works well for running carpool.

Finally, I ask you, if I am wrong about this whole makeup thing, then why is Revlon's Cherries in the Snow the best-selling lipstick of all time?

In Search of the Fountain of Youth

In the last few years, I have experienced a gradual and reluctant awakening to the inevitable fact that, alas, I am not quite the svelte, young woman I once was. For a woman who prides herself on her lack of vanity, I am astonishingly upset by this predictable and totally natural progression of events.

During the last few years, I have fallen into the trap many stay-at-home mothers fall victim to and have rather let myself go. I admit it. There just doesn't seem to be much point in worrying about one's manner of dress when the children you spend your day with are only going to spit up, throw up, or worse, on whatever article of clothing happens to be closest to their leaking orifice.

I have found it especially demeaning when one of my children, while being cradled in my arms, reaches down to wipe a runny nose on my shirt as if I am no more than a mere tissue in the Kleenex box of life, or when one of them reaches up to use the hem of my skirt to wipe off a milky mouth or sticky fingers.

For a number of years, my clothing choices were limited to how quickly shirt buttons could be undone to nurse wailing infants. The fashion world really only entered my life as an irritating, relatively minor constraint that I chose to observe only in the most superficial way. As long as I wasn't kneeling at the altar rail in my paint-stained sweatpants, I figured I was doing okay.

Occasionally, however, I was called upon to leave my small island in mommy world, and when I did socialize with a group of savvy, hip, childless adults, I was woefully aware of the inadequacies of my appearance. I am here to tell you that a wraparound denim skirt should never sit next to a Donna Karen original.

Recently, when I asked my mirror who, currently, is the fairest one of all, my mirror answered: "No one in your generation." Not one to give up without at least token resistance, I took a long, hard look in the mirror and was shocked to see my mother's body looking back at me. (Well, the mother I remember while I was growing up, at least. My mother is now a gym groupie with buff arms I can only dream of. I tell you, grandmothers look a lot better these days.) I don't know when it happened. Really. For years, I was one of the cute young things at the mall, and then— about five minutes later—I looked in the mirror and saw a hag straight out of a fairy tale. I had to open up a bottle of wine, call my best friend, and make a plan.

First of all, some hard truths had to be faced. I tend to wear whatever clothing is folded on top of the laundry basket, just because that is what comes to hand when I reach blindly into the closet while reading *The Battle of Little Big Horn* and repairing Cinderella Barbie's crown at the same time. From now on, I am going to take the time to search for cute clothing items I haven't worn for a while, rather than feeling smug simply because I have reached into the depths of a drawer and come up with matching shorts and shirt on the first try.

Secondly, I am going to throw away clothes with stains on them even if they are so comfortable I had planned to be buried in them. I admit that it is shameful that I can trace our last family-vacation itinerary simply by looking at the various colored stains on my summer clothes: purple spots from snow-cone juice, blue cotton candy reminders, and rust-colored blood stains from a small shovel-and-pail dispute on the beach.

Next, I am going to quit blaming the dryer and cheap-clothing labels for all my tight clothes and lose a few pounds. (However, if this involves serious chocolate deprivation, I am simply going to buy bigger clothes and quit pretending that I am ever going to look like I did before carrying nine-pound babies around in my tummy.)

I am going to exercise. Really. Like those women who own sports bras and black exercise pants. I hereby publicly confess that the leisurely stroll I call exercise, which I undertake while walking my children to school and back, doesn't exactly qualify as decathlon training.

Neither I, nor my reflection, could muster up much enthusiasm for the bran muffin–tofu diet or the sweaty, exercise changes in lifestyle. What I was really looking for, I decided, was more of a quick fix, a little pick-me-up. Something more along the lines of a new, life-changing lipstick color, a trendy outfit that makes me look ten pounds lighter, or a feel-better-about-yourself, you're-looking-ten-years-younger, new pair of earrings, rather than a genuine, heartfelt conversion to vegetarianism, crystals, and chanting.

Tragically, like many, many misguided women before me, I decided that what I really needed was to color my hair. I thought it would give me an instantly younger, more attractive edge to my appearance. Since this requires no actual waiting or dieting, and the suffering on my part would be limited to writing a large check, I felt I had found a bandwagon I could jump aboard with both feet.

What I didn't know, of course, is that when I emerged from the beauty salon, I would have hair the color of Morticia's from *The Addams Family*, that my hair would be dyed black to match my favorite pair of pants, and that I would frighten small children on the way home.

For the rest of the week, I avoided mirrors like a Jewish mourner and winced every time I had to go out in public. I think the Lord saw a wonderful opportunity with my little experiment to teach me, yet again, how little our outside appearances matter, but, frankly, I learned that little character lesson in the first five minutes. I sure wish the Lord had allowed me to wear one of those hair shirts instead. Never again will I boast about how little I care about my personal appearance. Apparently, I care much more than I knew.

I am not exaggerating about the humbling side effects of a bad hair-color job. My husband told me to find anyone, anywhere, and pay anything to get my hair back. One of my friend's husbands got on an extension while I was talking to his wife on the telephone and sang me a few bars of the "Elvira" song. He sure is lucky I have such a well-developed sense of humor.

As God is my witness, when I finally did wash all the shoe polish out, I vowed never to color my hair again. I did not give up on the quick fix—maybe a new shade of eye shadow or some of that glittery fingernail polish—and I decided to start using candles instead of harsh overhead lighting for my dinner parties. Tell the truth. Have you ever seen anyone who looks bad in candlelight?

I have too much respect for pain to ever consider plastic surgery, so I'm going to need a little beautification more along the lines of a fairy godmother. The real truth is that I wasn't looking for a talented hairdresser when I dyed my hair; I was looking for someone who was good with a wand.

After living with the humiliating results of my first foray into the expensive, ultimately futile, and rather exhausting search for the fountain of youth (where is Ponce de León now?), I have determined that my graying hair, spreading waist, and drying skin really aren't that big of a deal. I certainly never intend to spend another week of my life preoccupied with anything as fundamentally boring as the hair on my head.

I've decided to go for broke in the opposite direction. I am going gray. After all, I earned every one of these gray hairs. In addition, I am not ever going to wear tummy-control stockings again. I am going to let it all hang out—over well-pedicured toes, of course. I am going to enjoy this decade of aging. In fact, I'd like to point out that it beats the pants off the alternative.

Pocketbooks

Southern women don't carry purses. They use pocketbooks. This is not merely a semantic distinction. A pocketbook is more than a useful accessory; it is part of a Southern lady's persona. In other words, Southern women and their pocketbooks are not to be trifled with. They have some heft to them—in more ways than one.

To evoke the proper mental image, I want you to close your eyes and conjure up a picture of Her Royal Highness, Queen Elizabeth II. You can't picture her without her pocketbook, can you? You know the kind I mean—it has two straps, and she carries it on her arm, right at her bent elbow, in whatever color matches her shoes. Surely the richest woman in the world doesn't have to go around showing two forms of identification every time she whizzes in and out of Buckingham Palace. I certainly hope not. I'm willing to bet that Liz's pocketbook has the same things in it that any Southern woman of her generation carries.

First of all, there is a compact of pressed powder and a tube of red lipstick. If one doesn't feel like smiling, the theory here is that one can always paint on whatever look is appropriate—and, of course, *ladies* do not have shiny noses. Next is the inevitable hanky, fine linen or a used paper tissue—doesn't matter. There is also a comb that would never actually slide through hair that has been fixed with enough hair spray to withstand gale-force winds. In addition, you'll find two quarters to call for a taxi, or in the queen's case, a royal brigade armed with machine guns. Additional items are just puffery—maybe a few old breath mints or half a stick of gum for authenticity, but that's it.

So why does the queen schlep her pocketbook everywhere she goes like there isn't a legion of courtiers following in her wake with everything she could possibly need? For the same reason Southern women need their pocketbooks with the tissue, breath mints, compact, and two quarters bad enough to refuse being loaded into an ambulance without it.

No good reason.

Southern women in the over-sixty-five crowd need their pocketbooks just like the queen of England needs hers. In a way that baffles but intrigues me, our matriarchs' pocketbooks are somehow tied up with being well-dressed, properly turned-out ladies. Anyway, I can't see the queen or a Southern grandmother wearing a fanny pack, and I have to say, I think that's a good thing.

Never a Good Idea

There are some clothing selections that SWAGs should never make because they're just not a good idea. We've all been tempted by an outfit that isn't really appropriate for us, but, occasionally, surging hormones, or the lack of them, can lead us into dangerous fashion purchases which have expensive and embarrassing consequences. If you feel one of these inappropriate-clothing-purchase fits coming on, I urge you to consult the list below before handing over your credit card. Consider yourself forewarned.

If there are laces, ties, and leather involved, you'd better be rigging the mainsail for a boat because, at our age, a camisole with ties is just too complicated. Just think how unromantic it would be for your husband to put a loving moment on hold while he fetches his reading glasses.

Forget the stiletto heels. You are not a Bond girl, and you are never going to *be* a Bond girl. Accept it.

If you think the outfit you are trying on is too small, IT IS. No woman in the history of the world has ever *mistakenly* thought something was too small. If it doesn't fit, get the bigger size or move on. Weeping over your used-to-be size is a sign of weakness.

If the outfit wouldn't look so attractive to you if it weren't on sale, then it isn't so attractive. Mark my words: You're going to regret this purchase later. That outfit is just a future thrift-store donation with price tags still dangling from it.

If the outfit is something your teenage daughter would happily wear in public, then you have absolutely no business wearing it anywhere yourself. It is irrelevant how young you feel inside.

Don't buy toe rings, ankle bracelets, nose, eyebrow, or belly-button jewelry if you want to be taken seriously as an adult. If you are a SWAG, then you know better. If you are not, then thank God you had sense enough to buy this book and read this rule. I'm getting worried just sitting here thinking about all the things you might not know. I hope I remember to tell you everything.

If you are worried in the least little bit that too much of you may be unexpectedly revealed by your new outfit, then you will not have one bit of fun wearing it. You will be forever grabbing the front of your dress and hauling it up over your bosoms, so spare the rest of us that vision, and wear something you are sure will contain every inch of you securely.

If you say you "forgot" to wear panties with your new purchase, then you better be able to prove that you have Alzheimer's disease because that is the only acceptable excuse for that kind of behavior.

Unless you are genuinely beautiful in the league of Princess Diana or Grace Kelly (or any young beauty who is actually alive but doesn't pop immediately into my mind), if an entire room falls silent when you make an entrance in your new cocktail dress, then you need to rethink the entire ensemble. Something is definitely not right. First check the dress, then the makeup, then the hair. If you can't spot the problem, get someone you trust to check you from the back. If you still can't identify the faux pas, you might have to examine your recent behavior for any unbecoming slips of the tongue.

Finally, shop appropriately for the occasion. There's just nothing more off-putting than a woman who invites you over for a backyard barbeque and answers the door wearing a long dress and pearls. If you don't know what's appropriate, by all means ask. I promise you that there are at least ten women within spitting distance who are dying to give you their opinion on what you should wear to any occasion—from a missionary fund-raiser to a Mardi Gras ball.

The Swimsuit Dilemma

There is perhaps no other shopping experience as potentially wounding to the female psyche as the seasonal search for a flattering and stylish new swimsuit.

I have been known to wear bathing suits so out of date that they have come back around to being in style to avoid the crushed ego that is the almost inevitable result of an afternoon spent wiggling my way through a pile of new swimsuits.

In fact, I have worn swimsuits with bottoms so worn and picked from resting my fanny on the sides of pools that instead of nice, smooth, Lycra material, you would have sworn my backside was sheathed in shag carpet.

I have worn an old swimsuit with a top so stretched out from the tugging hands of small children that I had to hold it together with one hand when going underwater to avoid an indecent-exposure incident.

I have become an expert at pinning, repairing, hand-washing, and cosseting old swimsuits to avoid a fate worse than death—the search for a replacement.

I feel sure that I have worked off a few years in purgatory in the miserable penance I have served while trying on swimsuits. I must have been an ax murderer in my past life to have to pay for my sins in a hot, cramped, ladies' dressing room with an ever-increasing stack of swimsuit rejects.

First of all, no woman's body is at its best at the beginning of swimsuit season, and mine is certainly no exception. A season of Christmas goodies followed by Valentine's Day candy and Mother's Day treats does not make for pretty thighs. The inevitable creep of a few extra pounds of winter weight (indeed, I look like I've been storing insulation for the winter) does not give one an additional layer of self-confidence.

In addition, although I am intellectually aware of the health benefits of untanned skin, I am socially conditioned to believe in the innate truism that "tanned fat looks better than white fat." This is almost a sorority rite of passage. Unfortunately, I am a woman who tans while wearing the 45 sunblock for babies. Yes, indeed. I am so pale that I actually reflect light.

I hope you're getting the full mental picture here. Dry, pale skin that has been skillfully hidden under long sleeves for months of winter is now making an appearance, and it's looking like an all-day-at-the-beauty-spa emergency.

I know women who need prescription medication to go swimsuit shopping. Not me. I'm made of sterner stuff than that. I look at swimsuit shopping the same way I view the yearly gynecology visit—just one of those trials a woman must endure.

On the last possible shopping day before my children are dismissed from school for the summer, I screw up my courage, have a glass of wine with lunch and a commiserating telephone conversation with a good friend, and then it's off to the swimsuit crusades.

In the first wave of swimsuit shopping, I flip through racks of minuscule pieces of fabric with prices that seem to increase based upon how much fabric is being left off. I am amazed every year that people actually pay money to appear in public in such revealing attire. Most of the swimsuits for sale are more revealing than any lingerie I have ever owned. The way I figure it, the women wearing skimpy bikinis don't go home and put on their cotton underwear from Target. Their panties come from Victoria's

Secret or somewhere else that doesn't have red plastic shopping carts and doesn't sell car parts and bug spray two aisles over.

I usually discourage perky, young sales help. They can't sympathize appropriately when I whine, and their biggest swimsuit-trying-on worry is whether or not their fresh manicures will get smudged when they pull those wispy bikini bottoms up over their pencil-thin thighs. For me, trying on swimsuits is a solitary experience fraught with moments of deep remorse (remembered bags of chocolate bars) and personal frustration (surely one of these suits will come down to my knees).

Most of my conversations with young sales clerks begin with: "I haven't worn a two-piece swimsuit in my life, and somehow, after the births of three children, I don't really think this is the time to start—for me or any innocent members of the viewing public who might have to see this much of me on display." It has been my experience that most clerks in the under-thirty crowd will melt away at this point.

On the other hand, if I have a gum-popping woman over forty pulling swimsuits off the racks for me to try on, who doesn't bat an eyelash at my opening salvo, I know I've found someone who can go the distance—a sales woman I can work with, a woman who won't cringe at the sight of my spider-vein collection.

Next, it is time for "The Show." Once you are assigned a fitting-room cubicle, of course, you're committed. That moment is the official beginning of swimsuit season. There is no more time to diet and lose the last few pounds. There are no additional minutes to firm and tone before warm weather hits. The hour of truth is at hand.

After stripping down to my undies, the first harsh reality dawns on me. After months of not even glancing at myself in the mirror except to wipe off the accumulation of ballpark grime, cupcake splatter, and kiddie paint, this is the time I have to take a good, long look at myself in the mirror. Unfortunately for me, it's not a small, rose-colored mirror hanging above the sink in one of my bathrooms, which reflects my body in soft, flattering light. Oh, no. This mirror is full-length, with a 180-degree, three-way view, so that even when I look straight ahead, I can see every inch of my sagging behind.

Although it seems impossible that the woman in the mirror could be me, I'm afraid that department-store mirrors do not lie. It is at this precise moment every year that I decide to throw the swimsuit budget out the window. Standing there in my underwear looking at the full, IMAX view of myself makes any amount of money spent on a flattering swimsuit seem justified and, indeed, reasonable.

The next painful epiphany occurs when it becomes obvious that the stack of swimsuits in the same size I bought last year will no longer meet this year's needs. This necessitates a return to the racks for bigger clothes, which is in itself an inauspicious beginning.

It is about this time when the perky sales help (always a twenty-one-year-old, gorgeous girl with a pre-baby tummy, long skinny legs, and a face that is attractive without makeup) asks, "How's it going in there? Need anything?"

Inside, I'm thinking, "I need a new body. Or just my old body back again. Or your body. You'd probably look great in this suit. I have dinner napkins with more material than this suit."

Aloud, I say, "Everything's fine! Could you, perhaps, go to the linens department for me and get a tablecloth? Then we can cut a hole in the top, and I could wear it like a poncho on top of one of these swimsuits. Because that is the only way I'm going out in public in one of these!"

"It can't be that bad," says perky, never-been-pregnant-tummy girl.

"Wanna bet?" I mutter under my breath.

Another thing I wonder: Why the fluorescent lighting? Has anyone you have ever known looked good in fluorescent lighting? I look like I'm just recovering from malaria after a month working as a missionary in the Congo. Every wrinkle, line, and scar stands out in harsh relief under lighting that doctors use to remove suspicious moles. Does anyone ever say to the sales clerk,

"You know, I think I look radiant in this light"? I think not. I resemble a face under a sheet in the morgue. And no matter how cute a swimsuit is, trying it on over granny panties is a real turnoff.

Surely, there is a better way to buy a swimsuit. Maybe I could get away without buying a new swimsuit this year. The old ones really aren't in such bad shape. After all, who has to know that the orange suit actually started out its life in hibiscus red?

My First Gym Experience

Like thousands of others, I found myself at the gym in January trying to live up to the New Year's resolutions I hastily made at midnight amid confetti, champagne, and nostalgic melodies. Like many of you, I found the daylight examination of my new get-in-shape resolutions extremely harsh, overwhelmingly specific, and slightly nauseating.

As I stood outside my newly selected gym site in the wee hours of dawn without a smidgeon of makeup to hide my sleepless night and my eyes obscured by thick glasses rather than my usual contact lenses, I decided, with a shred of optimism, that the whole gym experience couldn't be *that* bad. After all, just about everyone I know works out in a gym. Probably, I thought, it would turn out to be fun.

Was I, perhaps, delusional? Clearly, I was a complete innocent to the world of gym groupies and entirely naïve to the fiercely competitive underworld of firm fannies and well-sculpted torsos. In fact, for my entire life, I have always held firm to the belief that exercise should be merely a part of recreation, a social activity, something that, even for adults, should be enjoyable.

My ideal workout is a long walk in the country. Picture the sun shining, wildflowers blooming, and birds twittering. On these excursions (think European walkabout here), I take time to examine interesting flora and fauna along the way, as well as the new curtains in the house down the street.

I've never enrolled in an exercise class. I have lived my entire life happily oblivious to aerobics, step classes, and all the other exercise crazes, and I haven't felt like I missed out on anything either. While I have always wanted to engage in enough physical activity to ward off a heart attack, I am more attracted to solitary exercise with the additional fringe benefit of time for thinking and reflecting. I have passed by rooms of sweaty women exercising wildly to loud music with a deafening beat playing on a lousy sound system and shuddered openly, wondering why anyone would voluntarily choose such an activity.

The closest I ever came to joining an exercise class was taking a yoga class in college, which was taught by an aging hippie who urged us to meditate while listening to ocean surf. I think most of my classmates napped through her class. I used that time to pray for everyone and everything. No kidding. It was very peaceful. Plus, the yoga class counted as a PE course, which was required for graduation, and we didn't have to change clothes or take a shower. Perfect.

Then, I got older and fatter. Although this was a natural progression of events I'd observed in others, I assure you that it looked much worse on me. So, I finally found myself approaching an institutionalized setting for exercise, a suburban cliché I had felt personally superior to all these years: membership in the neighborhood gymnasium.

It was worse than I imagined. On the first day, as I crossed the street to the entrance of the gym, I watched my fellow exercisers' cars squealing into the parking lot trying to outmaneuver each other for the closest parking spot. This observation stopped me dead in my tracks. Did no one else see the irony? I hung back a bit to let those black-legging-clad women with their own workout gloves and bottles of imported water get into the building first. They had a mean look on their faces that said, "I've gained five pounds over the holidays, and I've got to get in there and work it off right now!" They reminded me of women shopping the after-Christmas sales—a time I wouldn't be caught dead near a mall. (Well, okay, my vision of hell is mall shopping in general—I admit it.) Those women meant business. They were circling the door waiting for the gym to open like sharks headed into the shallows. I followed them meekly inside and signed up.

When I was growing up, ladies simply did not work out in gyms. I remember in the 80s when Chris Evert began weight training in order to compete with Martina Navratilova in their epic tennis battles. Not only was such training considered unfeminine, all the sophisticated equipment of today simply didn't exist. Athletes I knew growing up worked out more like Rocky in the first movie—you know, tin cans for weights and a lot of swimming and running.

I understand that those tried-and-true plans still work. In fact, it's kind of hip now to use a couple cans of creamed corn for weights when working out to a DVD.

I tell you this only to help you see, from my perspective, the sight that met my eyes when I went into the gymnasium for the first time. My first impression was that I was seeing the perfect marriage between the medieval torture devices you see in museums and the high-tech, stainless steel, white medical equipment I've seen way too much of in my OBGYN's office. First of all, there were bodies stretched out in every unladylike position imaginable—just like in my doctor's office. In addition, judging from the sweating bodies, grimacing faces, and all the huffing, puffing, and groaning, the similarities between the weightroom and the labor and delivery floor of the hospital were uncanny.

In another strange twist, I had chosen to join a gym in my neighborhood, which is housed under the auspices of a church, and some well-meaning soul had attached Bible verses to each piece of equipment. So there was a bit of an Inquisition motif to the workout. Unhappily for me, my eyes are so attuned to the written word that I couldn't seem to help myself. I continued to read those strategically placed Bible verses and to puzzle over their meaning. Was there a message there for me in particular? Was there supposed to be some connection between the Bible verse and the piece of equipment to which it was taped? If that was the intention, I don't think they matched up the Bible verses thematically well with the equipment. For example, if you're hanging from a chin-up bar, wouldn't you expect the Bible verse to be something uplifting? Those scripture selections definitely had an Old Testament ring to them.

I haven't even told you the worst thing of all. You will never guess in your wildest dreams who introduced me to the world of weights and treadmills. Nope. Not some handsome coed with hard-muscled arms and compassion for forty-year-old women. Not even my sister who is a veteran of every diet and exercise plan that has come on the market in the last twenty years. I hope you're ready for this. My *mother* taught me how to use the gym equipment.

Now before you fall out of your chair laughing, I want to tell you that my mother was only twenty-one when I was born. Still, I hope you fully appreciate how desperately out of shape I must be to go to the gym with my mother, for heaven's sake. As we walked around the track, I asked her to visualize herself in her forties being introduced to the gym workout by her mother. That mental image got her attention. She laughed so hard I thought she was going to throw up on her high-tech workout shoes.

I guess my gym experience was just another "never say never" lesson. I certainly never imagined a scenario that would place me side by side with a bunch of strangers riding bicycles inside (how silly is that?) and walking around in circles rather than through the natural world where I can explore what's around the next stand of trees, feel the breeze on my face and the wind in my hair.

You know what the bottom line is? A gym workout is just so unromantic. Not exactly a walk on the moor with Heathcliff, is it? You can't watch the sunrise or see it set over the water. Where's the joy in sweating in a room full of strangers you rarely even speak to? I can be gregarious, but I don't want to talk to anyone I didn't give birth to until I've put on my lipstick. Thankfully, I doubt any of the others in the gym would recognize me out in the real world with lipstick applied, normal hair, and that extra ten pounds safely hidden under a dress where it belongs. That's a good thing. I'd especially hate to run into that man who had to explain about the levers you use to change the position of the weights. I figured that was just a good place to put my water bottle.

Outside the Screen Door

Stealing Magnolia

Admit it. You have stolen magnolia leaves, or you know someone who has. I know. I know. It was necessary. Vital. Advent decorations were on the line. There were nude mantels with Christmas approaching. Whatever the reason, most Southern women feel that they have a God-given, constitutionally protected right to steal magnolia leaves from wherever they might find them growing—for whatever exalted purposes they might need those waxy green leaves.

My mother is one of the biggest thieves I know. She, like thousands of other well-bred Southern women, wouldn't steal a Sweet 'n Low packet from a fast-food restaurant. But she would not hesitate for one second to put on her gardening gloves, pick up her pruning shears, and head over to a neighbor's house in the dead of night to harvest a few magnolia blossoms.

I know. I have driven the getaway car when she has headed to a local residence that has some "magnificent" magnolias, which she has decided are "just going to waste." I have plotted all sorts of dire consequences for her when she finally has to go to a nursing home where, surely, she will not be mobile enough to steal magnolia blossoms anymore. I have pointed out the irony of stealing magnolia leaves from the church memorial garden only to be rebuffed with remarks like, "God made these gorgeous trees for everyone to enjoy. Besides, this arrangement is going on the altar!"

As for those women who have a supply of fully grown magnolia leaves just weighing down their yards, well, you will never, ever, hear one of them volunteer to share. She might want to. If someone ever comes right out and asks to cut some, she might even say, "Of course, honey. You come anytime."

What she won't say, of course, is that if you do come, she'll be waiting for you in the top branches with a shotgun. Ask for her pound cake recipe. Ask to borrow her husband for the weekend. Don't ask for her magnolia leaves.

Southern Women and Their Trees

Southern women love trees. In the South, it is not uncommon for architects to receive requests to carefully design house plans around choice trees and to strategically place windows to frame the most delectable views of landscapes. As you walk from room to room looking out the windows of our homes, you can view a kaleidoscope of changing seasons.

Because of relatively mild weather year-round, most Southern women view their yards as mere extensions of their homes, which means that yard maintenance is a hefty item entry in the family budget. I'd go so far as to say that while most of my friends have a deep and abiding fondness for their silver patterns, this affection does not approach the passionate attachments Southern women form with their tallest foliage.

Trees embody every characteristic Southern women admire. Small shrubs and flowers come and go, but trees endure for generations. Trees have inner strength; they're built to withstand storms and the light, trendy winds of lesser change. Our oaks, elms, dogwoods, sweet gums, hickories, poplars, pines, and magnolias are able to rise above all the choking kudzu, which attacks their trunks, branches, and roots like packs of hyenas after one magnificent lion.

Most importantly, to the outside world, our indigenous trees are identified with the South and our hot, humid, eccentric, maddening, and yet somehow endearing culture.

The most revered Southern tree is obvious: it's the magnolia, of course. I'll be the first to admit that no tree cliché is more impressive than the magnolia. The giant blooms are bigger than life, yet deceptively fragile. Like gardenias, magnolia blooms bruise easily and are hard to arrange.

Southern women are taught from an early age to use every part of the magnolia tree just like Native American women long ago used every part of the buffalo. I wouldn't be a bit surprised if some Creek woman on the banks of the Alabama River used a few magnolia-leaf arrangements to spruce up the village.

When I was a child there always seemed to be a magnolia tree in someone's yard that had boughs perfectly shaped for climbing in my bare feet. As an adolescent, I could usually find a sheltered spot under a magnolia to share some best-friend confidences, and by the time I'd been married a few years, like most Southern women I know, I could shape those waxy green leaves into a wreath, swag, or greenery arrangement to suit any social occasion. Without a doubt, the magnolia is the solid staple of any Southern woman's tree portfolio.

House sales have been won and lost based on the quality of the magnolia trees on the property. I've driven past many properties for sale way out of my price range, only to think to myself, "Well, I wouldn't give you two cents for that million-dollar house. There's not a magnolia in sight!"

When my father-in-law cut down a magnolia tree in his backyard because the leaves made such a mess, I thought I was going to have a heart attack on the spot. It's a good thing I already loved him because cutting down a magnolia tree is a pretty hard thing to forgive. And I hate to have to tell you this, but this is the same man who later pulled up some perfectly healthy wisteria from his yard. Imagine! That was about ten years ago, I think, and I'm not over it yet.

Probably the second most recognized Southern-atmosphere-associated trees are the moss-laden water oaks, live oaks, and cedar trees of Mobile, New Orleans, Natchez, and anywhere else along the gulf coast or mighty Mississippi where mosquitoes, alligators, and good fishing mingle. It's hard to find a postcard from the Deep South that doesn't feature moss-covered branches.

There's just something about Spanish moss that reeks of atmosphere. The briefest glimpse of those trees makes me want to sip on a Bloody Mary and walk through a cemetery gossiping about dead relatives and potential voodoo queens. When I attended a street party on an old block in Mobile, Alabama, I could barely remember my manners and concentrate on the throngs of guests babbling on about current events. All I really wanted to do was settle under one of those old oak trees and let all that ambiance seep into my pores.

You don't see Spanish moss hanging from trees as far north as Birmingham, where I live. I've always been told that it won't grow north of Montgomery. But if you live south of there, you can spread moss around merely by tossing up a few bunches in your trees. I've never actually tried that because I was born in the South, and I know how many chiggers per square inch call that moss home.

Somehow oak trees, cypress trees, and the peculiar, smoky smell of cedar trees reenergize me from somewhere deep inside. Southern trees provide the picturesque background for generations of feuds and fights, reunions and weddings, funerals and receptions—a living backdrop with roots that run deep under all of us and spread out in every direction.

I ask you: Who loves roots more than Southern women? The trees that dot our landscape tend to be grand in scale—like the live oak that serves as the hallmark of the Grand Hotel in Point Clear, Alabama, and the oak tree that symbolizes Sophie Newcomb College in New Orleans, two of my favorite places.

The Southern woman's love of trees may be a bit narcissistic since Southern trees and Southern women share so many characteristics. Our roots spread far and wide, sometimes breaking up driveways, upending sidewalks, and choking a few innocents standing in the way. Often, Southern matriarchs live to ripe old ages (or maybe it just seems longer than the average life span because they are such forces to be reckoned with) just like the hundred-year-old oak trees that line our front walks. Both the trees and the matriarchs look a little worse for wear over the years, but the lines on both seem, to me, to most often reflect wisdom, character, and humor. Southern women are enduring creatures like our trees, too—like Faulkner's well-loved Dilsey in *The Sound and the Fury*. Both our trees and our women bend with the breezes that come and go; blossom in the hot, sultry climate; provide shade and protection for others struggling to bloom underneath; and tend to serve as quiet, background beauty.

Of course, every once in a while, one of our grand beauties topples over in a hurricane and crunches everything in its path. And we can all name at least one Southern grande dame who has stirred up a hurricane or two.

Personally, I'm a bit partial toward the Southern pine in all its variation of species. Although I don't think pine trees are all that attractive as individuals, the smell of pine resin from freshly cut timber or pine chips is an aroma I associate with life in the South.

I think it is only fair to point out that it isn't only Southern women who have a deep fondness for local growing trees. My favorite priest actually named some of the trees he can see from the deck of his home. Knowing him, I'm sure he talks to those trees, too, and it wouldn't surprise me at all if they answered him right back. The man is a poet, so what can you expect? If he told me what those trees were saying as they swayed back and forth in the wind, I'm telling you, I'd be the first to believe him. First of all, he's a really good priest, so I wouldn't be surprised if God sent down a few messages through some conveniently placed pine trees. And, second, he's an especially fine poet, and, well, they're just different from the rest of us regular folk.

Anyway, I'm almost sure I can remember lying on my back in the grass as a child and looking up at the top branches of trees, watching them move back and forth in the hot summer breezes, feeling like they were singing me some sweet Southern song I knew by heart but just couldn't remember the exact words to.

Summer Whine

I'm sure you've heard the old saying, "Everybody complains about the weather, but nobody ever does anything about it." I hate to admit that I'm one of those weather complainers. Especially since one of my pet peeves involves individuals who have a propensity to wallow in negativity—the glass-is-half-empty crowd, those chronic naysayers who will probably lodge a dozen complaints about heaven with Saint Peter before he opens the pearly gates for them.

As usual, just when I was feeling a little too proud of my positive-attitude self, I was reminded of one of my failings. I am, I most shamefully admit, a hot-weather complainer.

I dread summer weather. I'd rather baby-sit sextuplets than sweat through Alabama's sweltering Septembers. I have no excuses to offer. I am a born-and-bred Southern gal and a native-grown wimp in my heart of Dixie. Even as a child, I can remember hating the feeling of a hot, sweaty face and hair stuck to the back of my neck. When the long days of summer settle in, I feel like going into hibernation. Before I had adult responsibilities, I could be found cooling my heels in the shade.

As I've grown older, I'm sorry to say that my tolerance for hot weather hasn't improved. In fact, now I have to endure the sight of my baggy arms in sleeveless, linen tops while my fortyish body cries out for long sleeves, a jacket, some kind of coverup.

I'm telling you, there's just no hiding a few extra pounds in summer clothes. In my winter clothing of many layers and lengths, I'm convinced I could smuggle a baby across the Mexican-American border if I put my mind to it. But in the summer, you can look at my thin cotton dresses and tell whether I had the no-fat dressing on my salad at lunch or the full-calorie bleu cheese.

Summer is just too much for me in every way: too much heat; too much direct, brazen, unremitting sunlight; too much unstructured time; too much togetherness with all the neighborhood children. Overwhelming!

In order to blossom, I need a season with a little more unpredictability. I crave variety. Give me a spring or fall with a bit of capriciousness. I'm not saying I look forward to hurricanes or tornadoes or anything dangerous, but I like a good thunderstorm to shake up the status quo. Nothing else quite clears the air like a few days of temperamental weather. I particularly delight in unexpected weather patterns—hail in the middle of summer or snow in March. I don't like for the meteorologists to be right all the time. I think it's good to confound them every once in a while and remind them of who's really in charge of the weather.

My favorite weather forecast calls for cold, windy days. Anything seems possible to me on those days. I'm tempted to check to see if the wind's in the east. Part of me believes Mary Poppins might just float by hanging on to the end of her umbrella.

I am astounded at how much time local-television news crews devote to the weather. They must have the most well-thumbed thesauruses in America because they can come up with innumerable ways to spin "hot, sunny days" and drag out completely uncomplicated prognostications. Once you've heard the forecast and cast your bets on percentages and aching joints, what more is there to say? I swear they spend as much time on the weather as they do on economic issues, politics, wars, and crimes all put together.

Obviously, I don't fully appreciate how important the weather forecast really is to some people. I agree that it's nice to know whether to plan a picnic, take an umbrella, or start boarding up for a hurricane, but otherwise, what difference does it make?

I am particularly dumbfounded by the fact that local-weather forecasts contain so much weather information about cities far away. Are there really that many people in Birmingham, Alabama, packing for a trip to Portland every morning? Why should we receive a daily taunting of "seventy-five degrees and balmy in North Carolina" when we're well over ninety degrees before our 8:00 AM coffee? I notice that it is usually California with some kind of "ha, ha it's great weather out here" forecast on days when my kids can't walk to the mailbox without sunscreen. Meteorologists have a mean streak, I think.

Have you ever noticed that old people, in particular, seem weather-obsessed? Maybe this is the reason the local-weather forecast takes up the first fifteen minutes of the news hour. All the blue-hairs out there call up their local-television stations and demand a city-by-city account of temperature differentials. On a more charitable note, maybe the weather forecast just gives our senior citizens something to talk about. Nothing is more socially acceptable than complaining about the weather. It's expected in our culture, a standardized form of neutral banter.

I, however, am not indulging in any sort of banter in my summertime moaning and groaning about how hot I am. I'm serious about my anti-heat bias. Hot weather is enervating. I can barely summon up enough energy to swat at mosquitoes—which I'm certain are trying to infect me with the West Nile virus (as if there isn't enough to despise about summer and mosquitoes already).

But in the winter, I want to put on a sweatshirt, climb on a ladder, and paint something; or gather wood and build a fire. I can be a productive citizen in winter. I'm enthusiastic—cheerful, even. I have tons of energy in cold weather, mental as well as physical, as if all my personal energy reserves have been stored up like whale blubber, just waiting to be called into action. Cold weather makes me want to drink hot chocolate and wade my way through *War and Peace* again.

Each fall, I gaze longingly at my calendar looking forward to the end of October when relief usually comes to us down South. Every time I open my closet, I'm convinced I can hear my summer clothes pleading, "Pack us away! We've had it. There's nothing left of us but rags! You can only wash us so many times before we fall apart. How many months can you expect us to be perky without a break?"

My winter clothes (all four outfits of mix-and-match pants, skirts, and sweaters) live nine months of the year smugly folded on my closet shelves just hoping for a change in season so they can get a little fresh air. The colors in my winter wardrobe never fade. They're almost never washed. They go out of style long before they're worn out. There's just no justice for anyone or anything involved in summer in the South.

I'm a nicer person in the winter. Really. It's a shame that I live in a part of the country where winter is so short because most people don't get a chance to see how delightful I can be. I'm up for anything in the winter! If I were a flower, I'd be a pansy. When everything else is huddled under a bed of pine straw trying to keep warm, I'm poking through with odd bits of color and excitement. Sleet, ice, snow—let her rip!

I read in *National Geographic* that people who live near the North Pole, and even parts of Alaska, who endure months with almost no sun, sometimes develop physical illnesses due to lack of sunlight and deprivation of day and night distinctions. There are well-documented studies showing that Americans across the country get depressed in the winter months when they are trapped indoors.

So far, I haven't met anyone who shares my summer depression. In fact, I don't think it's socially acceptable to complain about summer-vacation months. Figures. And since I firmly believe that happiness is often a matter of will, of blooming where we're planted and all that, I have to work on my negative attitude regarding the long, hot Southern summers. I was born here. I'm certainly not going to move, so I'm either going to have to develop a much sweeter disposition during the summer months or else look a whole lot cuter in my summer clothes when I'm whining about the relentless heat.

Some Things I Love About Summer

I love the smell of sunscreen and of wet swimsuits drying.

I love the clink of ice in a glass of freshly made lemonade and the smell of my hands when I pick homegrown mint leaves for iced tea.

I love that it never seems to get dark on summer nights, and friends don't feel like they have to rush home after a leisurely summer supper.

I love that my children are home with me, and we can read books in the swing until my voice grows hoarse.

I love even thinking about napping on a porch under a ceiling fan with the sound of water lapping nearby.

I love that there are fewer schedules and agendas that require my attention.

I love the feel of beach sand between my toes and the taste of salt spray on my lips.

I love that my daughter can spend an entire morning playing with one roly-poly on the sidewalk.

I love that, without feeling too guilty, I can finally read the stack of books I always have waiting in the wings.

I love to arrange sunflowers and zinnias in my bare feet.

I love to ride in the car with the windows rolled down and the air conditioner on full blast.

I love that in August, when the air is suffocating and thick, signs of fall begin to appear like lifelines into a new season.

Gardening at Our House

We are not really a gardening kind of family, but we have grandiose ideas and a highly exalted opinion of our potential, which is not in the least phased by year after year of lackluster blossoms. In actual fact not I, not my husband, nor any of our children can distinguish between a weed and a wildflower. We've had some lively debates over items that spring up in our garden, not wanting to bring about the demise of even a dandelion with ideas of bettering itself. We are, at best, spasmodic, superficially enthusiastic gardeners. We're sort of like Christians who show up for the big shows—you know, Easter and Christmas.

My gardening tools are a pitiful collection of garage-sale items. In the gardening realm, I have: a shovel, a trowel (an English term for the little shovel I usually give the baby to use), a rake, and, well, another rake. Nevertheless, my enthusiasm for spring planting is not at all dampened by my lack of equipment, knowledge, or experience.

This year, I have discovered a secret weapon. I found the most stupendous Mexican sun hat with leather straps that fasten under the chin so it doesn't blow off. And I want you to know that if I don't grow some prize-winning zinnias with this hat, I swear I'll give up sweet tea. I believe that I was born to wear this hat. I'm just not sure I can wear it in public.

When I tentatively showed it to my friend, she said, "Take

it back. Immediately." My husband started humming the theme to *The Big Valley* when I showed it to him. So, I guess I'm going to garden in my new sombrero because I don't think I have the guts to wear it to the pool.

Except for shopping for the hat, I garden without a whole lot of preplanning. I go for the gusto, plant as the spirit moves me, all the clichés you can think of. Therefore, the only people who will garden with me are my children. And it is just my good fortune that only one of them can read because I am not very big on following all those "plant so-and-so far apart and only so deep" directions.

I figure if birds can successfully scatter flower seeds across the country in their highly inelegant manner, anything I do is a step up. Anyway, have you ever noticed that the most gorgeous roses, hydrangeas, and wildflowers are usually found way out in the country, miles away from nurseries selling expensive fertilizer and pages of how-to directions?

My mother swears that people used to throw their old dish water outside the back door of their kitchens, and she claims this is why the old hydrangea and gardenia bushes are so beautiful, but she may be making that up. She does that sometimes just to liven up the week. Just in case it's true, I've been doing the suburban equivalent. I've been dousing my rosebushes with fish water every time I change the water in the kids' aquarium. I must admit I've never had so many blooms. Apparently, Confederate rosebushes love fish poop.

Last week, the children and I planted our summer garden. We worked hard. We planted about fifteen packets of seeds, and we were out there at least thirty-five minutes. The second I strapped on my new sun hat, I felt a new gardening confidence flow through my veins. As a true señora, I was in complete control of the hacienda and its garden.

When my son asked what kind of flower seeds he was pouring out of his packet into the one deep hole he had previously been digging to China, I fielded my first lack-of-gardening-knowledge question of the day. Although I could not even pronounce the name of the flower on his packet, I did notice that it was indigenous to only one small island in the South

Pacific, so I answered my son's genera-species question with hat-inspired attitude: "That, my son, is a *blue* flower." He was completely content with my less-than-fulsome answer because the flower pictured on his package was, indeed, blue. I sincerely hope that the one insect on this entire planet that is capable of pollinating this particular species of flower actually sees fit to anoint our little plot of earth, because my son has every expectation of harvesting a flower.

At first, I'd thought of planting with some attention to growth potential and the like, but after watching my youngest son pour an entire packet of seeds into one hole and then go on to plant another packet in the sandbox (after sharing a midmorning snack of sunflower seeds with one of our fat squirrels), I decided to let the kids do a little freestyle gardening.

We decided to go heavy on sunflowers. The first word on the back of a packet of sunflowers is "hardy." Perfect. One of my children brought sunflowers to fruition at preschool last year, so how hard could that possibly be? We also put in zinnias and coneflowers, plus anything else that looked pretty on the package. I do have some doubts about the orchids.

While we were all sitting in the porch swing recovering from our thirty-five minutes of intense manual labor, I couldn't help but observe that our garden looked like a bit of war-torn Europe or a field firefighters had been frantically trying to dig up to head off a forest fire.

I was worrying about how disappointed my kids would be if nothing we planted came up at all. Realistically, I knew it would take a miracle of Biblical proportions to make anything bloom in our wasteland of a garden. Parting the Red Sea was going to look like small potatoes compared to making our garden grow.

I was just gearing up to take off the sombrero and deliver a practical, real-life, gardening homily to my children, hoping to limit a few high expectations, when my son said, "Just look at our wonderful garden, Mommy. Can't you just see all the beautiful flowers? Use your 'magination!"

I was being entirely truthful when I said, "Son, I cannot even imagine what this garden is going to look like!"

Rules Children Garden By

Wetter is better. You can never water too much, especially if you have a new watering can.

Stop gardening to play with any worms that you find.

You can plant anything anywhere.

Try a bite of anything that looks tasty.

Don't wear shoes to plant your garden. You need to feel the dirt with your toes.

It is never too early or too late to plant flowers.

All plants are equally valuable, so mix a few dandelions in with your mom's roses.

Stop and smell anything that blooms. Take your time about it.

Plant flowers that attract butterflies. Spend time chasing the butterflies.

Lie down in the dirt, look up at the sky, and imagine how flowers feel.

Dig with your hands. If you need a tool, find a stick.

Be completely confident that anything you plant will come up.

Plant your seeds close together. Everybody needs a buddy.

All colors are fun. Don't limit yourself.

Don't chase squirrels and birds away. Everybody has to eat.

Water your feet. Squish the mud between your toes.

Follow bugs to see if you can discover where they live.

Check ten or twelve times a day to see how much your plants have grown.

Plant a few pieces of candy. Maybe you can grow more.

When it's your turn to use the garden hose, make sure someone gets "accidentally" wet.

Turn the sprinkler on. Play in it.

Make some decorations for your garden. You can never have too many decorations.

Dig up some of your plants to see what they look like on the bottom.

Stare out your window at nap time and imagine what your garden is going to look like.

Falling Leaves

Have you ever wondered who started the whole obsessive leaf-raking, manicured-lawn behavior? I don't think a woman thought of it, nor do I think any American male initiated this. I am convinced the Utopian-lawn crusade must have been a British idea. The term "lawn" just brings to mind polite English gentlemen wielding pruning shears.

Some women have become outdoor neat freaks about their lawns. We all know at least one woman who can barely wait for the pinecones to hit the ground before she is outside gathering them up. She can't walk up her front porch steps without spotting a weed in a flowerbed three feet away that simply must be pulled up by the roots immediately.

In the South, of course, we don't refer to "lawns" unless we are catering a really big, outside wedding reception with a white tent, professional landscaping, and a whole platoon of men to check that every blade of grass is growing in the same direction. Down here, we have "yards." You can tell just by the name that a "yard" (front or back) isn't anywhere near as nice as a "lawn."

Every fall, we all engage in the frantic, weekend activity of raking leaves. We begin with enthusiasm. It is, after all, a socially acceptable reason to wear a sweat suit in public. It is invigorating to be outside again without sweating. The leaves are swirling in the wind. All the red, yellow, and gold colors of fall seem incredibly vibrant. The air has a bit of crispness to it, and we know that soon we will be able to wear long sleeves again to hide our baggy arms.

Southern women who experience the spring-cleaning urge during the later season feel the need to conquer the great out-doors—to get out in the yard and bring some order to nature's chaos. To get those leaves raked, bagged, and carted to the street to ensure that—well…*what*, exactly? It is somehow im-portant that our yards have no leaves on them. Why? Is a yard without leaves somehow more aesthetically pleasing than a yard with piles of crumbly dry ones?

I don't know for sure how the yard-cleanup tradition got started, but it is time to put a stop to it. I say that a yard full of leaves is just nature's way of reminding us of the season. In case you've forgotten, you look out the window and get an instant calendar update. Who do we think we are fooling with all this leaf raking anyway? Do we really hope that someone is going to drive by our carefully manicured yards and say, "Look, honey, at that perfectly raked yard. It isn't even fall over there!"

How long does a good rake job last anyway? The leaves are usually still coming down as fast as we can rake them up. What a thankless task! Worse, it is self-imposed suffering. Tell the truth. When you look at your weekend to-do list, how high a priority do you give to raking? The reality is that we love to be outside, just to be part of the season, and for some reason, we feel the need to legitimize this activity by assign-ing ourselves a task.

I am putting you all on notice. I am through with this ri-diculous and unnecessary ritual of attempting to cleanup the current season and make it look like a season it is not. It is unnatural and probably not ecologically sound. Mother Na-ture and I have an understanding. She keeps the hurricanes and tornadoes from my doorstep, and I leave everything else she does pretty much as I find it. From now on, on fall weekends, I am going to make myself a big cup of cocoa and sit on my porch swing and watch those leaves pile up.

You should join me.

The Hydrangea

Hurricane season is mostly a weather-channel experience where I live, but, occasionally, we get a taste of what the coastal cities put up with on a regular basis, and I want you to know that storm preparation is *not* for the faint of heart.

When we got our first storm warning of the season, the first thing I did was to drag all the wicker porch furniture inside my dining room for a little interior storm decoration. Then I unhooked the hammock, tied up the garbage cans, and generally secured everything in sight that could become a projectile fired at my family by tropical-force winds. After that, I sat down for a well-deserved diet beverage and a brownie (my own personal diet plan which works for me, so I don't want to hear anything about it).

That's when, with a stab of guilt, I remembered the two steep corners of my roof where leaves, acorns, and assorted debris pile up like I'm creating compost heaps for the neighborhood. Of course, the gutters should have been cleaned out months ago, but I hated the thought of twelve inches of rain pounding those clogged crevices—just asking for leaks.

After inhaling one more brownie for stamina, I slipped on my oldest shorts and T-shirt, talked my husband into steadying the bottom of our tallest ladder, and made him promise to change me into something cuter if I fell off the roof and had to go to the hospital. Then I headed outside to secure the homestead and meet the great American gutter challenge.

It was soon obvious that my leaf rake would never reach far enough to remove months of debris, small tree trunks, and enough mulch for every flowerbed in the local park—in addition to a startling variety of insects. I decided that I would have to climb to the top of the ladder and stand right on top of the red, "DO NOT STAND ON TOP STEP" sign in order to hoist myself onto the roof.

When I was finally seated on the edge of my two-story roof with my legs dangling over the edge, I allowed myself a moment of self-congratulation. Then I remembered that what goes up must eventually come down, and, sadly, I couldn't think of any way to avoid the laws of gravity when I backed my fanny down the ladder.

My husband, the hero standing at the *foot* of the ladder, called out encouraging and helpful advice such as, "Well...be careful." After being chastised by me for crushing my favorite gardenia bush with the ladder, he was loathe to move it again and suggested that I "climb around" the roof to get to the problem areas.

I could see his point. I sure didn't want him to tax himself moving that ladder while I was up there cleaning live beetles out of the rain gutters with my bare hands. Briefly I wondered if I fell off the roof on top of him whether it would send both of us to the hospital or just him. Even-money bet, I decided.

You are not going to *believe* what I found up there.

Right in the middle of a pile of leaves, sticks, and who knows what all, a hydrangea bush was growing out of my roof. I'm not talking about a hydrangea sprout, branch, or sprig. It was two-feet tall, and it had glossy leaves like a pet greenhouse plant. In fact, it looked healthier than anything I'd ever grown on purpose in my flowerbeds.

I was completely taken aback. Even *I* know that hydrangeas are not supposed to grow on the roof. We don't do that kind of thing down here.

I slithered over to it immediately, grasped it by a long branch, and pulled it up by the roots. All the roof shingles came up with it like icing on a birthday cake when you pull out the candles. Never have I seen roots that long in my life. They were five feet at least and spread out in all directions like the tentacles of a giant jellyfish.

That hydrangea had been frantically searching for soil and water. I'm surprised it didn't burrow right through the roof and into my middle child's bedroom. Maybe it could smell the water in my child's fish tank and thought, "If I can just make it a bit further..."

Instinctively, I felt that this plant deserved to live. It was hardy—pioneer-like. It found itself in dry, barren roof tar and made the best of a tough situation. It was thriving. I began to feel sentimental about that hydrangea bush. I wanted it to become part of our home's neglected foliage.

Tossing it over the side of the house, I made my tentative, fearful descent down the ladder just as the first curtains of rain hit our house. Quickly, I began to dig.

My husband yelled, "What in the world are you doing? THERE IS A HURRICANE COMING!"

"I know that," I said, "I just have to plant this hydrangea."

"Have you lost your mind? You bought a hydrangea *today*?"

Balancing both feet on top of the shovel, I jumped up and down, trying to scoop out a big enough hole for my hydrangea and replied, "I didn't *buy* it, silly. I found it on the roof."

Spring Planting

Every spring, without fail, I feel the urge to plant flowers. For me, this means driving to a nursery, writing a large check, and returning home for the ever-hopeful planting. I fantasize my efforts will result in such an abundance of color and charm that it will cause a traffic pileup right in front of my house as people lean out of their car windows to drool over the brilliance of my window boxes.

The reality is that I will toss out a few annuals, which will eventually thirst to death in August. So, I am going to assume that the whole planting urge is an innate, estrogen-related response to the coming of spring. Even those of us with no gardening talent feel the sense of rebirth going on all around us in nature, and we want to be a part of fresh plantings and new beginnings.

For our Southern women-friends who are serious gardeners, spring planting is the culmination of winter months spent poring over coffee-table gardening books. For them, there are no casual strolls down nursery aisles and no random plant selections. Oh, no. Each selection has been carefully vetted for likely size, compatibility with other flowerbed friends, and overall blooming potential. The planning for the liberation of Iraq had nothing on these women for diagramming, strategizing, researching the local flora and fauna, and hours of stewing about what their gardens, window boxes, and planters will flaunt for the season.

Martha Stewart's spring planting can't compare to Southern women's flower-garden campaigns. Some of these women have specially written clauses included in the sales contract for their homes to insure that only the most worthy buyers receive the legacy of years of shared cuttings and prayed-over plants. When one of these gardening giants sells a home, she wants to make sure her yard is going to be in good hands with the new owner. If she discovers, after a few carefully phrased questions concerning fertilizing, mulching, and pruning, that the new owner is obviously not up to the job and doesn't show the proper inclination to learn from her years of valuable experience, well, we all know what will happen.

The ink won't be dry on the contract before that woman will be out in the dead of night in the yard of her old house doing a little landscaping. Anything that won't survive benign neglect by the new owner will be transplanted to a more worthy caretaker. She thinks of herself as a plant emancipator.

We won't even talk about who gets custody of Japanese maple trees in a buy/sell conflict. I don't think that issue has made it all the way through the courts yet, and we wouldn't want to prejudice any readers.

Southern women who buy a house from a true gardener know that there must be an offer made to the original gardener/seller to welcome her back for future cuttings, important floral arrangements, or to share blossoms that she planted that will only come to fruition after she's long gone. Obviously, a buyer who benefits from all the hard work of the gardener who came before her should at least offer to share future blossoms. It's the right thing to do. For example, a polite offer at closing from the buyer to the seller would be, "You must come back in June for some of those gorgeous roses! I know you always use them for your garden party."

"That is so sweet of you, and I will," is an appropriate response.

In addition, a certain amount of raving over a magnificent gardener's domain is required in the purchase of a home and its grounds. Even if the purchaser is not a gardener, such compliments will inevitably make the seller more lenient when negotiating a price, and the seller/gardener might, in a fit of charity, leave a few plants that she would ordinarily have dug up and taken with her.

As Southern women, we should also remember that some plants are more important than houses. (Bricks aren't alive, are they?) Rosebushes, magnolia and dogwood trees, and other green things that have been planted to commemorate someone's birth or death should be given a wide berth by buyers, sellers, and current occupants when considering additions, renovations, etc.—even if the honorees have been dead for years. Remember, we are a culture of multiple generations, so don't be shortsighted in your approach to a Southern woman's foliage.

Years ago, when I lived in my first house, a woman actually knocked on my door and demanded to inspect the dogwood tree in my backyard which had been planted to honor the birth of her mother. Before leaving, she made me solemnly promise never to cut it down. This I was happy to do, of course, since I know better than to cross a Southern woman holding pruning shears.

And if there is a magnolia tree on your property, don't buy a house with the illusion that you are the sole owner of that tree. There may be neighbors with a proprietary interest, who have been allowed for years to cut branches off that tree for all their arrangements, and the surest way to be run out of your new neighborhood by sundown is to thwart such previously held understandings.

In fact, before you do any pruning of "your" magnolia tree (or anything else in the yard that might be considered community property in some way), you would be wise to have a casual consultation with your neighbors on either side. If you are going to do some major landscaping, your neighbors may need a little warning; a chance to think it over, to schedule accordingly any outdoor events they may have planned, and to decide if the spring-planting color scheme they have chosen for their own yards is going to be adversely affected by your new landscaping. This conversation requires tact, flattery, and, sometimes, outright cajolery.

One of my neighbors has lived next to me for two years now, and I still haven't recovered from the day he moved in and plowed under the entire backyard, including a bed of the biggest, most divine white lilies you have ever seen in your life. I know the old lady who lived in that house for sixty years before him and who nurtured those lilies like babies must have covered her eyes if she was watching from heaven. To this day, every time I see him, all I can think is: "Lily killer!"

The Squirrel Wars

I am constantly amazed at the large numbers of wild animals I find flourishing in my own small bit of suburbia. Amidst homes, sidewalks, and streets crowded with traffic, we're breeding wild animals street savvy enough to hold their own in any game preserve in Africa. We have a small yard in front of our house and an even tinier patch of green in back, so I find it hard to believe that we can support as many species of squirrel, bird, bug, slug, locust, and opossum as we spot from our windows on a regular basis.

I can see the insolence in the eyes of opossums that knock over my trash cans searching for leftovers. They stare me down as if to say, "We were here with the cockroaches and dinosaurs, lady. This is our turf. We'll be here long after you and your weak offspring are carried off by mosquitoes." It's a trifle unnerving.

Although I haven't seen any zebras on the loose, just about everything else has found a home in the wilds of our neighborhood. And I heard the squirrels had a meeting about us, and they're planning a revolt, or at the very least, a class-action lawsuit. There are more squirrels than people, they figure. Squirrels were here first, they claim, and if they have their way, we humans are living here on borrowed time. If you look at one of our squirrels square in his shifty little eyes, you can see him

plotting. Those little suckers want to take us out. They're form-
ing unions and trying to get some birds in on the action.

I used to like squirrels. My impressions of them were formed
by early exposure to Beatrix Potter illustrations. I thought of
squirrels as small, dainty creatures, a bit delicate and shy. I don't
know what species of English squirrel inspired the drawings by
Beatrix Potter, but Squirrel Nutkin had clearly never met his
overweight, inelegant, Yankee cousin, the suburban menace,
because the squirrels in my neighborhood could make mince-
meat out of those hoity-toity, British-born squirrels.

The squirrels in our neighborhood are so fat and happy
that the branches on which they climb stagger toward the
ground trying to support their weight. Furthermore, our squirrels are enormously greedy. Time and again I've watched them
cram ten or twelve acorns in their mouths until I think their
cheeks will split. Worse, they're lazy. They refuse to make two
trips for nuts; they'd rather cram another nut in their mouths
on the first run.

There's no doubt about it. The squirrels in our neighborhood have a bad attitude. They have no sense of their place in
the food chain. They don't even pause when I walk near them;
I am no more frightening or intimidating than a pesky blue jay.
Eventually, if I get too close, they'll scramble up the nearest
tree in irritation, but only to sit on a bottom branch and shower
abuse on my head for interrupting one of their food-storing
frenzies by daring to walk out my own front door.

Our squirrels are the size of overfed house cats, and they
have irritable dispositions. Just the way they chatter at one
another is enough to make me despair of any two ever getting
along. They chase one another up and down tree trunks and
are so selfish they'll fight over one wrinkled old nut, even
though they have a bushel tucked away in the hollow of the
nearest tree. The truth of the matter is that squirrels do not
share well.

Most irritating of all is just how dumb squirrels are. I guess
that's what happens when your brain is smaller than a wal-
nut, but I ask you, is there any better visual definition of
dumb than watching a squirrel cross the road? I've had time to

paint my fingernails while watching suburban squirrels make mad dashes right, left, no, right again, run three-fourths of the way, then stop. Back across, stagger left, quick dart to the nearest sidewalk. No wonder so many squirrels become road kill. You have to work hard at *not* running over a squirrel. They are that dumb.

I used to think of squirrels as cute furry pets. I'm over it. We're growing them so big here that I see them looking in our windows and sizing up the furniture. I get the feeling they're thinking about moving in. They see lots of convenient nooks and crannies for nut storage in my kitchen, and I think *they* think we're pretty soft targets. My love affair with squirrels came to a screeching halt when they dug up every pansy I planted last fall. After digging them up, they tossed them on my front porch and left every one to dry out in the sun. The audacity of it! Finally, they buried their nuts deep in my planters. It's fair to say that the battle was on.

Last year, my family was harassed by a band of squirrels. My husband and I were asleep in bed, minding our own business, when we heard the mad scurry of tiny little claws running back and forth across our attic floor. We handled it like the city dwellers we are. We banged on the walls and yelled threats like, "Hey, get out of there!" We really scared those squirrels. Next we spent hours in our hot, stuffy attic trying to plug any small holes in a futile effort to keep the squirrels from setting up winter condos in our attic.

It was all to no avail. We'd think we had them. A night or two would go by, and we wouldn't hear them. We smelled victory. With our big brains and opposable thumbs, we had finally managed to outwit the dumb squirrels. Then, when we least expected it, they came back. This time they brought friends and relatives. You could tell by all the noise they had a full-fledged, squirrel family reunion going on in our attic.

"What are you going to do about this?" I asked my husband.

"Me? What do you expect me to do about it? I don't know anything about squirrels!"

I was astounded.

"I want you to get up there and get those squirrels. Didn't you ever watch *Designing Women*? I'm with Delta Burke. I think the man should have to kill the bugs!"

"Squirrels aren't bugs," my husband pointed out logically (as if this helped his case).

"You know what I mean! I want the wildlife out of my attic!"

"I'll see what I can do," he promised.

My husband called a wildlife rescue group. Apparently, they aren't all that worried about the suburban squirrel population. Now if we wanted to throw in an endangered bobcat or snail darter, maybe we could talk, they said.

We decided to try one of those "friendly" traps that allows you to relocate your squirrels to a sunny meadow far away. I was thinking Montana would be a nice place to set them free. I wanted a few interstates between us. I am sad to report that those squirrels were so dumb they couldn't even figure out how to get themselves trapped. They just sat outside the trap looking at the bait excitedly and chattering back and forth like two old ladies on a park bench who can't see eye to eye on anything.

My husband was beginning to look a little wild around the eyes from sleep deprivation and the constant pressure of trying to outwit lowly members of the evolutionary tree, but I was approaching a Zen-like peacefulness about the whole squirrel problem. In our last squirrel encounter, we were both in bed reading books when we heard a squirrel run across the ceiling. My husband flung one of those weighty legal texts toward a point where the sound seemed to originate, but I just continued calmly turning pages in my novel.

I had decided to learn to live with the squirrels. I am the mother of three young children, so I have learned to live with all sorts of obnoxious sounds that would drive a childless couple insane. I was tired of talking, thinking, and worrying about squirrels. As far as I'm concerned, they can have the attic. I'll invest in some gerbil toys, and they can set up a playground up there. I just don't care anymore.

The Family Gallery

Family Novels

One of my favorite presents, an 1891 silver dollar, was given to me by my best friend's father in celebration of my oldest son's birth. I have it safely tucked away to give to my son when he is old enough to keep it for longer than fifteen minutes without losing it. I thought I might make a key chain out of it for his twenty-first birthday, when he's old enough to appreciate hearing stories about the man who carried it in his pocket for years.

I still have the handwritten note from my friend's father that accompanied the baby gift in the mail, promising to regale me with incredible tales of this lucky coin. Unfortunately, as things often happen, my friend's father never told me those tales because time got away from him and from me. And before we made time to sit down and tell one another stories, he died.

So now, the lucky silver-dollar story line is dead, too. I can't tell you the stories about the lucky silver dollar because I never heard them. No one else knows the stories or remembers them. I asked.

Of course, my son knows stories about the man who gave him the silver dollar. I've sung him songs the man taught me and described the stories he would make up using real-life characters from our small-town cast in hilarious, improbable, and ridiculous plots that kept my friend and me roaring with laughter deep into the night.

A couple of years ago, when we were singing one of those songs, "Lemon Tree," along with the car's CD player, and I was recounting one of my childhood memories (again), my son asked, "When will I get to meet your friend, Mommy?" Because my friend's father had been dead for years, I almost drove off the side of the road while attempting to explain the permanency of death to my child.

"But, Mom," my son protested, "you don't talk about him like he's dead."

I tried to explain that so many people make up one's life, and even though some of them die along the way, in many ways they never really die in our minds.

When I look at pictures of my family, I see in my relatives' eyes what I most want to inherit. I want to be the keeper of their stories. I want to be the one who remembers, embellishes, exaggerates, adapts, blends, and lies, so not one of the people I have loved in my life will ever be completely dead.

I can't think of anything worse than not being remembered. I don't want to be remembered for heroic deeds, social or business achievements, or even great humanitarian works. I want to be remembered by my children and their children for some perfect snapshot of a day or moment we spent together. It could be as simple or ordinary as a shared book or walk, the intimacy of a private joke or joint experience that is unique to the two of us— one of those real, Kodak moments. I'd pick a perfect mental photograph that captures forever the specific smell, feel, and taste of a particular day, time, or second. It would be one of the few days when we are together, living perfectly in the moment. When I am dead, I want family and friends to talk about me like I'm not dead. That would, I think, be the ultimate compliment about how I had lived my life.

For a couple of years, I read nonfiction almost exclusively. The characters in novels seemed almost overwhelming in their nearness to reality, and I was riding safely on the nonfiction bandwagon until a friend tempted me with a particularly well-written, new novel. I was off my teetotaler phase and drowning in a sea of novels, neglecting domestic responsibilities and mommy duties with excuses like, "Sure, sweetie, I'll make lunch in just one second." I was back to reading novels about generations of families and all their failures, tragedies, joys, and triumphs. Every year, I spend lots of dollars buying books about other people's real and fictional families. Wouldn't it be great if we could purchase novels chronicling the lives of our own families?

Who wouldn't like to learn about their parents, grandparents, great-grandparents, aunts and uncles, and anyone else who has been alive and sentient at any time in their lives simply by reading about them? I'd like to read our own family history like a novel with as many points of view as there are family members. Imagine how the stories would unfold. Each tale would be a story—not *the* story, since no one person knows it all—and every story is part of every other, like rivers, streams, estuaries, and tidal pools that flow into one common ocean.

I would read the stories by the certifiably crazy family members first, just to get a feel for the margins. Then I'd read the stories recorded by the best-loved matriarchs or patriarchs. After that I'd start looking for the outcasts, the misfits, and then the storytellers without an ax to grind. Wouldn't you just love to read about the women who received numerous gentlemen callers, endured rushed marriages, and gave birth to remarkably premature babies?

The problem with family history is that the things I want to know aren't recorded anywhere. They don't involve marriage certificates, land deeds, birth or death records. What I'm looking for isn't preserved in staged studio portraits. All that information is available to any genealogy sleuth. I'm looking for something else.

The things I'm looking for—constantly searching for—are the things that really matter. What was my great-grandmother's favorite color? What was the happiest day of her life, and where was she? What was her daughter, my grandmother, like as a child? Who was the great love of her life?

What I find most frustrating about this search is that I know someone in my lifetime knew the answers to these questions. Had to. But somehow that information got lost. Eventually, we all get reduced to a name with birth and death dates on a piece of marble in a cemetery. Hardly seems enough. Over time, the personalities of relatives in our old photographs seem to visibly lighten and weaken until we are not even tempted to pause for closer examination as we flip through the family photo album.

I've made some attempts over the years to satisfy these desires. When my oldest child was born, I made up a list of questions I wanted relatives to answer in writing, so that I could fold some tangible piece of family connectedness into his baby book. Dismal failure. No one wanted to fill them out. Another time I bought a game about family history. Strike two. No one would play with me. It could be this family has some impressive Mafia skeletons. It is also possible, as has been suggested, that I am too nosy.

People are more interesting to me if they have a little history to them. In the last years of my grandmother's life, I could actually feel time moving swiftly. I feared each shared hour might be our last. I have a great-aunt who has almost perfect recall, even though she is old enough to remember riding in a horse and buggy. I love to pull up a chair and hear her stories.

No one seems to have time to talk about memories. Later, when there is time, a lifetime often gets wiped out by dementia or unexpected death. Then it's too late to share the memories, and the memories, as well as the person, are gone forever. I'm afraid that a lifetime of excuses not to reveal anything intimate renders mute years of joy.

I keep asking impertinent questions, and I assure you I receive precious few answers. It is up to my imagination to flesh out the dry statistics left from lives never revealed in shared memories. Sometimes even the touch of an object, my son's 1891 silver dollar, for example, brings back a flood of the sweetest memories and a bittersweet longing for more.

The Family Reunion

In the South, family reunions are annual events with compulsory attendance. To merit an excused absence, you must have a vital organ removed a scant few hours before family reunion kickoff time. No vaguely worded "we regret having a previous engagement" will suffice for a day of family martyrdom.

Blood ties bind down here, so don't start thinking that a few generations have diluted your genetic relationship enough to let you off the hook. If it is summer, there will be a reunion, and short of a lucky head injury, you'll be there.

There are a few people who really do enjoy reunions. My mother is an example, but really she is just a genealogy buff, and a family reunion gives her a socially acceptable excuse to poke around old cemeteries. When cornered, she'll admit the truth—she's much more interested in dead relatives than living ones.

When I die, if I somehow miss the pearly gates and go to…well, option B, shall we say, I am convinced that as my punishment, every day will be Family Reunion Day. I feel sure that I would gladly trade places with Atlas. A little job like holding up the world for eternity would be no big deal compared to attending a family reunion every day until the end of time.

As Southerners, we have a love/hate relationship with members of our multigenerational family. This makes it impossible for us to stay away from each other and tempted to shoot one another when we get together. Maybe it's the heat. I know I want to swat somebody when the temperature soars above ninety degrees.

Most Southerners spend 364 days a year dreading the next family reunion. We count down the last week like we're waiting for gum surgery and secretly hope for a viral infection that would give us a legitimate pass on reunion day. (You know how old people drop like flies during flu season—you couldn't risk infecting one of them.) We can all feel when the reunion date is closing in. Ghosts of family reunions past call across the years. Eventually, most of us give in and go, so I think it's better to capitulate gracefully, load the cooler, and fill a prescription for Valium on the way out of town. After each reunion, we announce to anyone who will listen: "I am never going to a family reunion again! Do you hear me? This time, I mean it!"

We pray desperately in the car on the way to the reunion site that the certifiable crazies won't be able to attend. There are enough of the merely colorful eccentrics in the family to jazz up the day without the family members who would undoubtedly melt if you accidentally threw a bucket of water on them.

Over the years, I have acquired some family reunion coping skills that I am happy to pass on to you. First, I always back my car into a parking space with a clear view to a major highway in case I need a speedy getaway from all the extended-family togetherness. I also make sure that my best friend has my cell-phone number and knows to call me with a well-feigned emergency if I haven't given her the "all's well" smoke signal by sundown.

Not even an act of God can stop the family reunion. If you have a family, they will come. This is because every family has at least one perky person who is in charge of reunion plans. The perky planner has enough energy to make the activity director on a cruise ship look dull. This is a woman who owns a badminton set and carries nametags in her glove compartment. Just when you think all the old-timers are too frail to risk another family reunion trip, and you can picture an end to the yearly forced assemblies, along comes the family's perky planner. This family member is usually some distant cousin (related by marriage—not blood) who happens to have a van and is just thrilled to go by every retirement home in the state loading up all the old relatives and their walkers. She leaves her garage at daybreak. As additional torture, she just happens to have a calendar, games, old home movies—color-coded by decade and cross-referenced for genealogy buffs—and a kitchen-duty roster.

As a Southerner, it is your familial obligation to pack up your immediate family and turn a perfectly nice, summer Saturday into a family daytrip nightmare. At least one child is statistically likely to be carsick on the way. It will be 105 degrees at the reunion site, and you're obligated to sit outside like a giant mosquito buffet while you shout into half-deaf ears to identify your particular branch on the family tree.

There will be a forced feeding about noon. Your great-aunt Olivia will back you into a corner to try a spoonful of her famous potato salad, which she proudly maintains has been loaded into her car and ready for the family reunion for three days. Family lore has it that Aunt Liv's potato salad was the governor's favorite food during the 1930s. It is widely rumored that her culinary specialty had something to do with his untimely demise the day after one of her famous luncheons—referred to within the family as "lovely affairs but a trifle deadly." When you open the Tupperware lid, that potato salad will actually have strands of bacteria strong enough to reach out and grab your spoon.

In a futile attempt to identify something safe to eat, you will whisper furtively to the one cousin whose company you still enjoy as an adult, "Who made this?" In the end, you will be content with the Cheerios you fish out from underneath the baby's safety seat.

You will be hugged until you gag. You will be asked embarrassing questions about how old you were when you outgrew that annoying stammer. You will speculate about your genetic connection to this unattractive group of people, and you will indulge in a few minutes of secret fantasy that you are really a long-lost member of an obscure royal family who was somehow dropped into the heart of suburban America.

Then, like every year, there will be one moment when you are actually glad you came. You'll hold a frail, aging hand for perhaps the last time while you recall an almost forgotten fragment of memory from your childhood, or you will look out across the lake and see your kids playing with cousins they see once a year as if they are long-lost brothers, and the whole mind-numbing, grossly overrated day will have given you one second of piercing joy that will make you remember what part of you came from this family. Of course, it will take weeks of therapy to sort it all out, and you definitely won't be coming back next year.

Questions to Avoid Asking at the Family Reunion

(Lest They Be Answered)

"Are you still married?"

"Are all those children yours?"

"When did you get so fat?"

"Are you dating anyone yet?"

"How much did that set you back?"

"What happened to your hair?"

"Did you have a face-lift?"

"Were your feet always that big?"

"You don't work anymore, do you?"

"Do you remember me?"

"Why don't you ever come visit us?"

"Do you remember _____? Yes, you do!
Well, he's dead."

"Are y'all married or just living in sin?"

Hands

My earliest memory of my grandmother is a crystal-clear mental snapshot of her hands. When I grew restless or bored during church services, she would allow me to play with her hands, and I would twist her wedding rings around and around her fingers with what must have been maddening repetition.

I was about three or four years old because I remember that I couldn't see over the pew in front of me. My hands were so much smaller than hers that my entire hand fit into her palm. I couldn't imagine ever having hands as big, wrinkled, lined, or blue-veined as my grandmother's.

What I didn't know is that my hands would grow large enough to throw a beautiful spiral football pass that any Southern woman would be proud of. I had no idea that my just-married hands with their smooth white fingers and perfectly manicured digits would develop creases, lines, and calluses over the years to reflect the work of my life.

Over time, I developed the dry, cracked fingers of a mother whose hands spend all day in water, cleaning solutions, and worse, trying to avoid the next round of throw-up viruses. I can remember the feel of my mother's hands when I was a child—hard, sure, work-worn, with the texture that snags stockings when you smooth them over your legs.

Years ago, my mother, grandmother, and I were standing at the rail of a deck looking out over a lake, and I noticed for the first time that my hands had become the hands of my mother. The three pairs of our hands side by side there on the balcony railing epitomized for me the entire life's journey of Southern women—from vain young women wearing Vaseline and gloves to bed to soften up our hands, to mature adults abandoning any pretense of homage to hand vanity to arrange flowers, clean up after sticky children, and prepare countless meals.

If you look carefully, the whole measure of a woman can be taken by a showing of her hands. I'm comfortable seeing my mother's hands on myself now, and I know there was no more comforting feel than the clasp of my grandmother's strong fingers on mine.

The Family Gallery

Like most Southern women, I have rarely seen a photograph of one of my relatives, living or long dead, that didn't make me want to look around my house for an empty spot to hang it for a little public display of affection.

My favorite photographs of ancestors are black-and-white, sepia, or hand-tinted. There is something about the sharpness of contrast between the harsh black and grays and the unforgiving white that makes people in the portraits come alive. The muted brown sepia tones seem just exactly the washed-out colors memories would be if we could actually capture them on paper. And the bright yellows and blues of hand-applied color add a richness and depth to photographs that probably surpasses the real character's hair color, dress color, and garden arrays.

It is often as interesting to notice what, or who, is left out of photographs as it is to notice how and where the most important subject in the photograph is seated, dressed, and composed. I swear some of those women standing behind men seated in big, claw-footed chairs look like they are trying to signal the photographer for help—frantic-looking hands clutch handkerchiefs; eyes seem to plead, "Get me out of here! Why in the world did I marry this man?"

Background scenery or props often offer fascinating insight into an ancestor's tastes or personality or serve as tribute to the rages of the day. It is hard to imagine a Southern woman today going out of her way to have a professional photographer snap a picture of her baby perched on a bear skin, but there was a day when that was haute couture.

I especially like it when I can distinctly see the eyes of the person in the photograph. It's remarkable, really, what you can read in people's eyes, the reflections of character you can see preserved forever in one flash of light at one moment in time. I look at pictures of soldiers from the Civil War and World War I, and I can so easily envision the horrors they saw. Their eyes seem to retain misty reflections of the terrible scenes they witnessed.

My favorite photographs are from the late 1800s, and I especially appreciate pictures that have something quirky about them—maybe a bird in one of those magnificent Victorian bird-cages or a pair of wedding shoes of elaborate design—some small detail that gives me insight into the person immortalized in the frame.

In my home, I never feel lonely walking down my center hall-way because there is always a host of relatives to greet my every coming and going. It's a good thing they can't talk because you can tell by looking at them that I am the descendant of a bunch of bossy women. Every self-respecting Southern woman I know can carry on a one-sided conversation with a long-dead grand-mother, mother, sister, or friend if there is a picture around that really captures her "just like she was."

Most women who love old family photographs seem to be looking for ostentatious displays of family importance—maybe a famous military man or a hint of royalty. Not me. I'd like to have a picture of a couple of horse thieves or a flapper or two, just to liven up my suburban walls a bit.

I am also starting to think of photographs as a nice foil, a reflection of earlier beauty for the Southern women in my family who have put on a few pounds, shed a few hairs, and felt the inevitable force of gravity pulling their previously pert, well-rounded selves down to the linoleum. In my mind, my grand-mother will always have smooth, taut skin and flashing brown eyes. I want my children to remember her from the photographs on my walls, not their personal knowledge of her as a frail, washed-out version of herself. I've concluded that we all need to pick out a few good photographs of ourselves that we want cop-ied and passed out in our senior years because we all deserve to be remembered in our glory days.

Of course, there are pitfalls to prominently displaying one-self (big oil portraits, for example) in one's prime for any and all visitors to see and comment upon. It can be a trifle embarrassing if the then-and-now contrast is too stark. In fact, being asked to verify your identity with a driver's license or a passport is guaran-teed to be insulting. Startled questions such as, "Is that really you?" coupled with reactions like, "You're kidding. You were so thin, attractive, or blonde," can be rather off-putting. Teenagers can be particularly brutal: "Mother, please tell me that you did not go out in public in that outfit. Did anyone I know see you in that? Birds could build nests in hair that big, Mom. Did you wear that on purpose? Was it supposed to look like that?"

Southern women are generally split into two schools of thought regarding photographs. On the one hand, you have Southern women who do not wish to have their photographs taken under any circumstances. These women are as elusive as groundhogs and seem to share the old Native American belief that taking their photograph somehow sucks the soul right out of their body. When these women are gone, their descendants have to resort to incidental, ghost-like photographic sightings of them. They point to the corners of grainy photographs and say, "That's her! You can tell by the hem of her dress. I'd know those knobby knees of hers anywhere." Unfortunately for these women, their children are left with an abundance of pictures of them as young girls, as solemn-faced children in white dresses with hair bows bigger than their heads, and then those vacant-eyed pho-tographs of them in a nursing home snapped by whippersnapper grandchildren.

On the other hand, you have Southern women who simply love to have their pictures taken. They can flash you a toothpaste-bright smile—in between bouts of throwing up—that Miss Texas would be proud to wear in the Miss America Pageant if they know you're taking pictures. My mother can produce that perfect, Southern beauty-queen smile at the drop of a hat. She sees this as an insurance policy against potentially ego-damaging photographs. She always claims that she doesn't want any unflattering photos hanging around after she's gone. Both of her daughters know she is only half kidding.

Friends who come to see me know that if you stand still long enough at my house, someone is likely to snap your picture and mount it on the wall somewhere like you are a member of the FBI's most-wanted list. In my own defense, I'd like to point out that I've always viewed photographs as a cheap way to accessorize. Around here you can fill up a hall table and not even exhaust one branch of the family tree. Of course, I have been known to get a little carried away with the whole world of matting and framing possibilities, but that is another chapter entirely.

Being surrounded by the faces that came before me makes me feel centered. I know exactly which ancestor to blame for the big nose, the thin lips, and all the other genetic characteristics that connect my family. I think, like most Southerners, knowing and being comfortable with where we come from are important parts of being comfortable with who we are today. Contemplating the wars, depressions, deaths, and diseases faced by the women in my family who came before me makes all that I face today seem bearable.

One day I'll be just another face on the wall in someone's hall. Knowing my children, they will probably use me to cover up cracks in the plaster.

SWAG Translations

"Where did you say you're from?"
Translation: "I know you're not from the South. Is there some
cultural excuse for your appalling manners?"

"Aren't you creative! Who would have thought
you could marinate that?"
Translation: "I see your husband shot another wild animal. I guess
it's moose meat for another year at your house, right?"

"Well, just put on a little more lipstick."
Translation: "Maybe nobody will notice the hole in your
stockings big enough to drive a truck through."

"I don't see a reason in the world why you can't cover those
boat cushions in that toile fabric you love so much."
Translation: "We all know you'd be making that toile fabric into living-
room drapes if your husband hadn't spent that money on a new boat,
and, anyway, toile goes with everything. Just ask your decorator."

"You just have to get used to her. She's like that.
All her people are like that."
Translation: "The whole family is crazy as loons. It's genetic."

"Well, aren't you smart! I never saw anyone steam green beans before."
Translation: "Get me some salt and a little ham, honey.
These aren't fit to eat."

"Don't give it another thought. We just went right
ahead and started without you."
Translation: "Consider yourself crossed off every
dinner-party-invitation list for the next fifty years."

"You are such a big person to be so gracious about the whole thing."
Translation: "You have lost your mind to put up with that husband of
yours. I'll hold him down if you ever want to take a swing at him."

The Porch Swing

There is something about a porch swing that exalts the most humble of homes. In most places, people congregate in kitchens looking for warmth, but Southerners head for the porch. Whether it's a family reunion or a Sunday dinner, it seems natural for a party to spill over into the outdoors, and the porch swing is the most coveted seat in the house. In fact, if I were a real-estate agent, I think I could sell any house as long as it had a picture-perfect porch swing. "Sure," I'd argue, "it doesn't have a bathroom, but this house has potential. Just look at that porch swing!"

The perfect porch swing is not the product of a quick trip to the hardware store. It takes generations of bottoms to break in a swing properly. Old wicker is the best choice because it naturally swells and mellows with the heat and humidity. Slap a coat of white paint on the swing every spring, and you're ready for company. Hanging a porch swing is no easy task, either. The perfect sweep is crucial—not so high you frighten the old people, but not so low you discourage youngsters looking for a wilder ride.

The ink wasn't dry on the sales contract for our house before I was out on the porch directing the installation of my husband's inherited porch swing. First of all, I wanted it to be strong enough to hold three generously proportioned Southern men, who have imbibed freely in the libation of the evening, without collapsing and causing the hostess—me—any embarrassment. More importantly, since there is always room in a mother's lap for children who want to pile on, I refused to accept any petty weight restrictions for my porch swing. Finally, I wanted as few holes as possible in my wooden porch ceiling, so hanging my porch swing was a once-in-a-lifetime endeavor.

Swinging is one of the few activities on earth that transcends all geographical and cultural boundaries. Buried somewhere deep inside our psyches is an urge to escape the constraints of gravity and soar. I can remember my first lesson in how to pump for myself. "Feet out—then, under." In the South, where mild weather permits all-year undulation, we've elevated swinging to an art form.

For children, the porch swing is an ever-present source of adventure. One day it's a pirate ship or well-fortified castle. The next day, Davy Crockett fires his rifle over the back of the swing in defense of the Alamo.

I've observed that adults swing according to their temperaments. I can walk by a swing and read the mood of its occupant at a glance. An angry swinger is easy to spot—jerky, energetic swinging, like a pilot on a strafing mission. Idle, hot-summer-day swinging is my favorite. The head lolls back on the swing with the face turned up to a ceiling fan. Knees are bent at the edge of the swing, and the height of the swing's curve is directly dependent upon the length of the lazy swinger's legs since only the minimum expenditure of energy is exerted.

Another time-tested swing is the rock-the-baby-to-sleep sway. This technique utilizes long, smooth arcs with no sudden jerks or stops and is usually accompanied by humming, singing, or indiscriminate soothing noises from an adult crooning to a babe in arms. This type of swinging is a highly effective cure for nightmares and tummy aches and has a proven therapeutic value for the adult as well as the child. Moreover, this natural soother is free and available twenty-four hours a day.

As long as you have a spot on the porch swing, you know you're part of a family. I like to imagine all the conversations that have taken place on our swing over the years, the heart-to-heart conversations that flowed naturally between the generations in the intimacy of shared seating. There is something healing about the repetitive rhythm of swinging back and forth, back and forth.

When I sit on my swing and close my eyes, I can still see the shoes of family members who shared their swings with me. I can remember the exact feel of their push on the floor to set the swing in motion when my legs were too short to reach the ground. I can hear echoes of their advice in the air blowing past my ears.

Within These Walls

If you've ever lived in an old house, you know that creaking floorboards are part of the whole quaintness package. Of course, you also get tree roots growing in your pipes and no outside electrical sockets with the deal. Unlike the irritating antiquities just mentioned, I've found that aging, ever-settling, noisy floorboards are rather pleasing.

Underneath those planks of oak and pine beats the heart of generations of families, and I'm convinced that if a house had a voice, and we humans were quiet long enough to occasionally hear it, the resulting sound would undoubtedly be the intermittent moan and groan of creaky stairs, well-trodden hallways, and stomped-upon foyers. In moments of fancy, I honestly think I can hear messages from our old house, like whispers in the tops of trees in a strong wind.

Unfortunately, my psychic abilities don't seem to translate any of the whispers into intelligible conversation. I haven't seen any ghosts or heard any open doors slam shut or any other stereotypical communication from one world to another, but I keep listening. It seems logical to me that an inanimate object that has served as a mute witness to so many families' secrets would be in some way affected by all the sheer living going on within its walls.

Aside from the obvious characteristics conveyed upon wood and plaster by decorating, furnishing, and the like, each house has its own personality; don't you agree? I've been in houses that felt sad on a gut level, as if not enough sunlight ever streamed in the windows to clear out the shadows or not enough laughter bounced against the walls.

I've been in houses that were exquisitely furnished but still remained lifeless and cold. They seemed to exist only as a backdrop or stage set for characters living out on the fringes, as if the inhabitants of that house had somehow lost their souls to the world around them. Those houses seemed to be only stopping-off places, not homes where you could relax and put your feet up. I've been in small, humble homes that radiated warmth and welcome and seemed to reach out and embrace every person who entered.

I have a theory that every house takes on the personality of its occupants, and even when they die or move away, a little piece of them somehow remains in the house. I'm constantly amazed that in the South, in particular, individuals can live an entire life span in one house. Yet when they die, we rush to bury them, clean out their closets, pass along their jewelry and odd bits of treasure, and within weeks, you can find no trace of the person who lived there for years and years. I, on the other hand, am somehow comforted by the idea of lives that were lived out in the exact same spots where I'm eating, bathing, sleeping, and working.

I wonder about the families who inhabited our house, and I speculate about them often. I look for traces of them in our house, and I am always amazed that there are so few. When I'm searching the attic or basement for some lost item, I stop to pick up old pieces of newspaper and read them, always looking for some sort of connection to the people who used to live here. I pull out a faded piece of Christmas tinsel, and I wonder what their holidays were like. Did they put their Christmas tree near the dining-room window, like we do?

I wonder about their children and imagine where they slept.

I daydream about those women kissing their babies and tucking them into bed, babies who have now grown up, moved away, reared their own children, and died. Did they pace the same long center hallway with sick children and make a long circle to the porch to try and catch a cool night breeze to soothe a fevered child? I think about them wrapping blankets around their children and making them line up outside to watch a meteor shower like I have done.

I wonder who lived in our house during infamous moments in our country's history. I will never forget the bed I was making upstairs when I saw the second plane crash into the World Trade Center on my television screen. I wonder who was living in my house on the morning of December 7, 1941. I imagine the former owners of our house standing at my kitchen sink washing breakfast dishes when they heard the news bulletin on the radio about Pearl Harbor being attacked. The events that shaped their lives were all tied up with the house I now look upon as my home.

I think about the former inhabitants of our house: running to the front door to greet company, helping elderly friends up the steep steps, arranging baskets of flowers on the front porch, picking that horrendous wallpaper for the kitchen, worrying about paying their mortgages, cooking food for their sick neighbors, dressing their daughters for weddings, sending their children to their rooms to think about some misbehavior—all of the daily facets of living that we take for granted but which connect us with those who have literally lain where we have lain.

I hope they loved their house as much as I have loved mine. I hope it was a haven for them when they were tired or dispirited. Somehow, I feel deep down that it was. This house *feels* happy.

Of course, it needs a new roof. For some strange reason, you can't run the dishwasher and the washing machine at the same time. If it sprinkles outside, the lights go out. All of the dining-room windows are painted shut. There are valves for coal furnaces and strange pipes that lead nowhere. There is a mysterious black box with switches that activate nothing we can identify. There is no den, no playroom. The front door dumps you right into the only common living space. You have to practically flirt with one of the toilets to get it to flush. Even though we're surrounded by the most beautiful old oak trees with trunks bigger than my arm span, I am fully aware that if a tornado ever topples one of them (a seasonal hazard where I live), our neighbors will have to come dig us out because we will unquestionably be squashed like insignificant insects.

Still, I love my house. It has character. In fact, I think it has a little piece of each character who ever lived in it. Judging by some of the bizarre quirks in my house, some of our predecessors must have been quite unusual, and I can't really say that we're any less odd. I'm sure the former mistress of this house would be appalled to know that we are storing a lawn mower, yard tools, and sporting equipment in her carriage house. I'm quite confident that she would hate the track lighting some idiot attached to her kitchen ceiling, and I know she wouldn't recognize her basement, which is now home to a television big enough for a pool hall.

I doubt that the creaking floorboards in this house have changed too much over the years. You learn quickly which stair to avoid if you want to escape detection when slipping from one sibling's room to another. Every adult knows to walk on the outside of the stairway from the second floor to the first if you want to avoid waking anyone downstairs. I have personally walked off my frustrations by stomping on the kitchen floor. It is quite possible to shake layers of dust and resounding echoes of disapproval down upon deserving heads in the basement.

I hope when we hand our house over to the next family of occupants that they can feel the good vibrations from our family echoing through the years because we have done so much living and loving inside these walls. We've made a happy family here. We've nurtured children in these rooms. We've worried about friends and relatives, cooked thousands of meals for loved ones, talked through many nights, cried together, and set out from this house to begin every new adventure. I hope there is evidence within these rooms, in the very air that blows through this house, that a family was here, an ordinary family living life to its fullest.

Southern Women & Southern Men

/

A Love Story

One of the sweetest true love stories I know has a ninety-two-year-old man and his eighty-eight-year-old wife as the male and female leads. They have been married for sixty-six years.

They have no children, only each other, and the old man now has Alzheimer's disease with only moments of clear lucidity.

They sit together all day, usually in one room. The wife still takes care of her husband with a little help, and they still maintain all the Southern trappings of gentility in their conversations with one another.

The well-read wife has kept a journal for over fifty years marking the important happenings in her life and her country. I know I am not the only member of her family dying to read those journals.

My favorite observation about their marriage occurred one day when the husband's vacant-looking face suddenly lit up with pleasure when he heard his wife coming down the hall to join him. "I hear those sweet feet," he said.

On another occasion, the wife related that, suddenly, out of the blue, her husband said, "Honey, you sure are beautiful."

She responded, "Now, you know I've never been beautiful."

He was quick to add, "You have *always* been beautiful."

Can you imagine your ninety-two-year-old husband saying that to you when you are eighty-eight?

In Love in a Movie

One of my favorite movie lines is uttered by Rosie O'Donnell, playing Becky, to Meg Ryan's character, Annie, in the 1993 movie, *Sleepless in Seattle*. Becky says: "You don't want to be in love. You want to be in love *in a movie*."

I know exactly what she means. Every woman I know wants to be in love in a movie. Movie love is perfect. Invariably, the romantic leads are gorgeous and thin with toned bodies that could (and sometimes do) model underwear in magazines. Every little hitch the romance runs into can usually be worked out in two hours. If not, and true love is destined to be cheated by death, self-sacrifice, world wars, the other woman, or some other tweak of fate, you just know those two souls are going to be together in heaven (or elsewhere) for eternity. In the meantime, you will thoroughly enjoy sobbing your way through the credits.

Of course, if it's one of those dark, depressing, social conscience–raising movies where everybody is going to die, give up, lose, fail, or get murdered, lost, or forgotten; if justice is destined to remain underserved, and moviegoers will leave hopeless and frustrated, well, just don't go to those movies is my advice. We're all familiar with the chronic-illness, cheating-husband, lost-your-job, beyond broke, misbehaving-children, regular-life dramas.

That's not entertaining at all. Most of us are looking for something more in two hours of movie escapism. We want to see people who are better looking than we are, characters that have buckets of money to lavish on their lovers, and problems that can be satisfactorily resolved by killing off the right people or serving up a pie in the face of those who are just asking for it. We expect the wrath of God and of vengeful lovers to come down on every villain in sight. We want our characters to get what is coming to them for good or for ill. That so rarely happens in the real world. As soon as the movie is over, we're all going back to regular life. Going to the movies is supposed to be *fun*.

It is obvious to me that some Hollywood types need a refresher course in fun. They need to work through their personal issues with a psychiatrist on their own time. If I'm paying ten bucks a pop to see a movie and eat Junior Mints, I want to have a little fun doing it. I think that Hollywood powerbrokers see themselves as a tad more enlightened than the rest of us. They're above *fun* in the sense that we, the people, understand fun. They think they know more than the rest of us—about everything. Just ask them. These days, they even tell us how to vote. Why in the world should I care about what some movie actor thinks about politics? For the record, I don't care what politicians think about movies either.

I'll never forget the first film my oldest son saw that didn't end in happily-ever-after bliss. A responsible parent would have warned him about the finale in *Old Yeller*, but I didn't. (He's our firstborn. We're learning as we go along.) "You mean the boy has to shoot his own dog?!" my son asked, askance. "This is a terrible movie! Why in the world would anybody want to *watch* this?"

"Welcome to the world of big boy movies," I replied.

Grown-up women never outgrow the need for romance in their lives or their movies. It's not just sentimental fluff for wispy ingénues. Even those of us who have been happily married for years and years still long to be in love in a movie. That's why we flock to all those chick flicks that our husbands don't want to see. Men want to see things blow up. Women want to see romantic movies that inspire deep sighing and wonderful fanta-sies. I guess the theory here is that if the need for romance isn't fulfilled in real life, then we're looking to make up the deficit with the big screen. (Yes, sometimes we want to see things blow up, too. A lot depends on the guy doing the blowing up.)

There is one day in every woman's life, usually when she's in her thirties or forties—even if she's happily married, has great kids, fulfilling work and friendships, the whole shebang—when she realizes: This Is It.

I had my This-Is-It moment one day when I was washing dishes in the kitchen sink. "How did this happen???" I wondered. One minute I remember saying, "I do," and the next minute I was washing four loads of laundry a day and going to Little League baseball games on my anniversary.

The This-Is-It moment is earth-shattering. Never again, the woman realizes, will she share a first kiss. (Well, okay, if her hus-band keels over or divorces her she might, but I'm not looking for trouble here.) Never again will passion be new. No man will ever touch her face again as if she is the most exquisite woman on earth. Odds are, her husband will only stroke her face if he's wiping hotdog mustard off her chin.

I'm not going to even address how the This-Is-It moment causes some women to fly off the rails into a full-scale midlife crisis. I'm just not qualified. These are merely my personal obser-vations on daily life, but remember—I pay attention. I'm not pass-ing out excuses for adultery either. All I am saying is that for some of us this never-again deal is BIG.

Even if you love your husband half to death like I do and wouldn't cheat on him with anyone on earth (assuming, and this is a big assumption, that there is someone out there who would be interested in cheating with you), the fact that all that romance is over except for vicarious experiences in books and movies, well, that just about breaks my heart.

However, in a column marked "Rare, Guilt-free Exceptions," I advise you to come up with a freebie list for you and your spouse. This is a list of four or five people who your spouse has virtually no possibility of ever actually meeting in this lifetime. If by some miraculous occurrence the two do meet, and that person is dying to cuddle up with your beloved, then you promise to grant that match freebie status. If, for example, the number-one name on my list, Pierce Brosnan—the prettiest man on the face of the earth—should by some inexplicable quirk of fate ever have occasion to place his perfect lips on mine, I have my husband's permission to go ahead and smooch him right back.

My husband has his own freebie list, naturally, and I have to say I am just mystified by some of his choices, but since they're *his* fantasies and I don't have to kiss any of them, what the heck difference does it make? My husband and I have talked many times about the movie *Indecent Proposal*. In this movie Robert Redford offers Demi Moore a million dollars to spend one night with him. That's right, a million dollars to become the lover of— not the neighborhood troll—but Robert Redford. Maybe after twenty years, my husband and I have just been married too long to get it. We can't see the problem, and we've spent some quality time discussing it. Now if it had been the husband offering the wife a million dollars not to take Robert Redford (who was probably way up there on her freebie list) up on his offer, we'd understand the moral dilemma.

My theory is that after years of living together, we love our husbands (those of us who've made it this far) more deeply than we ever could have imagined when we first married them, but I'm not sure about the "in love" part. I know there are times, moments, days or nights when the in-love part feels real, intense, and passionate like it did when we were dating, but it's not part of daily life anymore for most of us, and I think that is just a shame.

I have a friend who believes women actually go through a grieving process when they realize This Is It. No one else is ever going to gaze at us with the focus of a laser beam or sweep us off our feet for a night of no-holds-barred passion. This is assuming, of course, that any of us could actually be *swept* anymore. I'm afraid I'd have to be thrown over the average man's shoulder like 130 pounds of fertilizer, and that's just so depressing I don't know what to say. In a movie, on the other hand, I'd be swept into my hero's arms while wearing a particularly flattering, Medieval-styled velvet gown, which would trail along a flower-strewn path behind us on the way to our romantic bower. I'm almost sure there isn't a flower-strewn path within miles of here, and I don't know a single straight man who has ever used the word "strewn" or "bower."

The truth is that I wouldn't really change anything big about my life. (Well, okay the bank account has room for improvement, and I would definitely not have this nose in a movie.) Even though This Is It, I've discovered that "It" is pretty darn good. It takes years of living with someone, holding a cloth to their foreheads when they throw up—that sort of thing—to build a love that isn't dependent on beauty, good health, or money. Being married to a true friend is the best feeling in the world, but sometimes, when I read a great love story or go see an epic, big-screen romantic movie, I remember what it felt like to be young and in love for the first time. There's nothing else like it. I can't help wanting to feel that way again.

Writers have made fortunes penning self-help books on how to put the sizzle back into the sex lives of happily married folk, but what I'm talking about is much bigger than sex. It's intensity, really—an intimate, almost telepathic tunnel vision between lovers—that makes us feel beautiful, immortal, as if we could shoot right up through the stratosphere.

I have noticed that everyone knows at least one couple that defies the odds. They are the exception that proves the rule, and I find them utterly fascinating to watch. The couple I know seems, to this day, twenty years into their marriage, to remain besotted with each other. I love to watch the way that man looks at his wife. Every other woman in the room is invisible to him. (I admit, I find this a little irritating since he is exceedingly handsome, and I think we should all be able to enjoy him from a respectable distance without having to set our hair on fire to get his attention.) Like most happily married people, this couple is a great addition to a dinner party, but it makes me wistful to see the way they go out of their way to touch each other on the leg, the arm—nothing like a disgusting and juvenile public display of affection—as a reminder, a touchstone, an "I'm here" reassurance for one another.

Some romances are just bigger than life—Lucille Ball and Desi Arnaz, Anthony and Cleopatra, Paris and Helen of Troy. Of course, those self-absorbed romantics wrought a whole lot of havoc in other people's lives because of their single-minded pursuit of one another, but oh, my—to be someone's one-and-only for a lifetime.

Surefire Ways to a SWAG's Heart

Do something nice for her mother or sister. (This is sneaky but foolproof.)

Send her flowers for no reason at all. (Of course, I know how corny this is. It works. That's how it got to *be* corny.)

Clean out her basement, garage, attic—whatever is in dire need of excavation. (Here's the tricky part: Do it without being asked. Trust me on this one. Your wildest fantasies are about to come true.)

Ask her about her day. Listen attentively as she answers. Voluntarily contribute information about your own day to the conversation. Make eye contact. If you really want to go for broke, rub her feet while you do this. (This is worth a dessert of your choice.)

Reach for her hand, and hold it for ten whole minutes while walking down a public street. (The handholding must appear to be willing, spontaneous, and heartfelt. If you grab her by the arm because she's about to be run over by a garbage truck, it doesn't count.)

Look shocked when she flips through the family photo album and groans at the sight of her pregnant silhouette. Tell her she never looked more beautiful to you than she did then. (There is no limit on how many times you can repeat this compliment. Positive results guaranteed. Use freely with pre- and post-menopausal women.)

No matter what she asks you about her weight, her hair, her mother, or her sister (a) she has never looked fat to you; (b) her hair always looks great; (c) she is 100% right in every fight with her mother, sister, mother-in-law, or best friend. In fact, you should throw in that they are probably just jealous of the aforementioned great hair or light-as-a-feather weight.

Fix something around her house that has been driving her crazy for years—like glass doorknobs that fall off for no reason at all. (Be prepared for her to agree to marry you on the spot and offer to bear your children.)

Run a bubble bath for her; fill the room with lighted candles (make sure she's not allergic to scented candles, and avoid those that smell like food products—like peach, vanilla, cake batter—because they disgust me, and they *should* disgust everyone else). Place a glass of her favorite wine, a bar of her favorite chocolate, and a best-selling book on the side of the tub. CAUTION—Know your SWAG in book selection. If you pick a Tom Clancy bestseller, and you haven't noticed that she's not that kind of girl, you may have just blown the whole deal right there. For example, I'd be tickled pink with *National Geographic* or *Smithsonian* to unwind, but *Ladies Home Journal* is not going to light my fire, and I'm going to have to reevaluate our whole relationship if you are ignorant of this.

Attend to her motoring needs. Suppress the desire for adolescent snickering here. I mean (a) fill her gas tank for her when it's empty, so she doesn't have to fill up on her way to work and reek of gas fumes all day; (b) start her car for her in the morning, so it's warm and defrosted when she gets in; or (c) if you're looking for something a little more glamorous in the motoring category, buy her some great shades and a silk scarf like Grace Kelly wore for motoring in her royal convertible.

Notice how incredibly cheap, universally appealing, readily available, fairly quick, and totally painless the path of true love can be.

Feel free to thank me by the pound in milk chocolate.

The One Thing

In moments of Pinot Grigio–induced wisdom, I have been known to expound upon one of my core beliefs about a successful marriage. Although marriages come in all shapes, sizes, and flavors, I firmly believe that every pair of lovers shares The One Thing.

The One Thing is impossible to define. It can be as small as the endearing way a lock of hair falls across your husband's forehead or the indefinable comfort conveyed by the weight of a wife's hand resting on the back of her husband's neck. The One Thing represents the connection two happily married people feel. It is immediately obvious when a couple lacks this, and its presence makes those who long for The One Thing in their own marriages to gaze wistfully at strange couples in restaurants who have it. In their togetherness, these couples seem to embody all that is missing in those marriages that have lost their magic somewhere along the way.

I think The One Thing is what keeps us going when life throws terrible obstacles in our paths. The One Thing has probably saved more marriages than all the counseling sessions in the world. It is somehow impossible to remain angry with someone whose smallest gesture can reduce you to tears, and I think that's probably an innately good thing.

Recently, the husband of a friend who was trying to patch up a marital spat asked me the question that every woman I know has been asked by the husband of a good friend at least once in her adult life: "I just don't understand. What does she *want?*"

To answer, I always pour another glass of Pinot Grigio and begin by asking the husband to tell me about The One Thing in his marriage. Believe it or not, sometimes this actually works. Most of the time, though, the husband asks me something like: "So— you don't think this will all blow over if I bring her flowers or something?"

Sleeping With a Snoring Man

I have been married for almost twenty years. I have a long-term investment in my husband. I do not plan to ever divorce him. When asked about our marriage, I always say: "I may kill the man, but I am never going to divorce him." (I want to point out right here that this is *humor*. I agree with Jill Conner Browne, her majesty, the top-dog Sweet Potato Queen of the world, that "we really can't kill 'em even if they're asking for it." In fact, I agree with almost everything that Ms. Browne writes; I just don't have the nerve to say it the way she does. I'd have to wash my mouth out with soap.)

The very idea of starting over with another man, new in-laws and relatives, and all the other baggage that goes along with getting married again is enough to make me take to my bed with a box of chocolate and a good book. My hat is off to women who are willing to take on a whole new man project and train up another one starting from scratch, but I just don't have another round of youthful enthusiasm in me. If anything ever happens to my husband, I'm going to be one of those little old ladies who travels around in packs with her friends, drinks in the afternoons, watches television reruns, and wears sweatpants unashamedly in public. I think that'd be fun.

If I ever did divorce my easy-going, responsible, generally good-egg husband, it would be in a fit of chronic-sleep-deprived exhaustion, and I would insist that right there on the front of the final judgment, those divorce papers would cite in capital letters the cause of our irretrievable marital breakdown: SNORING.

Those of you who have lived with a snorer need no further explanation. You have walked in my bedroom slippers. You will not think it is unreasonable to divorce an otherwise delightful husband because he snores like a foghorn. Those of you who have never lived with a husband, father, or brother who snored as only a man can snore may need a little education about this issue. I am *just* the woman to provide it.

One of the most frustrating aspects of living with a chronic snorer is that snoring is an accidental, unconscious (literally) act of pure torture. To all outward appearances, the snorer is sleeping like a baby and cannot be accused of malice aforethought. (I know; I know; snoring can be a sign of sleep apnea, a serious medical condition, but that is another chapter. I'm not interested in the snorer's problems in this article. This is all about the snorer's *victims*.)

It takes my husband all of fifteen seconds to fall asleep at night. I'm not exaggerating in the least. It has been my experience that only men and innocent infants can fall asleep that quickly. You expect me to be happy for him, don't you? Well, I'm not. I know what you're thinking; you think I'm jealous, and you're right. I'm a big enough person to admit it.

I have great difficulty falling asleep, and I have a number of girlfriends who complain about the same problem. I think back over every conversation of the day, begin planning my to-do list for the next morning, worry illogically about every person I love, and require a little decompression conversation to wind down enough to flirt with the sandman.

Not true for my husband. That man is sawing logs before I can get my reading glasses off my nose and the covers adjusted to my satisfaction. So inadvertently, just because he was kissed by the genetic, good-sleep fairy and can fall asleep in mid-sentence, my husband enrages me every night by falling asleep as soon as his head touches his pillow and immediately commencing a snoring routine that sounds like jackhammers breaking up concrete. This behavior guarantees that there is no possibility that I will fall asleep—even if I am exhausted—because of the noise pollution on the pillow next to me. Even if the big lump stops snoring, my teeth are usually so tightly clenched by this point that I'm hours away from dropping off.

Perhaps the most irritating common denominator of snorers is that no matter how many times you shake them awake and tell them that they are snoring, they always deny that they were even asleep. I've talked to other women about this, and the typical scenario goes like this: Wife wakes up husband and says, not very nicely, "Roll over. You're *snoring*." Husband always replies—you guessed it—"I wasn't even asleep!"

Those are fighting words at my house. As far as I'm concerned, once my husband utters those words, the glove has been thrown down, and I'm free to get the fly swatter and smack him on the forehead every time I hear him snort. I've tried to reason logically with my husband regarding this issue. I've said, "Right, honey, for kicks I've just been laying here waiting for you to go to sleep so that I can make up a story about your snoring. That's really fun for me. Why in the world would I wake you up if you weren't really snoring???"

When whining to a friend about my snoring-husband problem, I confessed sheepishly that I was tempted to use a tape recorder to tape his snoring to play back to him in the morning, so he could hear how loud it really is.

"Did it," she said.

"Really?" I asked, "What did he say?"

"He said I was turning the volume up to make it sound worse."

Figures. Typical snorer denial.

Another obnoxious thing snorers do is to fall back asleep within seconds of being woken up and begin snoring *again*, before you, the injured party, can rearrange your pillow and lay your head back down to try and fall asleep again yourself. Snorers are utterly callous. This is the point when I usually lose every trace of civility. I leap out of bed screeching like a cornered monkey, pull the covers off my husband's snuggly body, and demand that he go elsewhere—anywhere else—to sleep. There is nothing like chronic exhaustion to make me lose my manners.

The most insidious thing snorers do is to vary the pattern of their snoring. At some point, every long-suffering spouse theorizes that maybe she can learn to live with it. The reasoning behind this theory is that, eventually, one can train oneself to tune the sound out—like city dwellers who no longer hear sirens and traffic noises and actually miss them when sleeping in a quiet location.

The problem with these sneaky snorers, of course, is that they never maintain a steady rhythm. They snore a few steady breaths and then fall silent. You begin to hope you've hit a lucky night, and maybe there won't even be any more snoring. Your mental defenses go down; you begin to relax, and then a loud, discordant, double-nostril snort starts the snorer off again. It's almost like they want you to stay awake and watch their eyelids reflect restful REM sleep mode. It makes you wonder if snorers are really just hogs for attention.

I'm ashamed to confess that I have lain awake, stared at my big snoring husband, and had all sorts of shameful thoughts float through my mind. I can't help but speculate about whether anyone has ever smothered a snorer in his sleep. You can see the temptation. If I drew a jury with at least six women with snoring spouses, I think I could get off without any hard prison time. In the daylight, of course, all this seems a tad over the top, but at 3:00 AM all bets are off.

Things Southern Women Find Suspicious

Anyone who dislikes small children or animals.

Perfectly healthy women who voluntarily choose to
dispense with wearing makeup in public
on a regular basis.

Sushi. We call that delicacy "bait" down here.

Southerners who eat fried chicken with a fork. We'd
like to see their birth certificates.

People who don't have any relatives we've ever met
socially, gone to school with, gone to church with, or
heard gossip about at the Piggly Wiggly.

Bartenders who don't know how to make
a good mimosa.

New husbands who have a "great" relationship
with their ex-wives.

Biscuits in a can.

Recipes from Yankees that claim "feeds twelve easily."

Children who fail to say "yes, ma'am" and don't
get scowled at when they forget.

Southern men who are somehow always free to go to football games on weekends but inexplicably busy when their wives' cousins are getting married.

Clothing labels that say "dry clean only." We just know we can wash anything.

Beauty treatments that promise to make us look instantly younger, healthier, or thinner. (Although if the price is right, we'll give it a try.)

Bottled water. I ask you, has there ever been a more successful case of international fraud?

Old people's cooking. It pays to check underneath those dumplings.

Grocers who say their tomatoes are "homegrown" even though they have Guatemalan stickers on them.

People selling "fresh" shrimp one thousand miles from the nearest body of water.

Call waiting. I mean, what's the point? You can't talk to both parties at the same time; that infernal clicking is just so annoying, and it's just so rude.

Dr. Stone and Wife

One evening, my husband and I went out to dinner with friends to celebrate our mutual wedding anniversaries. In the restaurant, my eyes were instantly drawn to a group of stained-glass windows across the room, obviously salvaged from a church no longer standing (I hope), which were appealingly positioned to catch the late-afternoon sun.

My initial response was to wince a bit at the juxtaposition of the church windows and the long bar of the restaurant. Although aesthetically appealing, it seemed a bit unseemly to watch someone belly up to the bar for a Corona in the filtered light of a church window.

I felt the urge to scoot my chair back a bit in case God decided to send a little lightning down to protest the way his sacred icons had been recycled for a bit of interior decorating. Surely, there are just some things that one shouldn't be able to buy at a garage sale—you know, blood products, newborn babies, and, perhaps, religious artifacts. I could just hear God saying, "So, you were looking for a little atmosphere with leftover items from one of my churches? I'll give you atmosphere!"

The sun was just setting, and the light created a kaleidoscope of magnificent colors. It wasn't until then that I noticed the most curious detail. At the bottom of the window where the dedication is customarily found, were the words "Dr. Stone and wife." Not "Dr. and Mrs. Stone," but "Dr. Stone and wife." I had to smile. Fifteen years ago that would have infuriated me. "And wife" was, of course, some flesh-and-blood woman reduced to "and wife" in stained glass for eternity. Now I see things a bit differently. I am willing to bet that "and wife" was a force to be reckoned with in her own right. I know she was much more than a nameless label or a mere appendage to her husband's name.

Southern women have always been particularly good at rising above their labels. After all, we all know women who are powerful forces in the community going about their business right out in public with names like Bitsy, Bebe, Mimi, Mamie, Sweetie, Bunny, Baby, Sister, and my personal favorite generational addition to these classics—Aunt Sister. These nicknames haven't slowed them down a bit. I guess if you begin your life with an albatross of nomenclature, you just have to toughen up early and develop some backbone.

Besides, in the South, even if you avoid a pet name, you are almost guaranteed to have a double name that will please both grandmothers and cement two sides of the family. You are bound to be way behind those Yankee first graders who can spell "Lisa" and "Sue" before you can measure out how much space you need to write your double name.

I guess that is why in the 1970s when so many women refused to take their husbands' names in marriage, it didn't catch on that fast down here. There was just already so much fuss attached to who you were named for and why, that adding your husband's surname to your own was simply a monogramming issue rather than a feminist debate. (After all, at least when you marry, you choose to take that particular man's name as opposed to keeping another man's name—your father's—just because you were born with it.) Anyway, I think most Southern women just couldn't be bothered with any more naming discussions, considering the fact that they would still be "Honey," "Angel," or "Sweet Thing" to every person within one hundred miles regardless of which last name they chose.

Southern women can rise above trivialities, and although I'm sure that Dr. Stone was probably a fine physician or academic, my guess is that "and wife" wore a lot more hats—wife, mother, housekeeper, hostess, community volunteer, church worker, school helper, the list could go on ad nauseam. In fact, I'll bet the farm that she was the one who ordered that stained-glass window, took the check to the church, and organized the dedication in the church bulletin. She may have arranged flowers and candles in front of that window for Christmas and for the weddings of her children or grandchildren.

Of course, I am merely speculating. She may have been a community saint. Then again, she may have had bats in her belfry. She may have divorced Dr. Stone, hired herself a crew of construction workers, and personally supervised the demolition of the church wall containing *her* window in a fury only imagined by those who have not personally witnessed a Southern woman throwing a full-scale fit.

We'll just never know what "and wife" was like, but it sure is fun to imagine.

Things a Southern Woman Could Live Without

Yankees who equate her accent with a low IQ.

Men who refer to her as "little lady" even
when she's forty.

Wedding invitations from people she has never met.

Snooty sales clerks who are too busy talking among
themselves to actually sell her anything.

Humid weather that makes her hair frizzy
and her face shine.

Hot summer days that make her want to take root in a
porch swing and have an admirer fan her.

Patronizing Southern men who interrupt her sentences.

Parents who fail to teach their children good manners.

Men—not gentlemen, of course—who wear hats inside.

Sales calls during dinnertime—or any other time.

People who don't write thank-you notes.

Drivers waiting for parking spaces who honk impatiently
at mommies struggling to fasten children in safety seats.

News crews who search trailer parks for women in hair
curlers and beer-bellied men in overalls to interview
about the state of the New South.

Dinner guests who say they're on a diet after she's slaved
all day cooking a divine, fat-gram-loaded,
deep-fried, Southern feast for them.

Are You a Kappa Kappa Gamma?

As an undergraduate member of a sorority, one becomes accustomed to college faculty members and administrators who are hostile to Greek organizations. It's one of those elitist intellectual snobberies that is often based on ignorance, sour grapes (no luck going through rush themselves), or, less often, genuine misunderstandings and, occasionally, heartfelt beliefs about social groups in general. I'd be a bit more sympathetic to these critics if they weren't such hypocrites—eager to use the Greek system's workforce whenever they need volunteers to organize, staff, and help run campus activities, but quick to dismiss or disparage the good things Greek organizations do for students and their schools.

Let me be up-front about this: I *loved* being in a sorority; it was a positive experience for me in every way. It was good for me academically. It was good for me socially. And it was fun. That's not a sin, you know.

Nowadays, when I run into an adult who is condescending about sororities, I rarely take the time to respond. I figure those people should take up their pet issues with someone who cares. Recently, however, I couldn't resist the temptation to set the record straight when a man I'd never met before eavesdropped on a conversation I was having with another woman about a new sorority chapter and interrupted us theatrically to say: "Oh, *please*, don't tell me you are one of those women who was in a sorority!"

I looked him over carefully, trying to give him the benefit of the doubt in case he'd had a few toddies too many. Out of the corner of my eye, I could see my friend backing away, shaking her head sadly at the ignorance of the poor slob who was about to be subjected to a little Southern-style consciousness-raising session.

"I'm a Kappa," I said in a neutral voice, giving him a chance to pull out of this nosedive if he wanted to.

"Oooh! Do you sing that *'Kappa, Kappa, Kappa Gamma, I am so happy that I am a Kappa Kappa Kappa Gamma'* song?"

"Actually, yes. I was teaching that song to my daughter just the other day, as a matter of fact. Why do you ask?" I questioned in my most frigid tone of voice.

"Oh. You have kids? I just moved here, and I'm looking for a pediatrician for my children. No one seems to be taking new patients. Can you recommend someone?"

"No problem. I know a Kappa who is a pediatrician. I'll call her. I can also find a heart surgeon, a real-estate agent, a school superintendent, a florist, an attorney, an FBI field-office director, and a state senator if I need them—all Kappas. You see, while all those fraternity boys were drinking beer and throwing things off balconies, we sorority girls were exchanging class notes, tutoring at-risk kids in the community, and building lifelong friendships. I can go anywhere in the world and find a group of Kappas who will help me."

"Well, I wouldn't want *my* daughter to be in a sorority!" the man added, not sure whether he'd just been insulted or not.

"Well, that's the beauty of the system. No one is forced to participate."

The man turned to walk away.

"By the way," I added, "If you ever need a marriage counselor, I know *just* the person."

(I was thinking gleefully of my militant feminist Kappa friend from California who would give this jerk a real earful about what it means to be supportive of women in our society.)

"I'm divorced," the man added.

What a surprise, I thought.

You Know You're a Bossy Southern Woman If...

You've ever tucked a strange woman's tag down inside her shirt for her—without being asked.

You've straightened pictures on the walls of your doctor's waiting room.

You've offered a stranger unsolicited advice about the present he is picking out for his wife.

You've talked about potty-training methods with a stranger while waiting in line for movie tickets.

You talk back to the radio and television and shake your finger at them in frustration.

You nod your head in agreement during church services.

You've forced a stranger's child to hold your hand when crossing a street.

After watching an inept employee bungle the job, you've offered to wrap your own present in a store that offers giftwrapping.

You can go into any nursing home in your state and feel comfortable striking up a conversation with someone else's mother.

You've told someone in the grocery store the best way to prepare some food item he or she is purchasing.

You feel the urge to bake a pound cake after reading the obituaries in the newspaper.

A Full Nest

Watching Caterpillars

Finally. I was finished with the monthly agony, the awful family chore of coordinating everyone's schedules on my calendar so that eighteen patriotic cupcakes arrived at the appointed hour in the appropriate child's classroom, etc., etc., blah, blah, blah. For the next hour and twenty minutes, I was free of extraneous and annoying household duties.

"Want to do something?" I asked my three-year-old from the mature auspices of my comfortable position on the porch swing. All I could see of my child was the backs of her legs, a hem that was partially coming out (mental note: fix hem), and white eyelet panties, size three. Her hands were supporting her weight on the floor of the porch, and her face was pressed low to the ground, getting a bug's eye view.

"I'm already doing somethin'," she answered.

"What are you doing?" I asked delicately so as not to offend.

"I'm watchin' this calerpillar," she said, as if speaking to a half-wit.

"What's it doing?" I asked, mildly curious.

"Mostly crawling. Sometimes stops and feels around for a while."

"Oh," I answered brilliantly, having exhausted my supply of

caterpillar conversation. "Do you want to do something with me?"

"You can watch calerpillars with me if you want to," she offered generously.

"Okay. Why not?" I decided.

"Sweetie, do they do anything else, these caterpillars of yours?"

A little face looked at me between white eyelet panties and dirty brown feet:

"Mommy," she said, "A little less talkin' and a little more watchin' with calerpillars."

Point taken. A simple summer pleasure. Time well spent.

Sounds of Children

Perhaps because I am so nearsighted that some friends have suggested I buy a dog and cane rather than new glasses, I have always been more attuned to the sound something makes rather than how it looks or feels.

On the one hand, this is a good thing because I can easily summon up sound memories of waterfalls, ocean surf, and other calming, naturally occurring sound effects whenever I need a moment of introspection in the midst of chattering children.

On the other hand, for people like me who are particularly sound sensitive, there's a fairly steep downside. Of all the parenting challenges I have faced, my children's tendency to produce repetitive, meaningless, and utterly baffling, nonstop noises is the one thing that may result in my eventual retirement to the nut house. Unfortunately, repetitive noises, in all their vast range of decibel and offensiveness, go hand in hand with children like spilled milk, snotty noses, and candy disputes.

Before I had children of my own, I assumed that children purposefully made noise constantly, and I resolved that *my* children would never make such silly and obnoxious noises. (That was just one of many pre-children resolutions that later provided comic relief for me and my husband.) After all, I reasoned—as a childless person living in a cocoon of luxurious silence on demand—how could human beings, even children, be so completely unselfconscious that they would not notice if they had been bouncing a tennis ball off their bedroom ceiling for forty-five minutes?

How, indeed, could a four-year-old tell the same knock-knock joke to his brother 137 times in a row and still find it wildly amusing?

Why do children ask the same questions repeatedly, without respite, for weeks on end, without any hope of receiving a different answer? You know the kind of question I mean, something along the lines of: "Can we have ice cream and Coke for supper tonight? Can we? Can we?"

How many times can a parent listen to the ABC song sung back to back before breaking out into a rash?

The tendency of children to make repetitive noises utilizing toys, furniture, and their own body parts, as well as those of others in close proximity, has made my eyes roll back in my head and the muscles in my face begin to twitch.

I defy any adult, while driving a car, to listen to forty-eight rounds of dwarf wannabes singing *"hi-ho, hi-ho, it's off to work we go"* without threatening to abandon the parenting ship.

If all other distractions fail, children trapped in a car will resort to counting how many times they can bang their heads against the backs of their booster seats before their parents' heads explode. Or they count how many times they can snap their fingers while making clicking sounds with their tongues. Or they experiment with how much saliva it takes to write their full names on the car windows in squeaky streaks of spit—*anything* to avoid silence.

Children are innately anti-silence. Before they are born, some mischievous angel whispers into their tiny ears: "Now remember, your job is to make noise—wherever, whenever. That is your mission!" If nothing else comes to mind, children will induce a coughing fit to fill up dead air.

In the grocery store—where I have been known to come home

with eggplants and bubblegum-flavored oatmeal for dinner—I have begged my children for a few minutes of silence with words like, "Please! Mommy needs a few minutes of quiet."

"Why?" one of my children asks suspiciously.

"Because Mommy can't think when all of you are talking to me, and we are going to have to make peppermint pancakes for supper if you don't let me find the ingredients I need," I reply.

"Well, we don't like peppermint pancakes, do we? Have we ever made peppermint pancakes before?" another demands.

"No, sweetie," I reply. "Mommy was being silly."

"I have!" my third child insists dramatically. "I've had peppermint pancakes about twenty-eleven times!"

"No, you haven't!" another argues.

You can guess how the conversation degenerates from there. On the days I go to the grocery store and spend $250 on groceries, we usually have cheese toast and yogurt for supper.

I never cease to be amazed that all three of my children can talk to me and to each other simultaneously, and they seem not to be the least bit bothered by the cacophony that results. I have a headache almost every day from the sheer concentration required to follow all the threads of their overlapping non sequiturs so that I may respond as quickly as possible to avoid the repetition of long, complicated stories that seem to go nowhere and make no point.

I say, "Hmm, that's interesting," *a lot*.

There are other earsplitting sounds that only human children can produce. The full-bodied wail of a mad, hungry, or frightened baby is a remarkable testimony to the power of human lungs. A baby weighing less than ten pounds can empty a restaurant, church, or waiting room in less than five minutes, and we're talking about adults who can easily tune out city sirens warning them of approaching tornadoes.

Fortunately, for all the bad sounds I associate with children, they produce some good sounds, too. The good sounds are, in fact, so pleasing that we adults are tricked into having more children and even into keeping the ones we have who continue to make irritating, repetitive noises. There is nothing in the world that compares to the months when your preverbal baby looks you straight in the eyes, sometimes grabbing your face or pointing emphatically with a chubby finger, while babbling some serious-sounding sentences of unintelligible baby talk with every expectation of being understood.

The first time you see a fat little cherub in a diaper crack up laughing aloud with an ear-to-ear grin and baby drool running down his or her chin, you discover a sound you will do almost anything to hear repeated. This results, of course, in obnoxious, repetitive baby talking by adults who croon to finger-sucking babblers, and the whole vicious noise cycle begins again.

When children first say your name, tell you they love you, and begin uttering the endless stream of questions that is the hallmark of toddlers worldwide, the noise level somehow becomes more tolerable.

If you dare to close your eyes long enough to appreciate the sounds of children playing in the ocean or building castles on a beach, their collective voice is at once stimulating and comforting.

One of the best sounds is of children playing outside on summer evenings. The ebb and flow of their voices calling to each other over the sound of crickets rubbing their hind legs together is the sound personification of summer in the South. The sounds children make as they learn and grow reflect the entire life cycle of humans—sometimes strident, often silly or disconnected or alternatively demanding and questioning. At their most charming, children make sounds that are the epitome of sweet innocence and abject wonder. I have to constantly remind myself that *all* of these sounds are a healthy part of growing up.

Who knew that child rearing would be such a noisy business?

Things Not to Say to a New Mother

Do you work? (May provoke violence)

Did you plan this baby? (None of
your business if you weren't in on conception)

Were you trying for a boy/girl? (Staggering sexism)

I'm glad he/she/they are yours and not mine!
(Generally, so is the mother)

Are all those children yours? (Offensive
unless you are a census taker)

When my children were young...(Snore)

He/she is hungry/tired/teething/thirsty. (Unsolicited
advice should be punished by instant death.)

Are you free for lunch? (In a galaxy far, far away)

Can he/she have a piece of candy? (Usually the choking
hazard is unwrapped and in the child's
mouth at this point.)

If he/she were my child...(Heard it)

Is he/she always like this? (Unless you mean
it in a good way)

Can I hold the baby? (After a brief medical history)

The Pear Tree

I am often reminded of the awesome responsibility of parenting, and the absolute nature of my power as a parent is frequently reinforced by a firsthand experience that does not reflect very well upon me. All I can say in my defense is that I am learning as much from my children as they are from me, and, well, I'm doing the best I can.

In one memorable episode, I was trying to finish baking cookies for a school fund-raiser when I was interrupted for about the millionth time by the slamming of my front door and the excited stammer of my four-year-old who wanted to know if I had seen the pears on our pear tree. Without even granting him the favor of looking up from my all-important mixing of the dough, I first admonished him for running in the house and then informed him that we don't have a pear tree in our yard—or any other fruit tree, for that matter. There was a moment of silence, and when I looked up, his face was completely crestfallen.

"But I see pears, Mommy."

I added, just to squelch the next inevitable question, "Son, we do not have a pear tree, so you couldn't possibly have seen any pears!"

My son looked at me for a few more seconds and then wandered rather aimlessly back outside.

A short time later, while I was changing sheets in one of the bedrooms, I could see my son and the neighbor's gardener having a serious conversation near the bedroom window.

The window was open just enough for me to hear my son tell him, "You see that? Those aren't bananas, are they? They aren't apples either, and they are not pears because my mama said we DO NOT have a pear tree."

I watched the gardener squint up into the branches of a tree, look back down at my son, and say, "Are you sure? Those look like pears to me."

"Yes, but they're not," assured my son. "My mama said they aren't."

And with that, he was off to play, and I was left to sit on my freshly made bed to contemplate the rather impressive boughs of a pear tree so heavily laden with fruit God would have been proud to plant it in the Garden of Eden.

Kissing that parent-of-the-year award good-bye for yet another year, I went to find my four-year-old to tell him just how wrong big people can be.

Together we found a ladder, picked a bountiful harvest from our pear tree, and peeled and sliced them together to make a pear cobbler. I like to think that pear cobbler tasted especially sweet to my son who was able to relate gleefully to anyone who would listen the story of finding a pear tree in our yard that his own mother didn't even know about, and how his mommy was wrong, wrong, wrong about that pear tree.

I like to think he learned from my crummy-parenting day the lesson that everyone makes mistakes—even mommies.

Your Mama Was Right When She Said

Date your friends. (You won't have to divorce a stranger later.)

Don't burn your bridges. (It makes them awfully hot when you have to cross them later.)

One day you won't even remember his name! (You'll just remember that he was a jerk.)

What goes around comes around. (It may take a while.)

Wear sunscreen. (You will one day discover that you are not immortal.)

A woman should dress her age. (Only two-year-olds are as young and cute as they think they are.)

Be nice to old people. (With luck, you'll be there soon enough.)

Treat others as you would like to be treated. (Or you'll likely get just what you deserve.)

Think before you speak. (Saves lots of groveling later.)

Chocolate never hurt anyone. (Recent Harvard study backs this up.)

Thank-you notes are important. (Every note you don't write will be remembered.)

Life isn't fair. (And it's a crying shame.)

A Point of View

One of the most frustrating tasks a parent faces seems so simple. I'm referring to the difficulties involved in capturing and holding a child's attention to convey a set of instructions that are, from the parent's point of view, absolutely vital, and from the kid's point of view, entirely trivial.

I'll give you an example. One of my children spends a great deal of his time in introspection. Frequently, when he is asked to complete some mundane task—to dress himself, for example—he reacts as if you have interrupted some Einstein-like deep thinking to make him eat worms.

My unreasonable parental instructions for the day usually begin with: "Time to get dressed, son."

Silence. I pop my head into his room. "Did you hear me?"

"What?"

"Ma'am? You mean 'ma'am,' right?"

"Ma'am?"

"It is now time to get dressed for school!"

"Oh. Okay."

Ten minutes pass. I check on my son, who now has on pants but no shirt, socks, or shoes. He is standing in front of his aquarium staring at our newest fish family.

"Son, are you planning to *just* wear pants to school? Now is the time to get dressed. *We are now getting dressed!* No more dawdling. I'm not kidding."

"Mom? Why can't you see the plankton in the fish tank?"

"It's too small, honey. Now get dressed! We can talk about plankton later."

Fifteen minutes later: "I'm ready, Mom!"

"Good. I like the pants, shoes, and socks, but I think you need to put on a shirt—right now!"

"Mom," my son asks almost mournfully, "Why are you always more interested in clothes than plankton?"

Sick Children

About 3:00 AM *on* a Friday morning, a mother awakes. A small person is breathing in her face and announces in a pitiful voice, "Mommy, I'm sick!" Before opening her eyes, she reaches out to pull the sleeper-clad body into bed with her.

As her child snuggles up, the mom comes to full attention and asks, "What hurts, sweetie?"

"My tummy," she hears through a sleepy haze. Immediately, her parenting-alert status moves to Defcon Three. She scoops the child up in one arm, vaults off the bed in a Heisman Award–winning move while asking, "Do you think you are going to throw up?"

They almost make it off the bed. Only the comforter is slimed before their feet hit the floor. Mentally, the mother begins shoring up her resources for sick days. One of her players is down. It will only be a matter of time before the virus remorselessly works its way through the entire house. Life as it has previously been known ceases to exist. The outside world has no meaning. Nation states can rise and fall unobserved from her household. For a while, everyone and everything will be viewed through a Lysol haze.

Even as these thoughts flash through her mind, the mom

murmurs encouraging words to the child who is throwing up: "You are doing great! You almost made it to the potty that time. I'm sorry you are sick. You can't go on the field trip, but you know what? We are going to have a great day! You can have ginger ale, and we are going to watch movies and read books all day."

The sick child is beginning to calm down, but he is on a hair trigger. As she changes the child's pajamas, the mom begins telephoning to find a substitute for the field trip and wonders for the millionth time why she is always the room mother.

The sick child is installed on the sofa to watch *Sesame Street,* while the rest of the children crowd around to stare and ask, "Is he going to get a shot?" This possibility sets the sick child off again, and the morning feed-and-dress campaign begins. It takes battlefield courage to face the day.

By 6:30 AM, the body count is still one. No one else is sick. The mom goes to the pantry to take stock of her weaponry. Although she doesn't yet know the nature of her enemy, the Motrin, Tylenol, and apple-juice armaments are standard issue. Naturally, she is out of everything. She decides to throw on some sweats and go to the grocery store before 7:00 AM when her husband leaves for work. That way she won't have to take the sick child with her. She needs the usual: bananas, rice, applesauce, soda crackers, ginger ale, and a hook—Popsicles, maybe, or some other bribe in case noxious medicine must be swallowed.

Since children only get sick at the start of the weekend or major holidays, she must decide by 9:00 AM whether or not this illness justifies a trip to the pediatrician. She places a call to the nurse and expects to hear back in three to four hours. Meanwhile, she can't leave the house, so she works out rides to school for the other children. She hands the baby a slice of toast and tells herself that it is perfectly fine for a baby to stay in her sleeper until nightfall as long as she periodically changes her diaper. The mom makes it official: she declares it a triage-parenting day.

Next she decides to change the linens on the sick child's bed. Soon she hears the unmistakable sounds of throwing up in the living room. She makes a mad dash for the couch and almost makes it in time to save her sofa. Seeing that her neat freak child is about to lose control because he has thrown up on his shirt, she begins a reassuring and meaningless monologue: "This is not a problem at all; we can change this shirt in two seconds, see? All clean. Now, let's get a new blanket. See this bowl? Remember: try to throw up in the bowl if you can't get to the bathroom, okay? But TRY to get to the bathroom. Then we can just flush it away."

She goes back to stripping the bed and realizes that in addition to her standard four-loads-a-day of laundry, she has added another two, and it is not even 8:00 AM. She runs down to the basement to start a load of clothes.

While she is down there, her oldest child mistakenly puts the child-safe lock back on the basement door and begins shouting for Mom to tell her that he has "saved the baby because someone forgot to put the baby lock back on."

Realizing that she is locked in the basement and that she has less than fifteen minutes before her oldest child needs to be in school, the mom contemplates her options. She *could* spend all day folding laundry and cleaning out the basement. It needs it. By nightfall, when her husband returns, she could go upstairs and search for survivors. She decides the fastest solution is to pry open a basement window, climb out, and beg one of the older children to let her in the back door.

She has one leg out the window and is just congratulating herself on her problem-solving ability when she looks up to see the freshly pressed, immaculate trouser leg of her single male neighbor who, she knows, thinks that every adult residing in her house is batty. He is nicely groomed for the day—complete with newspaper neatly folded under one arm and cup of gourmet-smelling coffee in one hand.

He is a Southern man and knows he must offer some sort of assistance but is clearly at a loss for an appropriate greeting when confronted by a situation for which he has no frame of reference.

The mom is wearing hot-pink sweatpants that are grossly

stretched out because she wore them when she was ten months pregnant. She has on her husband's old paint-dabbed sweatshirt, which she hasn't changed since the last throw-up incident, so she figures she smells pretty ripe. She wishes she had time to brush her hair (like it would have mattered), and she wonders how far the eye makeup she was too tired to wash off last night has streaked.

She hustles up the stoop to her back door and decides on a bright, "Have a great day!" for her neighbor. When she closes the door, he is still watching her in dumbfounded silence. She knows he is going to talk about her at work.

Meanwhile, she has missed the callback from the nurse. After checking to be sure the baby's mouth is clear of choking hazards, she finds the older children huddled against the front door as if they can't get away from the leper house and to school fast enough. Mom's friend calls from the sidewalk (she is not coming up to the throw-up house) to pick up the big kids for school.

Now the Mom is down to two children. The baby is happily tearing up mail-order catalogs, and the sick child is fine as long as Mom can hold him all day. She sits down with him and thinks dark thoughts about who did this to her family. She suspects a plot. Sure, it could be a random virus picked up at the grocery store or brought home from school to cultivate in her petri dish of a house, but her money is on the pale kid who came over to play on Wednesday. He didn't look too healthy. She makes a mental black mark against that kid's mommy. By about 1:00 PM, she is optimistic that the worst is over. She is going with the "it's probably just a twenty-four-hour bug" theory.

Then she gets the phone call from school. Number two child is throwing up and needs to be picked up. She grabs the baby, still in her sleeper, and straps her into her safety seat. Throw-upper-number-one can't stay home alone, so he and his bowl get strapped in next.

On the way out the door, she sees a scarf that she used to blindfold children in the last pin-the-tail birthday game, and she throws it over her current outfit, trying for a bit of style. It doesn't work. She looks like a bag lady.

Returning home with her children, the mom hugs everyone going in the house and begins her encouraging coach speech: "I know it was terrible to throw up at school! You are so brave. We are going to have a family day. You're going to love it! We are all going to rest, and by tomorrow, you'll see, everyone will feel better."

About 11:00 PM that night, the mom collapses on the bed, which is miraculously free of visitors. She is asleep before her eyes close, but her mommy radar goes off in about an hour when she hears throwing up from her bathroom—grownup throw up. She hears her husband calling, "Honey, I think I'm sick."

That makes two of us, she thinks.

Reasons Children Wake Their Parents in the Middle of the Night

To show how much they've grown

To explain that they fell out of bed

To point out an amoeba-sized injury that they fear
will become life threatening before daybreak

To inquire about the next day's dessert offerings

To explain that they are starving or thirsting to death

To ask if you are asleep

To offer to sleep with you if you are afraid

To ask if it is possible to grow up to be
a mentally handicapped person

To ask if they might have a future sibling who is
of another race or culture

To ask if it is still nighttime outside

To ask how many days there are until Christmas

To ask to be tucked in again

To ask the parent to pick up a toy, juice, or book that
the child threw on the floor in an earlier fit of temper

To tell a knock-knock joke they just made up

To ask if you want to sing in rounds

To see if you are still there

To ask what is going on in your room

To examine noises, shadows, etc. as if in search
of extraterrestrial life

To ask if there are any Popsicles left

To ask if you missed them

The Real Value of Money

For me, money is a necessary evil—never an end in itself—a social convention used to purchase things I consider life sustaining or luxurious. I don't give cash gifts, and I wish I could ignore money altogether, but that is only possible if one has much more of it than I do.

The whole concept of money alternately bores me to tears or leaves me with a slightly anxious feeling as if there is some important retirement account I should be attending to. Certainly I never thought I would find any aspect of cash hoarding charming, especially in one of my children.

I was wrong.

What I learned about money from my oldest child remained true for my other two children as well, so I think it is probably true for most little people. Children love money. As an adult, I immediately frowned upon this tendency and assumed it was some sort of instinctive greed. It took me a while to catch on. See, I've been an adult too long to view money through the eyes of an innocent.

For children, money is fun because it jingles. More money is logically more fun because it jingles more in your pocket. If you stand up and allow coins to fall through your fingers, they make a light tinkling music.

Paper money is to be disdained. In fact, my pious child once asked me rather indignantly why he had to give four whole quarters to God every week when all I ever gave God was folded-up pieces of paper. Believe me, in the eyes of my children, checks are the only monetary symbol more meaningless than paper money.

Although paper money is deemed worthless in play value, coins are precious because they are shiny like treasure, and they can be stacked in tall towers. My children explained this to me in a painstakingly clear and overly simplistic voice, as if they felt sorry for me—a person who had reached such tall stature to become so obviously slow witted.

As everyone who has lived with small children knows: Bigger is definitely better. Little kids will choose a nickel over a dime any day. The best prize of all is a silver dollar—*huge*.

My oldest child received a bag full of half dollars for his pirate-themed birthday once, and it was buried as stolen treasure all over our yard for a year. It would never have occurred to him to spend it.

To retrieve a penny from the street, children will risk being run over by a car. Money from different countries is especially interesting because it has funny writing and pictures on it.

Once again, I have been humbled by the ability of my children to find beauty everywhere—even in something as innately crass as money.

Mama Drivers

One day, I looked out the window of my big ol' mama mobile and noticed occupants of other cars staring at me like I had lost my mind. Eventually, I realized that they could not see the heads of children in my backseats and assumed (correctly, upon occasion) that I was talking to myself.

It occurs to me that some of you might be curious to know what kinds of earth-shattering questions mama drivers answer as they pass out juice boxes, snacks, and wet wipes while admiring preschool artwork (still wet with paint) and recently acquired skinned knees. All this, of course, occurs while the driver tries to decipher birthday-party directions printed in a tiny font in the middle of a clown's belly.

Mama cars are busy places. Not just anyone can climb into the hot seat and hit the highway. We've all seen the chaos created by drivers who don't know the proper carpool pick-up lanes. Drivers must have the concentration and nerves of an Indy 500 racecar driver. They must be able to change lanes to a cacophony of noises that closely resembles stadium roars during the Iron Bowl. Drivers must have highly trained psychoanalytical skills in order to negotiate peace settlements among minor combatants trapped like paratroopers in their five-point harness restraints, who will actually bite one another in rage. This must all be done without taking their eyes off the road.

In order to figure out the maddening intricacies of six different child-safety seats for one field trip, drivers will preferably have undergraduate degrees in engineering.

Mama drivers must maintain an immediate mental recall for all calendar events at all times so that they can responsibly promise delivery of fifty cupcakes to a frantic room mother who knocks on the driver's side window at a stoplight.

Mama drivers must have the athleticism of football wide receivers to retrieve dropped toys, juice, and other necessities for children who have a three-second patience limit. To qualify as a mama driver, you must be able to open food and drink with your teeth and pass it back to children who will clearly thirst or starve to death in the three blocks it will take you to return to your well-stocked kitchen. Even worse, you must be willing to lick dust bunnies and carpet hairs off dropped candy so that you can give the choking hazards back to squalling toddlers in their safety seats.

If you are wise, you will have already mentally mapped out the quickest route to the emergency room—just in case.

Mama drivers must have ears that can tune out the shrillest screaming while they listen to National Public Radio, the only news source of their day, to make sure that war has not broken out. They also need NPR so they can discuss something of substance at the next dinner party other than the pest-control leaflet they leisurely perused.

Mama drivers must be able to referee "he's touching me" wars without turning around in their seats. They need to be prepared to answer questions such as:

"What if a meteorite lands on our car?"

"Why don't ships sink to the bottom of the ocean like rocks?"

"When am I going to catch up to how old my brother is?"

"How can God and Joseph be Jesus's father? Is Jesus adopted?"

"Why don't people ever wear shoes to bed?"

The next time you see a mother talking and gesturing wildly in her car while making mad grabs under her seat and over her shoulder, give her a wide berth and don't honk at her at the stoplight. She may be addressing a great metaphysical question or, at the very least, dividing a stick of gum into three equal portions.

Letter to My Son's Kindergarten Teacher

I am entrusting my oldest child to your care. He has a tender heart. I think you are lucky to spend the better part of every day with him. His siblings and I will miss him. Here are some things you should know:

He is sad when it is not a school day.

He would rather read books than eat candy.

He has the negotiating skills of a Middle Eastern diplomat.

He is kind.

He loves babies.

He can hack his way into NASA on the computer.

He will be close to death before he will admit being injured.

He has the verbal skills of an Ivy League graduate, but he has just learned to tie his shoes.

When he is invited to a birthday party, he saves part of the candy from his treat bag for his little brother.

We have a no-hitting rule at our house—for little people and big people.

He loves knights, pirates, and cowboys.

His feelings are easily hurt.

Don't debate theology with him. He has humbled priests far and wide.

He has a broad musical repertoire, which includes the Beatles, Jerry Lee Lewis, and the Hallelujah chorus.

He is very patriotic and will correct you if you miss any words to "The Star-Spangled Banner." He is the only five-year-old who knows what ramparts are.

He can sound out any word. So if you wouldn't say it, don't spell it.

He has an Old Testament sense of justice.

He is excited to try new things.

He is a bit shy and listens intently.

He has hair untamed by any brush.

He responds well to praise.

He has friends of all ages.

He has an unfettered imagination.

He thinks fine dining involves macaroni and cheese.

He loves museums, concerts, and movies.

He believes anything is possible and is impressed Santa knows his size.

He has never ridden in a car without his safety seat.

He is the reason his mother quit teaching other people's children—to be with him all day.

He was loved before he was born.

He will remember you for the rest of his life.

New Car Woes

I would be hard-pressed to find a topic less interesting to me than the kind of car I drive. In my personal fantasy world, I would live in a small rural town somewhere and walk or ride a bus with all the locals to do my daily marketing and errand running. Of course, in the real world where I actually do live, I bring home approximately 130 bags of groceries every month to feed those bottomless pits called growing children. I'm quite sure that bus ride would get long and uncomfortable with all my children in tow. Plus, the locals might not like holding all my grocery bags on their laps or helping me haul all those bags from the bus stop to my house.

Still, I like the idea of riding mass transit without the responsibilities of car purchases, repairs, and parking spaces. However, since I live in the United States, and life as we've signed on to live it necessitates the ownership of a car, I have one.

When I purchased my most recent car, I don't think the car salesman knew what to make of me. He kept changing tactics, trying to win me over.

"What are you looking for today, little lady?" was his opening shot.

Strike one. In my mind, I said, "I have to buy a new car, *little man*, and I'd rather have gum surgery, so let's get down to business here." But aloud I contented myself with a hard stare in his direction.

"I meant, what did you have in mind today?" he plowed on while looking at me hoping for some hint on how to proceed with this sale.

"I want a car that will start every time I get in it. It must have air conditioning. I prefer that it have every safety feature known to man and an air bag for every living thing. I have to be able to install, without an engineer or mechanic, six child-safety seats in the back, while wearing pearls and a freshly ironed linen dress, without breaking a sweat. I want the monthly payments to be appreciably less than my home-mortgage payments. Other than that, I don't much care. Oh. And my husband is about a foot taller than I am and 150 pounds heavier. He'll have to drive the car occasionally, too, so bear that in mind."

Those were my complete instructions, which were crystal clear to me.

"I see," the salesman said, not nearly as cocky as before. "Well, ma'am, [I thought the fact that the well-dressed twelve-year-old salesman had switched to a respectful 'ma'am' from 'little lady' was a step in the right direction] did you have a particular model in mind?"

"No," I replied, patiently. "Just bring me whatever you usually sell to forty-something-year-old Southern women with three children, you know what I mean—something that will cart around lots of children, half their friends, groceries, golf clubs, and donations for the church bazaar—and make it snappy. I've got to pick up carpool in about twenty-five minutes."

"In your new car?!" the salesman fairly squealed.

"Of course in my new car!" I answered, "Isn't that the whole point of having the new car?"

Honestly.

"We'd better discuss some options," the salesman said as he nervously led me to a cubicle the size of the ladies' bathroom stall in most fast-food restaurants.

Opening a glossy brochure, he started reeling off color options that were remarkably unrelated to the actual colors of the cars. For example, "silver sand" was really brown; "coolest dew," was, surprisingly, green; and "deepest kohl," was—I guessed this one correctly—black. I felt like I was choosing a new fingernail-polish color.

"Listen to me," I said. "Just bring me a blue, black, or white mama car, and I'm out of here, okay? By the way, did I teach you? You look familiar."

"Yes, ma'am, you did! Freshman composition. I didn't think you remembered me!" he said, brightening up a little.

"I'm sorry to say that I didn't recognize you right off, and I'm even sorrier to say that it was your penmanship that gave you away," I confessed, pointing to the illegible writing on his clipboard.

"Yes. Well. You don't need perfect penmanship to sell cars, you know," was his witty comeback.

"Obviously," I replied. "You'd better write me up so I can get out of here, and remember, it would be an awfully sad thing to take financial advantage of a former teacher," I added for good measure.

"Yes, ma'am," he muttered, looking a little worse for wear as he chewed the end of his pencil and slunk off to get some higher-up's approval.

I swear it took me at least an hour and a half to buy a new car, and that is time I will never get back. Gone forever. Poof. What a waste.

The sad part about buying a new car if you have children is that the "new" lasts about fifteen minutes. For years, I drove an impeccably clean car. Really. As a rule I am a highly organized and neatly ordered individual.

The family car is an area where I have completely given up control and blown the bugle to sound a full retreat. The resulting mess is a disgusting, smelly, potentially lethal combination of old food and discarded junk that never fails to horrify neat freaks who open a car door, glance inside, grow deathly pale, and promise to follow me in their own cars.

Recently, I had trouble with one of the retractable seat belts in the backseat, which had been stretched all out of shape because of the unnatural acts required to install child-safety seats. I took it in for repair, and you're not going to believe what I found to be the cause of this mechanical failure. There were so many squashed raisins, crushed Cheerios, and melted pieces of candy down in the seat-belt mechanism that the parts were too gummed up to work!

What's worse is that I wasn't even embarrassed when the mechanic explained the problem. He was kind of twitchy, shifting his weight from one leg to the other, too nervous to look me in the eyes. I could tell that he was downright afraid to tell a Southern woman to her face that her car was so dirty that it actually impeded its mechanical function. I just thanked him for the repairs and gave him a big tip since I figure digging out melted Gummi Bears from between the car seats went way beyond his job description.

On any given occasion, our car has been known to contain: an assortment of half-eaten snack items; empty soda cans; three or four slightly wet, limp lollipop sticks; loose change from countries all around the world; overdue library books; crayons and markers; small cars, Lego pieces, and Barbie shoes; assorted rocks and minerals representing every parking lot we've visited in America; wet swimsuits left to mildew; baseballs caked in red mud; spare underwear—just in case; Batman Band-Aids; a box of tissue and one of wipes; assorted backpacks and cleats; bits of glitter and globs of paint reflecting the most recent holiday; a picnic blanket (you never know); church bulletins; odd socks; and enough receipts and pieces of paper to keep a recycling plant busy until the next millennium.

Indeed, there have been instances where we have had to track down a noxious odor to its source in a hidden crevice, corner, or pocket. I won't test your constitutions with a more detailed explanation in this area.

Furthermore, these are just items you might find in my car on an average day. I won't even tell you about the time I carried sixty-dozen dyed Easter eggs and had to stop on a dime, or the time we had to restock the fish tank, and one of the tiny hands holding the fish in a bag slipped, sending slimy goldfish all over the backseat. I won't mention the time we tried to take our cat to the vet at the same time as our elderly neighbor's dog, neither of which favored the idea of traveling in pet carriers. The devastating result of that little adventure had us all hanging our heads out the windows of the car all the way home and took me an hour with the garden hose to clean out.

Suffice it to say that the new car smell didn't linger in our vehicle.

Something to Tell You

Few phrases have the power to induce deep-seated panic in the heart of a seasoned parent more quickly than: "Mom, I have something to tell you." The odds are slim that you will hear anything after that phrase that could be remotely classified as good news. Children rarely feel compelled to utter such emotionally bracing phrases before imparting cheerful news like, "Hey, Mom, I got a college scholarship!" or, "I just felt like cleaning out my closet, Mom."

When I received a late-night telephone call from a friend whose twenty-two-year-old son had just called her to ask her to meet him for lunch because he had something important to tell her, I smelled trouble. Although I knew my friend wouldn't get a wink of sleep all night after that telephone call, I tried to reassure her anyway.

"Don't borrow trouble, sweetie," I said. "It's probably nothing. You know how self-important a twenty-two-year-old is. He's probably dyed his hair or pierced something or changed religions. I doubt it's anything to worry about."

"Anyway," I reminded her in my bossiest voice, because my friend tends to be one of those smothering mothers, "he's a grown-up man, and you're going to have to get a hold of

yourself, regardless of what he says." Frankly, I'd secretly worried for years that he would brandish a crucifix and a wooden
stake just to get her to back off a little.

My friend agreed with me, but she and I both knew that her
reply was just socially acceptable verbiage. My friend's son is her
whole world, which is one of the sweetest things I've ever seen
and at the same time, one of the most worrying. Why, I doubt
that boy ever picked out an L. L. Bean sweater without his mother
choosing the most flattering color for his eyes. She means well,
but she's just a little too involved, if you know what I mean.

Naturally, as soon as I hung up the phone with my friend, I
called that boy in his first-ever post-college apartment to get the
lowdown.

"Seven minutes," he said when he answered the telephone.
"I've been waiting for your call. I had a bet you'd call in less than
five."

"I would have if I could have found one of the thirty-seven
pairs of reading glasses I have stashed all over this house so I
could look up your telephone number.

"Now. What in the world is going on? You have your mama
scared half to death. Are you going to make her wait an entire
week until Saturday's lunch to put her out of her misery?"

"Actually," he said, "I'm going to make you both wait. I want
you to come with her to lunch. She's going to need you. You
know she'd call you five minutes after I left to tell you everything
anyway."

"Well. I'll have you know that I am a highly regarded confi-
dant, thank you very much, and there is precious little I wouldn't
do for my friend, your mother, and that includes you, her son, by
extension."

"I know," he said. "I'll see you at noon on Saturday at the
restaurant. By the time I get there, I expect you to have Mom
mildly sloshed."

"I can do that," I said.

And then that boy, who has been reared with impeccably
nice manners, had the audacity to hang up on me! I was offended

and would have told his mother on him if she hadn't already been so upset (and if I could have admitted to having called her son right after she talked to me).

My friend and I spent the next week scaring each other with hypothetical scenarios to explain the ominous "something to tell you" foreshadowing.

Because we are Southerners, we immediately guessed that he was dying of some incurable disease. We worried that he had cancer or leprosy. We speculated that maybe he'd picked up some strange disease when he went on that last college internship to the Amazon River.

We decided that—best-case—he'd shaved his head, sold his sterling-napkin-ring collection, and joined a cult. We considered, briefly, inviting our priest to join us for lunch but thought that would be awkward if the news was something different entirely. We contemplated asking some of his high-school friends who went on to play college ball to wait for us by the car; our theory was that, if necessary, the friends could muscle him into the backseat of our car so we could take him to a deprogramming facility. Because we have no idea where any of those places are, we worried some more.

By Wednesday, we'd decided that it would be best if he were a drug addict. We were pretty sure it wasn't alcoholism because this is the South, and, well, no Southerner would consider alcoholism to be real earth-shattering news. There's a very fine line between the social drinker and the alcoholic in the South. I wasn't sure I could spot a male alcoholic if he wasn't stumbling around, making unwelcome advances, or bragging about something. Where I come from, if a woman orders tonic water with a twist, you can safely assume she's pregnant, unless she's obviously postmenopausal, then you suspect alcoholism right away. Not many Southern women voluntarily give up booze. The only reasons I can think of for teetotaling are: being prepped for surgery the next morning, performing surgery on someone else the next morning, having been embarrassed half to death after four vodka tonics at the last party, or having to drive the baby-sitter home.

If he was a drug addict, we felt we could cope. This is familiar territory. Heck, there are advertisements for rehabilitation centers on cable television; plus, we both have enough physician friends and relatives to get that problem handled.

My friend and I were actually kind of rare in that we'd never been in rehabilitation or gone to counseling ourselves. Personally, I never felt any real pride in that fact since I'm sure we'd both have benefited from those experiences (who wouldn't?), but we were too cheap to ever go that route. Do you know how expensive counseling is? You could build yourself a therapeutic beach house, go down and meditate every weekend, and still come out ahead.

The next thing we thought of was that maybe he'd killed somebody. He is the sweetest boy in the world, but we worried that maybe he'd snapped in a fit of passion or something and accidentally killed someone, or been high—if he was also a drug addict—and not even known what he was doing. Either way, we agreed that if he did the crime, he would have to do the time, but we planned to alternate weekends visiting him if he had to go to the big house.

The week seemed to creep by. When I'm worried, I organize things, and by the end of the week, I had organized our household Band-Aids by size and shape, and I was seriously thinking of buying one of those battery organizers you see for sale on late-night television.

Finally, Saturday arrived, and it was time to pick up my friend for lunch. I drove so that my friend wouldn't have to count her Bloody Marys. When she came out of her house, I could tell how nervous she was by the way she was dressed. She'd pulled out some big-time Southern jewelry, and there was enough money in antique cameos, old pearls, and vintage platinum to keep your average burglar in liquor and guns for a year. She had on makeup that you can't put on in the rearview mirror while waiting for the light to change, and she was wearing linen pants she'd taken the time to press. I could tell she meant business.

"Ready?" I asked.

"Absolutely not," she replied. "Did you bring me a drink?"

"Of course. Check the cupholder, and don't slosh it all over the upholstery."

"You know I only did that one time when I thought you were going to run over that nun in the crosswalk. If you can drive decorously, we won't have a problem."

"Do you want me to go with you or not?" I demanded.

"You know I do. I'm nervous as a cat."

That boy kept us waiting fifteen minutes. If we'd still been in college, we'd have been halfway back to the sorority house. Ladies do not wait on gentlemen in the South. We'd had two Bloodies each, and we'd eaten enough French bread to feed the French-resistance army for a month.

Finally, he breezed in, kissed us both on the cheek, and slid into his seat. My friend was nervous, so she kept pestering him with questions about his new job, his apartment, and the menu until I finally decided enough was enough.

"Spit it out," I hissed at him across the table. "Your mama is about to die of a heart attack right here in this restaurant, and this is what you're going to remember: two aging Southern women in too much jewelry and rouge, worried enough about you that we both put on control-top pantyhose just to meet you for lunch. What's *wrong* with you?"

He took a deep breath, reached over and grabbed hold of both of our hands, looked his mama in the eye, and said: "Mama, I'm gay."

That's when my friend fell over in a dead faint like some sort of Southern-gothic heroine in a dime-store novel, which was just about the tackiest thing you have ever seen.

I couldn't decide who I was mad at the most—my friend, who had just crumbled at a rather crucial parenting moment, a reaction I felt sure she was going to regret as soon as she regained consciousness, or her son, who had made his mother wait, worry, and wonder about some big news that wasn't new to anybody except, apparently, Mr. twenty-two-year-old I've-just-discovered-myself.

When we'd both sort of heaved his mother back into her chair and shoved her head between her legs, I leaned over her back, put my hands on both sides of that boy's face, and said, "I cannot *believe* you made us worry like this. You have *always* been gay! This is not news to your mama. You think just because nobody ever brought it up, we didn't know about it?! All week we thought you were dying! A criminal on *America's Most Wanted*!

"Now, help me get your mama to the car. I appreciate what you are trying to do, and so will your mama when she has time to really digest it. Your mama loves you no matter what. As soon as she wakes up, she'll tell you that."

Honestly. All this fuss over being gay or straight, like we don't have enough to worry about with terrorism and fat grams and the bird flu. People just don't have their priorities right.

The
Church
Halls

Waiting in the Church Halls

I am a patient person, but I did not come by this attribute naturally or easily. Giving birth to three children in less than six years taught me patience. My choice was either to become patient or go stark raving mad. I say this not to boast but merely to explain a strange affinity I have for unexpected…waiting. I know this isn't normal. It may, in fact, be un-American, but, as I see it, being kept unexpectedly waiting by someone or something is like a little present—a few minutes of stolen time. (Of course, this philosophy comes from a woman who also believes that if you buy a dress on sale, whatever you saved on the sale price can be used to purchase matching shoes, so follow my counsel at your peril.)

When I am caught unexpectedly waiting, there is nowhere else I should be, no other task I have to feel guilty about not doing, and best of all, none of it is my fault since I have arrived in a timely manner only to be kept waiting by something outside my control. I consider such time a bonus. If none of my children is hanging from my arms like Christmas tree ornaments, I feel almost giddy. I am usually afraid to close my eyes for long because, like most mothers, I live in a perpetual state of exhaustion that I only realize when I sit down for a moment. When I dare, I love to lean my head back and revel in the luxury of thoughts free to roam amid the silence. I *love* to wait.

Waiting allows me to indulge in another favorite pastime of mine—guilt-free voyeurism. I like to observe people in public places, especially those living lives completely different from my own. You'd be amazed by what you can learn through silent observation. Of course, one day I just might get a punch in the nose, but, honestly, other people's lives are just so *interesting*.

When I was forced to wait in the hall of our church offices, I was intrigued by how interesting a bit of celestial eavesdropping could be. Don't worry—even someone as naturally nosy as I am would observe these offices with the utmost decorum. I positioned myself on the floor, in between individual offices, so that I couldn't actually hear the conversations going on in each office. So those of you looking for juicy church confessions will have to search further afield. Every detail I could hear was strictly unclassified.

When I closed my eyes, I could hear bits and pieces of the different lives going on around me, and I let them wash over me in waves. It reminded me of standing on a street corner in a bustling city and hearing little snippets of conversations, arguments, and monologues coming from the warm bodies crammed together for one moment in time waiting for the light to change.

I was astonished by how busy church offices are. If you are as nosy as I am, I recommend a few hours of observation in your local parish, strictly for the human-interest angle. You know how fascinating it is to sit on a bench in an airport, park, or shopping mall and simply watch the variations in humanity walk by? This is better. Really. More drama. People coming into church offices let their guards down a bit more than walkers in the mall.

I have always felt a bit wary of fancy church offices. I am deeply suspicious of preachers, priests, and other self-proclaimed do-gooders who drive fancy cars, keep bankers' hours, and have elaborate offices with ego walls that look as intimidating to the average churchgoer as the entrance to Vatican City.

The offices of this church were markedly humble, warmly informal, and looked more like professors' hideaways or temporary offices for the Red Cross. I liked that. I bet many people visiting church offices are nervous enough just opening the doors. Surely they shouldn't feel like they're headed to a CEO's boardroom.

In a single day as an accidental observer of the church offices, I learned that the vocation—as opposed to the job—of ministry is alive and well in at least one place. And if that's true, you just know the spirit is alive all over the place. It was a good thing to learn. I felt lighter inside. I have always been one of those people who doesn't want to know the priests too well. I don't really want to see their failings—an inevitability if they are viewed too close up, like family members. I think big-haired television evangelists have given priests and preachers of all faiths a bad name.

I saw a great cross section of America walk in those halls. I saw grieving people who headed to priests' offices for words of comfort and peace. I saw a young mother clearly looking for more tangible help. I saw church members eager to share something—time, money, food, and talents. I lost count of the number of times I heard, "Do you know anyone who needs_____?" One person came in to talk about a funeral, another a baptism. From what I could see, the church is a sort of good-deed clearinghouse.

There are three priests whose offices open on the hall where I sat. Like any three people, they each have particular gifts. The head honcho at this church, called the rector by us Episcopalians, has one obvious talent. He is the best listener I have ever known. I noticed that whomever he talked to—from the preschooler who ambled in for a little chat to those who had left "urgent" telephone messages, including the altar guild member who frantically exclaimed, "We need more wine from the cupboard!"—everyone got his undivided, complete, and unhurried attention. He never once seemed rushed.

I wish I had that gift! If I'm talking to you on the telephone, and one of my children interrupts to ask for juice while another is shouting for homework help, and the third is explaining that I must come immediately to get a ball out of the street before a car runs over it, I *sound* rushed. When I am forced to run full speed down the stairs to more evenly distribute a load of towels in my washing machine, which is thumping so loudly it is threatening to walk across the floor, and make a quick detour to answer the doorbell to tell the salesman that I can, actually, live without his cleaning products, even if he is working to keep kids off drugs, where I find a note from my husband to please pick up his dry cleaning before 9:00 AM...well, I feel, look, and sound frantic.

I never realized how big a business the church is. They feed hungry people, match up the haves with the have-nots, and counsel a flock of people busy living their lives as best they can. When visitors left the hall, most of them looked calmer, happier, and more content.

I enjoyed my time waiting in the hall. I was left with the impression that good was being attended to; church news was being exchanged; mistakes were being made and rectified; and that, ultimately, life was being lived—full speed ahead. I was rather comforted by the fact that in every religion, in every faith, in every denomination, we have good books, inspiring leaders, and dedicated souls. I left feeling I had spent the morning in a good place, and I enjoyed the waiting. Really.

Things SWAGs Should Never Wear in Church

Thong underwear. Nothing is more distracting to worshipers than seeing the waistband of a hot-pink thong peeking out over the top of your skirt.

Outfits you have previously worn to cocktail parties.

Jewelry flashy enough to have been worn by one of the Gabor sisters.

Hats with brims so wide they obscure the vision of churchgoers for three pews around you.

Flip-flops or any other footwear that smacks loudly against the floor as you tramp up and down the aisles.

Perfume in such vast quantities that individuals with allergies carry doses of epinephrine to church in case they are forced to sit by you.

Any article of clothing traditionally designated as beachwear.

Skirts hemmed so short that your Sunday panties are displayed every time you kneel at the altar rail.

Blouses designed to emphasize cleavage of a magnitude only appropriate for pornographic movies.

Any dress that fits your body so tightly that those around you fear seams may split if you reach for a high note during the closing hymn.

The Child Behind Me

One Sunday, someone else's child terrorized me for the entire duration of the morning worship service at my church. I cannot imagine what terrible sin I must have committed to deserve such torture. Whatever it was, I paid a high penance for it here on earth.

I'm not exaggerating a bit. I have kids, and I know typical bored-kid behavior. This child was way over the top. He was *horrible*. He could have inspired an eighteenth-century cautionary tale for children about bad little boys going straight to hell in a handbasket. Naturally, out of all the pews in the church, he chose the seat right behind lucky me.

The least offensive thing he did during the church hour was to repeatedly fold and rattle his church bulletin so loudly that it was all I could do not to turn around and look to see what he was making. (I'd just watched a television special about inmates at San Quentin who fashioned spears out of rolled-up magazines, so I was genuinely interested in his weapon-making potential.)

After I was jabbed in the back of the head several times, it was obvious to me that the kid was up to more than paper airplanes. He was working on a paper arsenal, and the back of my head was the target directly in his sights. I tried to scrunch down in the pew to make myself as small a target as possible. Who knew what kind of heat he was packing back there?

Next, he spit on me. Repeatedly. He spit tiny, church-bulletin spitballs into the back of my Sunday hairdo. *I'm not making this up.* He was spitting on me right there in front of God, his parents, and everybody. I hoped God was looking. I wanted a record of this behavior.

Worst of all, the entire time he was indulging in his juvenile delinquency, he kept up a steady stream of sharp soccer kicks at my solar plexus. The kicking proved to be a relentless, jarring, painful irritant to my lower back and a dangerous blood-pressure elevator.

The boy's parents stared straight ahead; they seemed oblivious to my increasingly pointed, over-the-shoulder glances in their family's direction. You and I both know that right there they broke the social contract. You know the one I mean. It's the same one we all ascribe to in movie theaters. A pointed look over one's shoulder in a movie theater is the international language for, *"Be quiet. You are ruining the movie for the rest of us."*

My kids know quite well what The Look means. They've been on the receiving end of it many times. The Look is the way we parents control our kid's behavior from all the way across a room. (In fact, I'm proud to report that one of my children confessed to just imagining The Look an iffy choice would receive from me, which caused him to rethink a situation from another time zone when I was blissfully sleeping in my bed in another state! I call that a parenting success story.) The Look demands good behavior *immediately,* and an accompanying raised eyebrow promises swift retribution and Draconian consequences if self-correction does not instantly occur.

My kids intercepted The Look, and they were edging away from me on the pew, sliding their fannies quickly down to each end. They fully expected the wrath of God—or worse, in their minds, the wrath of Mom—to descend on the little criminal any minute. They could feel the tension radiating from my posture and knew full well that I was seconds away from introducing some adult supervision into that bad boy's world, and they didn't want to be taken out by friendly fire.

Two weeks. That's all I would need. Two weeks with that child, and I could return him to his parents a model citizen. Of course, we all know that not everyone makes it through boot camp.

SWAG Rules for Children in Church

You must *sit* in the pew. You may not lie down, stretch out, or nap on your neighbors.

You may not bring your one-dollar offering in pennies so that you can place them in the offering plate one clinking coin at a time.

You may not fold your church bulletin into the shape of an airplane and sail it around the sanctuary at the backs of adults' heads.

You may not bring electronic toys that beep annoyingly throughout the service.

You may not bring a novel to read during the sermon as if you are sitting in the lobby of the public library. You must pay attention or, at the very least, pretend to pay attention.

You may not amuse yourself by making faces or obscene gestures at the well-behaved children seated near you.

You may not get up to go to the restroom twelve times during the sermon. Go before or after. Only rare exceptions to this rule will be granted.

You will not aim soccer kicks, repeatedly, at the pew in front of you. If you do, you will be held responsible for any lower-back injuries sustained by the adults sitting in front of you.

You may not: make rude sucking noises with your mouth, conduct a burping contest, pretend to be over-come with hiccups, roll your eyes, snap your fingers, rock back and forth in your seat, or indulge in any other socially unacceptable behavior that would be commonly demonstrated by patients in the state mental institution.

The Wedding Director

We've all met at least one. If you were as unwise as most of us and didn't elope, you probably had one at your wedding. Most likely, you didn't know her very well, but your mama did. You certainly had no idea that underneath all that lace and monogramming beat the heart of a marine. Surely, you remember your *wedding director.*

We really should give these women the credit they deserve. Who else would volunteer (well, sometimes there is gentle persuasion involved that would make a mafia assassin's blood run cold) to choreograph twenty or so predominantly single people whose sole goal in life is to have a party weekend no one will ever forget? Oh, yes, and each of whom is pleased and honored, blah, blah, blah, to take part in his or her friend's most special day.

The wedding director is a woman who insures that no matter what time the pre-wedding festivities ended and no matter what was used to toast and roast the bride and groom, all participants will be bathed, dressed in their frilly prom dresses and ill-fitting tuxedos, and assembled at least one boring hour before the service begins. That way they can sit around gossiping under her watchful eyes to insure that no catastrophe befalls a wedding under her command.

This is the woman who cares that you dyed your bridesmaid shoes to match your dress even though you and the clerk at the shoe store had to look twice to make sure it was possible to dye off-white to ecru. (One does not, of course, wear undyed shoes anywhere, under any circumstances.) The wedding director is not above asking to see your dyeing work-order receipt, and the date better match up with the current wedding.

The wedding director is a woman who will strip you naked in front of ten other girls to make sure your stockings are the nude shade requested, and your slip is the appropriate length. Before you get anywhere near walking down that center church aisle, she will check the color of your manicure and whether you have on the simple pearl earrings she requested or have tried to pull a fast one and wear some diamond additions.

She will examine your hair and makeup and finally pop a breath mint into your mouth before shoving you down the aisle with a final admonition to "Smile, and walk slowly. This is not a race!"

By this point in the wedding, members of the wedding party no longer care what the bride or groom wants. They just don't want to do anything that might bring down the wrath of the wedding director upon them. Bridesmaids know what the wedding director is thinking: "Honey, you are just another twenty-something pretty face. We can send you home to your mama and replace you with a relative the exact same size as you with a more cooperative attitude in about ten seconds flat."

All veteran bridesmaids know that you do not mess with the wedding director. The only person who gets a little slack is the matron-of-honor if she's pregnant and had to order special panels of fabric to make her dress big enough. She is allowed to lounge in the bridal room of the church eating M&M's until it is time to balance her extra-large bouquet on the top of her round tummy, have her body pointed toward the altar by the wedding director, and try to waddle on down the aisle. No other bridesmaids get to sit down. They might wrinkle.

Even the bride is not spared. The wedding director will be in her face in a minute if she sees any last-minute panic in the whites of her eyes. The director always has a supply of fine linen hand-kerchiefs stuffed up her sleeves and a prescription of Valium on hand for real emergencies.

This paragon has spent her weekend keeping representatives of several fraternities from brawling. She has placated hotel man-agers and sweet-talked fathers into writing an endless stream of blank checks. She has personally knocked on the hotel-room door of every member of the wedding party to make sure that all brides-maids and groomsmen are resting appropriately.

This is a woman who knows how to get a forgotten bridesmaid's dress Express Mailed from Antarctica to Hilton Head and have it hand-delivered to a panicked sorority sister with min-utes to spare before the service starts and without the bride ever knowing a thing about it.

The wedding director knows how to make estranged family members share a small pew in an unairconditioned wooden church on the Gulf of Mexico and make them look like they are enjoy-ing it. She knows how to seat the mother of the bride in pink and the mother of the groom in red and make it all look like part of a higher plan. The wedding director can wax loquacious about caterers, in-laws, and stepparents in such a saccharine sweet voice that it will be two weeks before they realize that they have been roundly insulted.

Usually, the wedding director has the bride and groom well in hand before the wedding. She simply adds the final *coup de grâce* by reminding them just before the rehearsal that they are really just props, the most important props, to be sure, but they are merely the dress-up part of the party. The actual wedding has little to do with *them*, personally. These two have already been cowed by a round of parties, teas, showers, and receptions. They are young, in love, and new to all the fuss and bother. Their sole aim in life is to get the whole thing over and done with while making the fewest family members angry with them as possible.

It will be years before they realize how easily duped they were by families, friends, caterers, musicians, and assorted well-wishers. For a long time, they will just gaze in a rather mystified manner at pictures depicting dresses they couldn't possibly have picked out, food they don't remember ordering, and guests they specifically remember requesting *not* be invited.

When asked about the advisability of inviting some young relative to participate as ring bearer, flower girl, or junior attendant, wedding directors always begin by tactfully saying how charming children look in their bare feet and in rows and rows of lace and ribbon and then advise against inviting them to participate. If this gentle discouragement doesn't work, directors move to Plan B. They recount wedding horror stories where children stole the show, and not necessarily with their Kodak-moment preciousness. If there is still pressure to ask so-and-so's child to be in the wedding, the wedding director capitulates with good grace, makes sure the child is appropriately dressed for a Southern wedding and that the child's mother or father is placed within swatting distance, and moves to her final plan to ensure a peaceful ceremony.

Just before a ring bearer or flower girl walks down the aisle, the wedding director leans down and whispers in his or her ear. No one knows exactly what is said. Even those of us who participated in weddings as children can't remember, but we are left with a vague terror of wedding directors that follows us to adulthood. I suspect that she threatens to make sure that no man or woman will ever write a rush recommendation for that child if he or she puts one bare foot wrong in the next forty-five minutes, but there is no way to really know. It may be a more immediate threat—for example, "If you misbehave, I am going to hold your face under that lime-green punch until your eyes spin around in your head." Whatever it is, it works.

Even the members of the clergy who have been around know not to fool with the wedding director. They are in charge of the sacred vows, but she is the boss of the wedding. The minister simply provides learned expertise, no more important than the musicians or the bridal party. During the rehearsal, you will see the minister defer to the wedding director several times with comments like: "I think we'd like the bride and groom to..." while waiting for the almost imperceptible nod of approval from her before moving on.

Wedding directors are like disaster-relief workers. They can take huge sums of money and spread it around effectively. They can make members of hostile groups work together for the common good. They can force everybody to play nicely regardless of extreme differences, and, most importantly, they make it all seem effortless.

The next time you go to a wedding, look for the ghost at the entrance to the church, and take her a big glass of wine when you get to the reception.

She will have earned it.

Southern Wedding No-Nos

Don't forget to RSVP in time to make a difference in price-per-head.

Don't bring a guest without written permission. (No matter how cute he or she is.)

Don't rearrange place cards. (Turf wars have been fought over seating.)

Don't dress your children in cheap lace or anything else that will require explanation when the wedding album is viewed.

Don't compliment any female guest more than the bride.

Don't omit seafood from your menu.

Don't bring a present to the wedding or reception. (We will know you were born above the Mason-Dixon line, and do you really want to advertise that?)

Don't forget to put your engraved calling card inside your gift so that you can be marked off a list somewhere.

Don't send a clever gift no one can identify that will require a crafty thank-you-note response. It's mean.

Don't overindulge yourself at the reception and forget that you are not one of the cute young bridesmaids or groomsmen.

Don't forget to ask the unattached, the elderly, and all little girls to dance.

Don't forget to give your spouse the "heck yes, I'd do it again" look when you hear the happy couple exchange vows.

Southern Women and Cemeteries

Southern women have an innate affection for cemeteries. To me, this is such an accepted premise in my life that I never paused to reflect upon it until one of my Yankee friends asked me, with a scrunched-up face and a turned-up nose like she was asking about a possible sexually transmitted disease in my family: "What *is* it with Southern women and dead people?"

I was instantly defensive and unaccountably offended considering this is not a Southernism I have ever spent any quality time indulging in or reflecting upon. I recognize that it is true that any Southern woman I know could wake up on a Monday morning with a to-do list that reads something like (1) go to grocery store (2) pick up dry cleaning (3) write thank-you notes (4) go by cemetery. This doesn't strike me as the least bit unusual, but, apparently, cemetery visits are not a regular part of errand-running life for Yankee women.

As you might suspect, I have a theory about all this. Because we live in a region of the country where the past and the present are intertwined, the cemetery is, for us, still a point of social activity—a gathering spot, a community touchstone something akin to the family church, school, and neighborhood ballpark. After all, in the life cycle of the Southern woman, we pretty much hit all those places at some point or another.

Cemetery-plot maintenance and flower arranging fall into the responsibility bivouac of the Southern woman. I have personally witnessed an otherwise sane and rational Southern woman take her car across three lanes of traffic without a signal because she spotted an overturned urn of flowers on her mama's grave. Everyone knows that children who allow dead flowers to lay around on their mothers' graves—or pots of dried up poinsettias to sit around until March—just broadcast to the world what ungrateful children those women gave birth to. One of the hottest conversation topics at the blue-haired bridge parties is when the players deplore the sad state of so-and-so's burial plot: "You'd think those children would do something about it!"

Maybe it's because those names in the cemetery never really die. There is always at least one child named after the person six feet under. This child is free to run barefoot over grave markers while being reminded of where he or she fits into a long line of ancestors, the people the child was named for. Most Southern children can tell you which dead person is responsible for the horrendous big ears or the Neanderthal foreheads in the family by reciting an endless parade of stories, histories, and lies so interrelated you can't tell fact from fiction.

The best family storytellers are usually women with strong cemetery connections who can make long-dead ancestors come alive like characters in a play, so that all the children absorb genealogy into their pores without even being aware of it until adulthood. I realized only recently that everyone doesn't have pictures of their great-grandparents on the wall, and that this is, particularly, a Southern way of looking at the passage of time—always to have the dead spoken of and about as if they are part of the living generation.

Recently, while folding laundry, I listened as my five-year-old's friend asked about a picture of a stern-looking man that fell out of one of the many photo albums that are crammed into every available nook in my house. My child answered his friend's question matter-of-factly with the name of that long-dead relative and added that he hurt his arm at the Battle of Murfreesboro. The other kid wasn't impressed, but I was.

A friend of mine from Wisconsin who lived in the South for a few years pointed out the incredible presence of the Civil War in Southerners' lives today. Although I am not of the generation of Southerners who refer to the Civil War as "The War of Northern Aggression," I don't think I can remember a week of my life when there wasn't some sort of reference to it.

Old photographs, especially the tin ones, fascinate me. My children and I often sit in the swing and look through stacks of them, examining carefully the eyes of the people in the oldest photographs, speculating about what their lives were like, and talking about the times in which they lived. I am fascinated by the physical changes in people over their lifetimes, and I love to imagine all their joys and trials and how they were affected by the happenings in their world.

In one delightful old photograph, one of my relatives is immortalized in a fancy wedding gown and hat. The children love for me to tell them how she sold her bonnet for three dollars to buy a dining-room table. I think I would have liked her. In another old photograph, you can see the gnarled, claw-like hands of an old woman who was obviously afflicted with debilitating arthritis. My children always maintain that she must have been "mean like an old witch." Amazingly, that is reputed to have been true.

Since cemeteries offer the only concrete (literally and figuratively) connection most of us believers have with the afterlife, we tend to pay attention to our graveyards. On holidays, special feast days, birthdays and the like, we decorate the family plots. If it's the Fourth of July, we might place a flag, especially for our veterans. If there is an anniversary of note or some big family news, we are going to swing the car by the cemetery for a few minutes of conversation, meditation, prayer, or tattling—whatever the needs may be. No one, not even the dead, is exempt from conversation with a Southern woman who needs to get something off her chest.

Family plots are sometimes a tender subject for Southern women, so tread warily when asking one of our matriarchs where she will be buried. Maiden names, first marriages, and long-dead infants weigh rather heavily on our minds. In fact, there is just no telling where a Southern woman may ask to be buried, what name she may want on her tombstone, and what date of birth she may elect to concede to for any and all to read for eternity. A Southern woman's need for historical accuracy and her strong streak of vanity often collide spectacularly.

Southern women who have had to live through funerals involving all sorts of divorced-name-subtractions and remarried-name-additions tend to be especially touchy about their own funeral arrangements. They have witnessed, firsthand, some unsightly, God-awful tacky statues of angels praying, singing, dancing, and who knows what all else, strewn across the gravesides of parents, former spouses, and cousins-in-law that they know would have made the deceased cringe in horror for being associated with anything so vulgar.

These are the women who order their plainly engraved tombstones when they're in their early fifties and still jogging five miles a day, just to make sure they don't get hit by an early case of dementia, which would allow some daughter-in-law with a vendetta to pick out a valentine-shaped tombstone to mark her mother-in-law's final resting place.

Fresh flowers are a necessity for most Southern women, and I know one woman who has commissioned a specially sized urn to be made for her family plot so she can plant boxwoods in the winter as well as fresh flowers in the spring and summer. She left work in the middle of a hot June day to meet the rest of her family at the cemetery for a few minutes of plot consultation. Again, this did not strike me as the least bit strange, and she and I went right from that conversation to discussing where we could get the best fried chicken for lunch.

For most Southern women, plastic flowers are the ultimate faux pas. If you really want to scare up a ghost, put some plastic daisies on a Southern woman's grave in December. I can almost guarantee you a haunting. I swear I wouldn't ride home in the same car with you. I don't make a living Southern woman mad if

I can help it; irritating a dead one is beyond my imagination.

I distinctly remember my grandmother taking me to see the newly arrived grave marker she ordered for herself years ago when she was in perfect health. I was absolutely horrified, and she was huffy all the way to the Piggly Wiggly because I had not admired it properly. To her, there was great comfort in having it correctly engraved to her satisfaction and exactly placed by my grandfather, without any tacky embellishments extended family members might be tempted to make in a fit of unbecoming grief.

In the South, the family cemetery plot is not a place to be avoided. It's just a part of the great circle of life, the jumping-off place for the last great adventure. Being able to visit a specific place that holds all those who came before us for eternity is a great comfort for some of us. Watching our own children trace the names and dates of births and deaths on the tombstones with their fingers helps us feel connected in this world to those who have gone before us and reassures us that we won't be forgotten by everyone when we die. If you're horrified that we enjoy the occasional ghost sighting as well, I can't really explain. It's one of those cultural things that defines life in the South.

Rules for Burying a SWAG

Bury her in the same lipstick she wore her entire life.

Bury her in the peignoir or the suit—depending on her age and what Southern city she's from.

Do not use plastic flowers. For anything. Under any circumstances. No matter what.

Do not dress her children, grandchildren, or great-grandchildren in tacky clothes for her funeral service.

Do not invite the new preacher to be part of the service if he did not know the dead SWAG personally.

Make sure there is plenty of food to feed everyone, so that the dead SWAG will not have to worry about the head count from heaven.

Make sure she is quite dead and not just bored into unconsciousness.

Do not squabble among your siblings over her china.

Do not let the grass grow so high over her head that you will need a map to find her grave.

Do not play recorded music. Find a pianist.

Make sure you know her favorite passages, prayers, beliefs, and pet peeves.

Cry because you'll miss her, but remember that you are not standing at the Wailing Wall.

Remember the very best little things about her and tell your children. When someone asks about a picture of a long-dead favorite SWAG on your wall, make sure your children can answer, effusively.

Thank-you Notes

As *civilized members* of a society that requires a token or minimal amount of social correspondence, I am sad to report that there has been an ever-increasing number of social atrocities regarding the sacred institution of all correspondence: thank-you notes.

I am astounded, confounded, offended on numerous levels, disgusted to the tips of my toes, and righteously indignant over what people are passing off as thank-you notes these days, and the concept of a cavalier omission of thank-you notes entirely has caused me to feel short of breath. I refuse to even contemplate the idea that any well-mannered person reared in polite society (anywhere below the Mason-Dixon line) would ever consciously, deliberately, and/or cold-bloodedly decide not to write thank-you notes for any graduation, birth, anniversary, wedding, housewarming, or other occasion for which some well-meaning soul actually took the time to purchase, wrap, and deliver a present.

We are not going to even discuss the fact that thank-you notes are not necessary, that the do-gooder would have purchased or performed said service with or without the thank-you note. *Of course*, that is true but entirely beside the point. Thank-you notes are not optional, and I don't know how anyone, anywhere, ever came to think that might be the case.

If there is someone out there who missed out, entirely, on a childhood of forced thank-you-note sessions, let me be the first to tell you that they are still required. There are no acceptable excuses. None. The only variable is the time limit. Six months is the generally agreed upon time period in which you should complete thank-you notes for most occasions, but there are situations in which time extensions are universally granted: mudslides that bury entire villages, an outbreak of the plague that kills one-third of the population, multiple births, or houseguests who come for the weekend and stay for the decade. Still, you should eventually write thank-you notes. Wait until the nuclear fallout clears. We will simply all understand that yours will be late.

I promise you this: every thank-you note you *don't* write will be remembered. I know a woman who is now a bona fide senior citizen who never wrote thank-you notes for her wedding presents, and twenty-six years later, I heard a disparaging remark about it at a reception. I'm not making this up. The fact that she went on to cure some nasty disease, adopt two homeless children, and donate her house to the city to be used as an orphanage went a long way to smoothing those ruffled feathers, but nobody ever really *forgot* it.

Thank-you notes are certainly not old hat. People still want to know that you received the present they mailed, that you like it (or can write a convincing lie that you do), and that you appreciate the fact that someone thought of you. And no, it is not enough that you verbally thanked your benefactor in the frozen-tater-tot section when you ran into her at the Piggly Wiggly. A telephone call or, worst of all, a secondhand "tell so-and-so how much I liked the gift" will not suffice. Such references are nice supplemental gestures to the handwritten note.

Perhaps we need to review some basics here, just to make sure we are all on the same page. (I have grown wary of making basic assumptions about manners only to discover that many individuals, who appear to be well-adjusted adults on the surface, clearly were secretly reared by wolves in a Siberian forest; from what I can gather, the packs spent little time on thank-you-note instruction.)

To compose a proper thank-you note, you first need to be thankful or, at the very least, be able to pretend nicely. I know that some brides have actually reached a point in the pre-wedding panic when they don't want to open another Neiman Marcus box because it will require a thank-you note, and they are "all caught up." Such a situation is, of course, just the shortsightedness of youth. That is when bossy matrons like myself really come into our own as we pour a glass of iced tea, sit our big fannies on the sofa, and dictate an appropriate thank-you note to an overwhelmed girl who can't imagine why she will ever be thrilled to open her sideboard one day and discover that someone gave her a set of sterling-silver crab forks as a wedding present.

Everyone needs a supply of "informals" or single cards always on hand to write thank-you notes. These should not, under any circumstances, have the words "thank you" written on them. These notes should have your monogram or name, beautifully engraved or nicely faked, or if that is a tad pricey, simple white or cream paper is appropriate. You may, in accordance with your age and attitude, diverge from the conventional *if* you are ever mindful of the tacky temptations that lurk on the fringes of any social endeavor.

Squelch any urge you have to tear out a piece of notebook paper from one of your kid's composition books. Observe proper rules of letter writing, and if you don't know them, look them up! Benjamin Franklin made libraries available to every American. Get out there, check out an etiquette book, and show some backbone!

You must then write several (these are minimum requirements, remember) sentences in which you mention with specificity the gift or service and create a descriptive phrase honoring its use, decorative attributes, timeliness, or last-ditch answer to prayer. Mention the thoughtfulness of the benefactor in some way, and, please, sign off appropriately. "Love" is not an appropriate closing for most correspondence. Think before you toss those words onto the end of a thank-you note to the Rotary Club for the scholarship money. "Fondly" is the preferred Southern closing for women that is quite often an affectionate and appropriate friendly parting, but "Sincerely," and "Best regards," are always in good taste.

The date is usually scribbled on the bottom left of a Southern woman's informal thank you, but the upper right is still perfectly acceptable. (This is one of the small snobberies we won't occupy ourselves with today in light of the serious transgressions that must be addressed. After all, we seem to be in a thank-you-note crisis.)

You must then actually stamp the notes and take them to the post office, or get your lazy rear out to your own mailbox and undertake the arduous task of lifting the little red flag for the mail carrier to relieve you of your heavy burden. Writing the notes is not enough. They must be mailed to be truly useful.

For those of you who are chronic procrastinators, do not make up elaborate stories about the post office losing all of your thank-you notes and the neighbor's dog eating the second batch you wrote. No one believes those stories. Just own up to the truth, and mail those baby-present thank-you notes after you drop the kid off for his first day of kindergarten. At least people won't be able to say at your funeral that you never wrote your thank-you notes.

I am not unaware of the innate unfairness involved in the thank-you-note task. I know I write three hundred notes for every one my husband writes. I have made some headway in my own home, and I urge all women to get a supply of nicely monogrammed stationery for the men in their lives. Some notes men must write themselves—notice I did not say dictate. I can't tell you how much I treasure the handwritten notes I have received over the years from gentlemen. I know it's not fair that men get praised for writing ten thank-you notes in twenty years—like they have come down off the mountain with the Ten Commandments—when every woman I know writes fifty between December and January. I can't change the world, you know.

I do believe that good thank-you-note habits start early. Every little boy and girl should write his or her own thank-you notes.

If they can hold a crayon, they can scribble a bit on the bottom of the notes you write until they can legibly write their names. They should write a few per day until every birthday and Christmas present has been acknowledged—even if you have to stand over them with your hands on your hips. I prefer simple bribery myself, a straightforward candy transaction in the true capitalist tradition. Later, when children can actually write a sentence or two, they know how to produce a written expression of gratitude—a good cure for those greedy Grinches engendered by our commercialized Christmases.

You'll be surprised by the response of those receiving children's thank-you notes. They are so rare that I'm tempted to write a thank-you note for the thank-you note, just to encourage such good behavior. Just think of the lifelong service you are doing your children by teaching them how to show gratitude appropriately. Remind yourself of some of the worst thank-you notes you have ever received—typewritten "thank you for the gifts" and other mortifying endeavors—that make you wish someone had cared enough to teach those high-school graduates some basics.

My first outing after my oldest child was born was to pick up engraved calling cards for him, and when he heads to college, he'll have more than a blue blazer and a good dictionary. He'll have engraved stationery and an etiquette book marked with paper clips showing examples of appropriate thank-you notes, invitation acceptances and regrets, and condolence notes, along with a Hershey bar for when they're all mailed. Knowing him, he'll probably use one of those notes to write home requesting "adequate funds to meet his current needs."

Gifted Flower Arrangers

Some people have a natural flair for flower arranging. It is truly a God-given gift, encoded somewhere in their bodies on a strand of DNA. I have observed that this genetic gift occurs more often in Southern women and gay men, but I can't begin to explain the phenomenon.

We all know at least one of these gifted flower people. They often add insult to injury by denying their gifts and claiming, "Anyone can arrange flowers! There's nothing to it. Just stick the stems down in the vase!" Comments like these are enough to make the less-gifted arrangers among us want to run for the Waterford vases. Those of us without a great deal of raw talent go for presentation and distraction.

If you leave a gifted flower arranger alone on the frozen Alaskan tundra and tell her that you really need some wedding arrangements for an Inuit couple who are tying the knot in about an hour, this woman will be able to come up with something to knock your socks off. She will be able to take two snow flowers, some local brush, and a few berries the caribou haven't scrounged up, arrange them in some native bit of pottery or genuine horn of a large indigenous animal, and have the nerve to exclaim that she "just used what was there, and isn't it amazing what the local landscape can inspire?"

I long to be one of these women, but really I am just a flower-arranging wannabe. Put me in a room with exquisite roses, fresh lilies, some lilacs, and enough greenery to cover up any gaping holes, and I'm a flower-arranging princess.

Of course, it will take me a couple of days to round up the proper equipment: three or four frogs of various shapes and sizes, some interesting or priceless vases in case my arrangements need a little help or distraction for the eye. I will need lots of statice and fern to stuff into unexpected holes and, of course, a variety of wire cutters, florist wire, foam, mosses, ribbon, etc. My pre-arranging potting bench looks like it has been arrayed with surgical instruments for open-heart surgery. The proper equipment, I theorize, will make up for any lack of talent.

Finally, after a small fortune has been spent on the infrastructure and technical support for my flower arranging, I am ready to begin. Meanwhile, my friend from the tundra, who came over to offer moral support and gossip while I arranged, opened my back door, walked down the length of my porch a few times, occasionally stooped to pick a green leaf or two (without ever having to actually climb down off my porch), and decided she had enough to arrange "a little something" to help me out.

Now, watch out when a Southern woman starts making "a little something" understatements. Doesn't matter whether it refers to "a little something" flower arrangements, "a little something" to eat, "a little something" to say, or "a little something" to buy. This expression is code for some serious, big-time, get-married flower arrangements, buffet food that will feed every adult in Vermont, a diatribe of a speech that she has been secretly rehearsing for days, or "a little something" gift that has "sterling" stamped on the bottom and hand-engraved initials on the top.

In other words, my friend picked two weeds, a dandelion, a few blades of monkey grass, and put together an arrangement *Southern Living* would be proud to photograph. I, on the other hand, spent two days assembling my top-of-the-line equipment and two more hours arranging blossoms I specially ordered from a local florist in the dead of winter only to have my arrangement look like one of those horrors you fear an out-of-town wire florist will send with your name on the gift card when you order flowers over the telephone. (I always fear that wire florists have sent red-and-white carnations in a yellow smiley mug with a big candle in the middle instead of the tasteful, loosely arranged group of seasonal flowers in a mass of different but complementary colors that I requested.) When someone ten states away takes my meticulously worded flower order over a toll-free line, I can almost hear her snicker, "Yeah, *right*," before I hang up the telephone.

I guess I will have to settle for being an enthusiastic arranger because I'm certainly not using any of my arrangements for important entertaining events. I want my friend with the dandelion bouquet to use her magic fingers. It is even worth it to have to listen to her tell me how easy it is.

Women Who Sew and Women Who Do Not

In the infinite number of ways one can categorize Southern women, I have determined that there are two types that will never meet on any common ground. I am referring, of course, to women who sew and women who do not.

I will not allow this dialogue to get bogged down in the finer details of smocking, French handsewing, basic construction, wedding-dress design, costuming, or the innumerable variety of sewing snobberies that divide women who sew into caste systems that can only be transcended through some type of Buddhist reincarnation scenario. For the purposes of this discussion, if you have a sewing kit that doesn't have the name of a hotel stamped on the front, and if you can sew on a button without working up a sweat, you can sew.

As you have probably guessed, I am a woman who doesn't sew, and I am getting a little bit tired of having friends whisper that fact to one another as if it is some sort of contagious disease. I am also beginning to feel faint when those around me who do sew tell me that, of course, I can learn, and they didn't start sewing themselves until they just had to....

I think these late-blooming seamstresses are genetically predisposed to fine needlework. Skeins of silk and smocking plates call to them as they walk past small boutiques. In fact, I have observed that if you question these "just picked it up" needlewomen, you will discover that they have a mother or sister who made lace for some obscure royal family, and a convent of nuns in Sicily regularly asks for crocheting advice.

Clearly, I had gone to the concession stand when God handed out the sewing DNA. To make matters worse, my mother is an accomplished seamstress, so I must be some sort of spontaneous mutation or genetic throwback, the exception that proves the rule. How depressing.

Like all mothers who, at some point, rebel at the idea of writing another large check for a handmade clothing item for a child who is guaranteed to outgrow it in three months and who will drool red lollipop down the front of it at the first opportunity, I *dabbled* in sewing.

I have a friend who hounds me periodically to learn to sew and offers to teach me. I have always known deep down that it would be a futile effort, but the idea of it was just so tempting: two friends sitting on the porch, sewing contentedly for their fantasy children frolicking on the lawn. Our real children interrupted the sewing lesson every fifteen seconds to demand juice, snacks, and to ask how can you tell whether earthworms are girls or boys. (A hard task for experts, I explained.)

I knew within the first thirty seconds of my lesson that it was not going to work. I watched as my friend threaded her needle and knotted it with one hand. I can tell you right now that this small test will separate those who sew from those who do not sew, will not sew, cannot sew, and those who might as well go home.

My friend continued working on her child's dress, putting in sleeves and a yoke, while chatting away for the rest of the day. When she paused to check on me, I was still threading my needle. There was a mound of sad little threads at my feet, and I had switched to red thread. (That ecru was just too hard to see.) She tried to hide her shock, but I know her really well.

"Would you like me to do that for you?" she asked in that pity-filled voice one uses when offering to cut up meat for a drooling institutionalized moron.

"Yes," I answered, not in the least proud. "Do you have any wine left in the refrigerator?" I asked, assuming that any slight inebriation could only help my dexterity.

My friend then offered to do the first few rows of smocking for me, just to get me started. "Fine with me," I answered. I began flipping through coffee-table books with pictures of children wearing divine, handmade clothing.

"We could make that one," my friend said, pointing to a photo, "that's what I always do—just copy the pictures."

"You mean to tell me that you taught yourself to sew by looking at pictures?" I asked. I was astounded. "That's like learning to be an architect by examining pictures of Frank Lloyd Wright buildings!"

"It's not that big of a deal," my friend assured me. She had finished constructing both of our dresses, and she was doing some sort of invisible hemming that was really fascinating in an odd sort of way.

"Haven't you ever heard of double-sided sticky-tape?" I asked. "You know, staples would show, but nobody but you and the Lord would know about the sticky-tape."

My friend gave me a hopeless look and decided to at least instill within me a proper appreciation for fine needlework. She began a sewing homily, a life lesson, her own special seamstress mini-sermon: "You just smile the next time you write a big check for those Easter outfits. You see how much work this is! Sewing is a labor of love, and it is even worse if some would-be seamstress does the fun needlework part and then hands the whole mess over to someone else to put together. If you don't sew, you just don't understand. Fixing other people's sewing screwups is like working in a sewing emergency room and resuscitating some poor sod who got run over by a log truck. It is *work.* Now you remember that the next time you are standing there in your dress from Target, and you be grateful for every handsewn stitch in your children's clothes," she finished.

Four hours later the children were cranky because they missed nap time. We had fed them bagels and bananas for lunch, and there were no prospects for supper simmering on the stove. My friend had completed two dresses. I *almost* threaded a needle.

Maybe I will learn to sew for my grandchildren. My eyesight should have degenerated enough by then that I won't be worried about the minor details, like both sleeves being the same length, or sizing that is remotely reminiscent of the actual child.

The worst aspect of sewing for children is, of course, their total lack of appreciation. They whine about having to try them on while you are making them and then about having to wear the final creation. They climb trees wearing delicate, see-through batiste and tear holes in lace that gets caught on teeny-tiny bracelets. They would rather wear Batman and Barbie clothes from Wal-Mart. It is enough to make me want to take to my bed with a wet cloth on my forehead.

Southern Women and Monogramming

A *Southern woman* will monogram anything she gets her well-manicured hands on: earrings, bedding, a baby's underpants, church hangings (with the Holy Trinity's monogram, of course— although you *might* see a few ecru threads on the back, initialing and dating the Southern woman's fine needlework, for posterity).

I confess to ordering a local bakery to monogram the petit fours for each of my children's christening parties—pink script for the girl and light-blue icing with block letters for the boys. One of my Yankee friends still hasn't recovered from being served a monogrammed dessert. "I cannot believe this! You even monogram pastries down here," she said in that mystified-by-Southern-eccentricities voice Yankees often use when commenting upon evidence of our civility.

The monogramming urge that bubbles up from a Southern woman's soul seems to be an innate drive to name, possess, classify, and distinguish. As a rule, we are downright passionate about monogramming. After all, monogramming ties together two aspects of our lives that we consider important: family names and fine fabrics. I guarantee that if you are talking to a Southern woman, and you notice that she has stopped listening to the fascinating minute-by-minute recital of your last doctor's visit while she fingers a bolt of antique linen you brought for her inspection with her head cocked slightly to one side, you can rest assured that she is trying to decide how she'd like to monogram your new shower curtain.

Whatever the purchase, if it will stand still long enough, you can bet there is a Southern woman out there who has tried to monogram it. I've personally owned monogrammed purses, towels of all sizes, chair backs, hair bows, shoes—you name it.

Monogramming mania can easily spiral out of control and require some sort of sorority-sister intervention and twelve-step program. During the teenage years, the constant monogramming by giggling adolescents is just plain obnoxious, but most grown-up SWAGs have learned to monogram in moderation, with discretion, and more selectivity than a child with a Sharpie and the will to use it.

As a fairly representative member of my Southern culture, I am deadly serious about monogramming. I prefer hand-monogrammed items, naturally, but since I am not willing to spend fifty dollars monogramming my child's book bag, I have bowed to the inevitability of machine monograms. I am still decidedly picky about the machine's work. I will examine the back of my monogramming order like Martha Stewart with her magnifying glass counting the number of threads per square inch. I want to see how the edges are finished.

When I see pinpoint oxford cloth on the men in my life, my eyes naturally stray to the cuff, pocket, or collar to see if they have been monogrammed to my satisfaction. Frankly, fine cottons are just the jumping off place for a Southern woman's monogramming obsession.

I will never forget one occasion in college when I asked my date to use his handkerchief to wipe something off my dress. I was absolutely astounded when he could not produce a nicely monogrammed white square. I knew right then and there that I could never marry a Yankee.

Nothing says wedding or christening present better to a Southern woman than sterling-silver anything with hand-engraved initials. We treasure baby cups, goblets, pitchers, and bowls as if they served hors d'oeuvres at the Last Supper. We prize those items with initials of long-dead relatives most—especially if the silver rattle has a few family teeth marks on it. Best of all, of course, is when a baby of the current generation eats smashed bananas out of a porringer monogrammed for a baby a generation or two before him who bore the same name. It is just this sort of situation that reaffirms for the Southern woman that all is right in her world.

Master engravers are hard to find these days. They do all their work by hand and command exorbitant fees that often far outweigh the value of the piece they are engraving, but their work is true artistry. Most Southern women can spot hand-engraved jewelry from halfway across the room. In my state, I only know one master engraver. He is said to be the only one in the Southeast, but I have doubts about that since I figure that in New Orleans and Natchez alone, there is just way too much sterling silver for one man to cover.

The engraver and I are on a first-name basis. When he sees me coming down his hall, he knows his electricity bill is paid for the month. My children may eat black-eyed peas and rice for a few weeks, but, by golly, they'll be doing it on hand-engraved sterling silver.

Bob, the engraver, didn't bat an eyelid when I brought in a one-inch-long beauty pin for my brand-new baby girl for him to engrave with her four-letter name. Bob took one look at me, a Southern lady with a freshly hatched baby girl in her arms, got out his magnifying glass, and quickly decided on script instead of block letters. Bob knows better than to fool around with a hormonal Southern woman and her monogramming.

Last year I was forced to find a new monogramming source for my linens, and I was highly stressed. There was a real wedding-present crisis around here until I tracked someone down in Montgomery, Alabama, who understands the emotional connection between Southerners and monogramming. I called her up on the telephone for the first time, and we talked for forty-five minutes. The next day I sent her an envelope full of my engraved calling cards to keep on file. When I get an invitation, she mono-

grams, wraps, (using lovely wired ribbon, of course) mails or de-
livers my present, and sends me the bill. In addition, she sent me
an exquisitely monogrammed hand towel when I placed my first
order, just to show me she knows what she's about. She is definitely one of us.

My linen person told me that when she started her
monogramming business, a little sideline out of her home, she
placed an order for materials with a supplier in New Jersey. A
few days later, she got a call from their sales representative asking if there had been some mistake. The orders for materials were
just far too *excessive* for a town of her size. What, they wanted to
know in New Jersey, were all those women in the South doing
with all that monogramming?

Eventually, she was transferred up the chain of command to
the president of the company, who required a little education
regarding the necessity of monogrammed items in the daily lives
of Southerners. I am told he actually accused her of making things
up. These days, the president calls her and puts her on speaker-
phone so that everyone in his office can enjoy her accent, which
she lays on pretty thick. Apparently, she has had no more problems with her New Jersey supplier.

I've wondered about this urge Southern women have to label
things. Is it merely an indication of a possessive streak that would
embarrass a two-year-old? (I envision a Southern woman ironing
her husband's monogrammed dress shirt, shouting "Mine! Mine!
Mine!" over the top of her iron.) Is our obsession with
monogramming merely a continuation of our love of nomenclature in general? The act of naming in itself is very powerful. Maybe
it's the physical act of naming someone or something that reaffirms our connectedness to those who have come before us, as
well as offering some tangible assurance that there will be some
mark from us on what we leave behind.

After all, as many times as you've heard your mother say,
"When I go, I'm taking those silver goblets with me!" we all know
that isn't actually possible, and heaven doesn't seem to encourage
carry-on luggage for those arriving at the pearly gates.

Maybe because for so many years Southern women were respected only for their hospitality talents rather than their other virtues, the women who came before us assured, for themselves at least, a footnote in future generations' celebrations by engraving their initials, names, or important dates on treasured items. At the very least, one of us would think, as we sip mimosas out of one of her goblets at a party, "I wonder what she was really like?" Or we might think, as we hand-wash each piece of silver after a christening party and rub the monogram dry with a soft cloth, "Was she happy, this woman who came before me?"

Things a SWAG Might Monogram

Her dog's collar

Her child's hair bow

Her bedding, your bedding, her in-law's bedding,
her child's bedding, the dog's bedding...

The backs of her chairs

The middle of her shower curtain

Hand towels or bath towels for anyone of any age
and for every occasion—including the Fourth of July

Every piece of silver she inherits, buys, or steals

Makeup boxes and jewelry (for any part of the
body that is *traditionally* pierced in our culture)

Her luggage

Her pocketbook

Assorted clothing items, including lingerie *and* the
lingerie bag in which the monogrammed silks reside

Desk accessories

Bookmarks

Her husband's garment bag, belt buckle, or other
male accessories, if he'll let her

Her wedding cake

Napkins, tablecloths—the whole linen world of possibilities

Stationery

Paper plates and napkins for a highly organized
yet seemingly spontaneous picnic

Shower wraps, bathrobes, etc.

A matching ring, pendant, and earrings—the whole obnoxious set

Baby books, photo albums

Tombstones

Glue-gun Adventures

In the past century, a new weapon has made its debut to the glee of craft-obsessed women all over the world. I'm referring, of course, to the new staple of any Martha Stewart wannabe: the glue gun. There has been little fanfare, no CNN feature stories, and no FDA trials. I'm telling you that a deadly weapon has sneaked under the radar of every safety-obsessed mom in America and made it to a cozy spot in the junk drawer of every kitchen on the block. Soon, glue guns and the small plastic sticks used to refill them will be standard issue at wedding showers because we are fast becoming a culture that can't live without them.

I am here to raise a little consciousness regarding this dangerous development. Do you realize that you don't need a license to buy a glue gun? There is no five-day waiting period. There are no background checks. Any idiot with five dollars and access to the local discount store can buy a glue gun. Currently, there is no legislation to protect minors. Every preschool in the country has a sticky shelf piled high with glue guns. Purportedly, only teachers are allowed to wield glue guns, but who really checks these things? I'm sure there are four-year-olds out there hot-gluing beads and eyeballs willy-nilly on art projects.

Maybe glue guns are okay for other parts of the country. I'm sure that in Texas, a concealed glue gun won't even raise eyebrows, but I'm convinced that the inventor of the glue gun had to be a Yankee who had never met a Southern woman and therefore had no idea of the inherent dangers involved in arming one. My guess is that the inventor really had it in for Southern women and the South as a whole and hoped this invention would cause the entire social structure of the South to collapse (again) with no possibility of that "rising again" nonsense.

Either way, I am sure of one thing: Southern women should never be allowed to purchase, borrow, or even gaze longingly at a glue gun. There is just no *good* that can come of it. Cheap, white, hot glue always ready at the tip of a small pistol is just too tempting for Southern women.

You know how Andy Taylor allowed Barney Fife to carry a gun but made him keep the bullet in his pocket? Same thing here. If that bullet was chambered, Barney inevitably put a hole in something. If you give a Southern woman a glue gun, she's going to glue, and possibilities for her gluing services are downright terrifying.

Somewhere in the South is a Southern male who has had his hairpiece glued on by a helpful wife. I just know it. You can see how tempting that would be, and I don't want to even think about the denture possibilities.

For some reason, Southern women are especially attracted to artificial flowers when holding a glue gun, and I am just too embarrassed to tell you some of the places my own friends have glued fake foliage, but I advise you not to look too closely at some of those funeral arrangements.

I speak from personal experience. I have an abnormal fondness for my glue gun. I admit it. The moment I spy a household-repair job, I heat up the glue gun and start aiming. Mothers like me don't get much instant gratification in our lives, and glue-gun repairs offer immediately satisfying results. Baseball trophy lost an arm? Bring it here and let Mama glue it. Picture on the wall crooked? Glue that sucker to the wall. Chair leg broken? Hot glue it. No need to call the repairman—Mommy can fix it.

It is easy to see how this behavior can spin out of control. When my daughter recently pulled the hem out of her dress for the 447th time, I reached for the glue gun and was shocked to see her run screaming to her room. What an overreaction! *Of course,* I would have taken the dress off of her before I glued it.

Interior-decorating challenges take on an air of simplicity with the aid of a glue gun. I am convinced that what I lack in artistic talent I can make up for with some really skillful glue-gunning.

On one occasion, after a fruitless search for a Mardi Gras wreath for my front door, I decided to draw my glue gun and make my own. Turned out not to be one of my better glue-gunning days. Every time I pointed the tip of my gun to the wreath, long strands of glue stuck to the counter, my clothes, and my fingers. After each application, I spent a few minutes peeling glue off my fingers and furniture before it could harden to the consistency of the bricks used to build the Great Wall of China.

At the conclusion of the morning, I had a pitiful-looking wreath. It looked like someone had drizzled a bottle of clear glue over it. To be completely honest, I also have to admit I received some rather severe burns on my fingers and arms that probably deserved a quick trip to the emergency room—a scene I decided to skip after realizing that I would have to explain that the cause of the burns was my own beloved glue gun. Who knows? In these crazy times, the emergency room staff might actually try to take my glue gun away, and then where would I be? Lots of holidays and birthday parties coming up. Plus, I think I'm really getting the hang of it now. I'm considering having my glue gun monogrammed and maybe making a cute little bag to keep it in.

A SWAG's Checklist for Obsessive Behavior

If you have any of these signs, it's time for a twelve-step program:

You have an almost uncontrollable urge to whip out a needle and thread and add a bit of embroidery to the skirt of the woman seated next to you in a restaurant.

You run out of oven space, counter space, shelf space, pantry space, and freezer space when you bake Christmas cookies.

The only time you ever missed your weekly hair or manicure appointment, you were in active labor.

You become so engrossed in the book you are reading that you fail to realize the house has caught on fire until the pages of your book become singed.

Your children hide their Easter baskets and Valentine's Day candy from you just in case you have a dieting lapse.

You schedule a surgical procedure around your favorite football team's game schedule.

You go to the library to check out a new self-help book and realize that there is nothing on the shelf that you haven't read.

You forget to eat meals and wake up in the middle of the night with ideas for your next project.

The Ultimate Paint Chip

Those of us who have lived through major house renovations become lifetime members of a not-too-selective club. Astonishingly enough, some of us choose to join this club of our
own free will. In moments of vodka-induced enthusiasm, our rose-
colored reading glasses tell us, "When it's over, you'll be glad you
did it."

I can't believe I ever fell for that.

That's the sort of logic that we women routinely use when
psyching ourselves up for a hysterectomy, or when we are forced
to entertain obnoxious relatives, or when our husbands have talked
us into traveling to parts of the world that don't have running
water or toilet paper.

Others of us had no choice about house renovations because
hurricanes or tornadoes tossed trees onto our roofs or flooded
our living rooms. Membership in the house-renovation club is
instantly awarded to any woman who has to climb on top of her
roof at 3:00 AM and spread out a blue tarp to protect her great-
grandmother's linen press from leaks impressive enough to inspire music for Walt Disney's *Fantasia.*

Regardless of how each of us is first initiated into the club,
the end result is always the same: We may be glad it's done, but

nothing on earth would make us do it again. We'd rather live in one of those shameful portable classrooms or a double-wide trailer. After we perform a little landscaping magic around those metal boxes, you'll swear you're in a big city's botanical gardens.

House renovations remind me of first weddings. All that fuss is fine when you're young and powerless, but if you ever remarry, you'll elope and then throw a fun party with people you actually like who will get along and have a fabulous time wishing you well.

Even the simplest choices in house renovations are fraught with the opportunity to make expensive, unsightly, monstrous mistakes. Let's consider the maddening dilemma of paint-color selection, for example. I'll be the first to admit that there are a few paint-selection goddesses out there who know instinctively just the right shade of yellow, blue, or green paint chip to pick. Those women are born that way—rare sports of nature—and it's a gift that weighs heavily upon their shoulders because friends call constantly for decorating advice. Those poor women can't sit down for supper without answering at least two frantic calls from the paint store with emergency paint questions from friends who have painters breathing down their necks waiting to buy paint and contractors who have steam coming out of their ears. These workmen have no time, interest, talent, or enthusiasm for exploring the fine distinctions between linen white, arctic white, and bisque.

It is nearly impossible for an average woman to view a two-inch paint chip and imagine what it will look like when it is splashed across twenty-seven feet of dining-room wall. Lighting can make all the difference in the world. I know a woman who made her entire family stretch out full-length on her kitchen floor three times during the course of a day—morning light, high noon, and sundown—to help her decide whether or not the pink color she had chosen for her walls was going to be too "shrimpy."

When a Southern woman finally finds the color she has been searching for, she has no respect for personal privacy, property laws, or human dignity when obtaining her sample color. I have personally had to take off a blouse that was "just the right shade of off-white" so that my friend could take it to the paint store to find matching paint for her foyer. As much as I love her, I was a little put out to have to drive home in my slip—even if it did look like a camisole—because everyone who knows me knows that I would never wear a camisole by itself because I have jiggly arms, and, well, I am just too old for that sort of thing.

I have known women who have mugged perfect strangers on city streets and demanded that they surrender articles of clothing, purses, magazines, umbrellas, etc.—all in the name of choosing the perfect paint chip.

I once watched a friend hold a paint chip up to the back of a woman's hair in her quest for the ultimate "warm brown" (every woman has an envelope in her purse with paint chips which are currently under consideration). We were standing in line for movie tickets when it occurred to my friend that the color used to dye that woman's hair would be just right for her bedroom walls, and she demanded that the woman reveal her top-secret salon formula on the spot. Unfortunately, that woman hotly denied dying her hair at all, and I was afraid a fight was going to break out right there in the line. If I hadn't been able to distract my friend with the chocolate-brown bow tie on a passing gentleman, I think the situation would have deteriorated even further. I couldn't bear to watch as she chased bow-tie man into the lobby of the theater. He was at least a foot taller than my friend, but he was old and had a cane, so I figured it was a fair fight.

Every woman knows you have to buy three or four different paint samples to paint on the wall and live with for a few days before you can commit to years of a chosen paint color. Buying the paint without allowing for these live-with-it days has resulted in paint choices so offensive that a woman gets mad all over again every time she has to walk through the room.

During the live-with-it phase, everyone who walks in the front door is asked to voice an opinion on which paint-color selection is best for the room. My best friend has been known to bring herself a sandwich, sit down in front of the paint samples, and ruminate for a whole hour before rendering an opinion, but my husband gets twitchy after about thirty seconds of viewing.

"I don't get it," he says. "They're *all* green."

"Yes, of course," I say. "We've decided on green. But *which* green? That's the question."

"Whichever green you want is fine with me," my husband says.

Wise man, my husband.

A SWAG
Business Glossary

Receipts: Small pieces of paper that can be found in endless supply in out-of-season purses. Receipts are perfect for jotting down telephone numbers, email addresses, or for leaving a hastily written note in a friend's mailbox.

Profit: Money left over in the grocery budget after feeding your own children, all of their friends, and other strangers at the ballpark. Often discussed and highly sought-after item that is rarely seen by SWAGs.

Reserves: Money stashed away in a SWAG's lingerie drawer for cash-flow emergencies when initial monetary expectations do not meet current fashion needs.

Taxes: Money earned by SWAGs that the law requires to be turned over to large, state-run bureaucracies to waste as they see fit.

Business License: This is Mafia-style shakedown money. It is also another excuse to make SWAGs stand in line at the county courthouse every year.

Cash Flow: Cash only flows in one direction—out.

Tax Deduction: Very tricky. Children are the standard tax deduction, but since the child tax credit wouldn't keep a one-year-old in diapers for a year, it's hardly worth the stretch marks.

Service: The work SWAGs routinely perform for family, friends, neighbors, churches, schools, charities, communities, etc., usually without compensation and way too often without acknowledgment or thanks.

World of Work

The Big Red Cleaning Machine

Manual labor is not my forte. It's not that I'm too good for it or anything—I'm not a job snob. In fact, I actually like to perform a number of menial chores—silver polishing, for example—because of the instant gratification involved. Few things are more satisfying than watching dirty windows clear up as if by magic, with nothing more than a little vinegar, water, and elbow grease.

The problem is that in most types of manual labor, I'm just so remarkably untalented, so obviously lacking in some genetic gift, that it is embarrassing. Clearly, I was not educated to use any part of my anatomy other than my brain with any degree of skill, and, apparently, I have no natural aptitude for manual labor, either. I've certainly approached elementary plumbing problems, lawn maintenance, and small home repairs with an awful lot of enthusiasm, instruction reading, and a deep-seated need to prove to the world that I am not entirely useless when separated from all modern conveniences by the occasional power outage.

Regardless of numerous past failures and expensive checks written to professionals to cover up my inept attempts to fix something myself, I remain optimistic. After all, I have a number of friends who can change the belts on their own vacuum cleaners without calling in NASA technicians. Am I so different from the other women in my life? Surely not.

When a friend mentioned, in the middle of a telephone conversation, that she had just cleaned her carpets with a professional, carpet-cleaning machine—by herself—I was instantly and overwhelmingly jealous. Why, I had no idea that there were such machines available to members of the general public! I assumed you needed to take a course or two, obtain a license or something. Obviously, it had never occurred to me to try such a thing by myself.

In my own defense, she caught me in a particularly weak moment. I was expecting eight people for dinner within twenty-four hours, and the carpets in my boys' bedrooms were dirty enough to rival cave floors in Afghanistan.

I felt the familiar tug of manual-labor temptation. I was positively *inspired*. My friend was raving about her success, and I thought—mistakenly, of course—in terms of those famous last words before disaster strikes: "I could do that!"

In laboratory tests, even lab rats learn which levers bring pleasure and pain, and they change their behavior accordingly. Not me. I seem to live in a delusional world where anything is possible, confident that I will somehow awake one morning with the repair skills of a building superintendent and the technical expertise of a mechanical engineer.

To my credit, I didn't rush right in. I showed some discretion.

"How hard is it?" I asked my friend, cautiously, the memory of a previously rented floor sander still fresh in my mind.

"There's nothing to it. Anybody can do it. Simple," she maintained.

"We're talking about me here," I reminded her. "Do you think *I* can use that machine?"

"Oh, yeah...well...I *think* so. Sure. Why not?"

My friend seemed increasingly reluctant to commit, perhaps remembering that I am the only person she knows who had to call in professional painters to repaint the living room in our first house because the edges were so poorly painted on the ceiling that it made people seasick to sit on our sofa and look up. You had to keep your eyes fixed on the fireplace mantel—sort of like the horizon—until we could get someone to fix that mess.

My friend then spent the next ten minutes of our telephone conversation talking *herself* into allowing me to use the machine that she had rented for the day after she was finished with it. I'd already arranged flowers for my party, planned the menu, and done all the fun jobs. There was nothing left to do to get ready for my dinner guests except serious bathroom cleaning, which I was happy to delay for any distraction that I deemed more worthy of my attention. In other words, I was primed for a little steam-cleaning adventure.

After my friend gave me additional last-minute instructions that I pretended to understand fully, I hung up the phone only to have her call me back twice to try and clarify a few points. All this before I was free to jump in my car and run by her house to pick up the mother of all machines, which she promised would be waiting for me on her front porch.

When I got to her house, I admit to being initially intimidated by the sight of the steam-cleaning machine itself. First of all, it was huge and red. The color red just screams "danger" to me. I think of disposal boxes for sharp objects in doctors' offices and stop signs: Beware. Danger. Do not touch.

Luckily, my friend knows me pretty well. She had anticipated my initially overwhelmed first impression, and she'd taped a package of chocolate-mint brownies to the handle to lure me up her front steps and closer to the machine—kind of like the carrot hanging out on a pole urging the dumb donkey forward.

It worked. This particular friend is one of the best cooks I know, so I would have approached plutonium products for her baked goods. I sat down on her front porch to eat my diet-blowing goodies and contemplate the big red cleaning machine.

Basically, as I saw it, I had two choices. I could eat the brownies and run, but I'd have to endure some big-time taunting from my friend who is much braver about everything than I am, a woman whose patience is constantly tested by my reticence in almost every new endeavor. That choice didn't hold too much appeal. My second choice was, of course, to grab the darn machine by its horns—handles, actually—and go for it.

The odds were with me, I thought. So far that week, I had experienced an unfortunate run-in with my son's rock tumbler that resulted in an unlimited number of tumbling days since I couldn't figure out how to turn it off. Plus I'd had a rather embarrassing conversation with the vacuum repairman (he knows me by name) who greeted my cheery "Hello!" upon entering his shop with, "What have you run over this time?"

I decided to pretend not to notice his tone.

"Metal soldier. Civil War, I think. Can you fix it?"

The way I looked at it, I was overdue for a successful machine interaction.

Just getting the thing to the car required all of my higher-education degrees. It simply would not push forward, so I had to pull it backwards down the driveway. Unfortunately, my friend's driveway is so steep that the machine kept picking up speed until it was quite out of control. I was saved when I was fortuitously pinned between the machine and the front of my car. Ever the optimist, I decided to look at that as a lucky break. Both the machine and I were still in one piece, so no harm done, I thought.

Lifting the machine into my tall mama-car was another Herculean task, and I congratulated myself on my recent gym workouts that enabled me to manhandle that sucker into the backseat.

Mixing up the cleaning solution wasn't as easy as you'd think either. There were so many warnings on the machine that I decided to make a cup of tea and read all the labels and instructions before attempting to turn the thing on. I was especially proud when I unearthed a plug adapter that we'd used for Christmas lights, which was necessary to plug the machine into the wall.

Once I got that thing going, there was no stopping it. It was actually kind of fun, sort of how I imagined a riding lawn mower might feel. I enjoyed myself, and I really found my rhythm right about when it was time to change the dirty water. I had no idea we were such a filthy family! In fact, up until that point, I had lived quite happily completely oblivious to how dirty our carpets really were. Frankly, I can't see that it did me one bit of good to find that out. Now I'm just going to have to keep renting that big red cleaning machine, and that's just one more job to add to my list. Of course, if there are a few brownies taped to the handle, it might just be worth it.

Ten Good Reasons to Clean House

To prove that you are not conducting sinister science experiments in your kitchen or slicing and dicing anything inappropriate for the family freezer.

So that the Department of Human Resources isn't called in by your neighbors to remove your children from an unsafe environment.

To evict all the new diseases which have recently hopped a plane out of the rain forest and are now stateside and setting up lawn chairs in your basement.

So that your children no longer look nostalgically at the cobwebs on your dining-room chandelier while reminiscing about Disney World's Haunted House.

To enjoy the day *after* you clean, which is the only day in the entire year when you really don't have to feel guilty about not cleaning your house.

When friends are forced to hold their noses to ward off the foul stench emanating from your suburban squalor when you fling open your front door to greet and invite them in.

When you are so overwhelmed by your dirty house that you no longer bother getting up off the couch when you throw used tissues at the trash can and miss.

When your mother-in-law is coming to dinner.

When you no longer remember the last time you cleaned your house, but you distinctly recall that your child was wearing a smaller shoe size at the time.

So that you can declare yourself too exhausted to cook dinner and take everyone out for something fattening, forbidden, and delicious.

The Coffin

I've finally found it—the one thing that every woman wants. This week, I'm going to get a memo out to every mother I know. In fact, I'm thinking about buying some commercial time on cable television and renting a few billboards. This is big news. I have personally invented a brand new, life-is-more-pleasant household item on par with ice machines and disposable diapers. I am now the proud owner of the biggest custom-built laundry hamper on earth, and I am about as excited about it as I have ever been about anything in my life. I would put this laundry-hamper acquisition up there with contact lenses and opera-length pearls as one of the finest things I have ever owned.

First of all, if you aren't in my four-loads-a-day laundry orbit, never have been, and never plan to be, then you should stop reading right now. This chapter isn't for you, and, frankly, you haven't earned the right to benefit from this life-changing laundry parable. You won't appreciate it properly, and, to be honest, that might really set me off, and nobody around here wants that.

However, if you have children, pets, and other relatives and friends who dribble red wine across your tablecloth on a regular basis, plus others who come to visit and leave you with endless loads of dirty sheets, towels, clothes, sports uniforms, etc., then I advise you to do what I did. Get on the horn, find yourself a good-fairy carpenter, and hire him or her to build you the hamper of your dreams.

I take laundry personally. My husband can clean a bathroom to a fare-thee-well, but laundry is my own little sandbox, and no one else does it to my satisfaction. Laundry sorting is one of the first family chores my kids learned. My children could be professional laundry sorters for the snootiest royal valets in Great Britain. Before they could tie their shoes, they knew the difference between beach towels and monogrammed guest towels, and they knew that *nothing* gets washed with towels except more towels. I promise you that one-year-olds can sort accurately by color, and if they know what's good for them around here, they can make the fine distinctions between light pink (goes with lights) and fuchsia (washes with bright colors). They can easily field the laundry curve balls involved in sorting oranges and yellows before they are out of diapers. I distinctly remember my middle child taking his pacifier out of his mouth so that he could concentrate more fully on his sock-sorting assignment.

Because I have three children who play sports, it is not uncommon for them to go through six outfits on any given day. I am here to tell you that shorts and shirts worn by small boys running wind sprints in ninety-degree weather smell to high heaven. Uniforms with all their grass stains, ground-in dirt, blood, Gatorade spills, and other stains you don't even want to know about need their own bin. No woman wants her delicate blouses to simmer in a laundry basket with reeking football uniforms waiting to be washed.

The stains on baseball pants actually defy description. What can you expect when the kid is actually encouraged to slide in red dirt and mud? Whoever decided sliding was a reasonable strategy in baseball? Outrageous! I guarantee that whoever started that practice was not in charge of the household laundry. No woman would have *ever* encouraged a child to deliberately and repeatedly slide a white-coated baseball leg along the ground. Women would have required those baseball players to *take turns* running to home plate. Simple. Democratic. *Clean.*

As a member of my Episcopal church's altar guild (the group

which takes turns to set up for the Eucharist, arrange flowers, and wash linens), I am completely distracted from praying at the altar when I watch our priest stuff a white linen cloth into the bottom of a chalice to soak up the remaining red wine. All I can think about is how many days that napkin will have to soak before it can then be hung to dry, starched, ironed, and returned to a drawer in the sacristy. I swear it's enough to make me switch religions.

The biggest challenge with laundry is, of course, that it is never completely finished. Unless our family joins a nudist colony, there will always be laundry waiting for me like the legendary troll under the three billy goats' bridge. I'm convinced that big laundry pieces mate in the dark and produce small laundry pieces. There is just no other way to account for the quantity.

I can no longer view a new clothing purchase as a mere fashion statement. I see laundry pitfalls in every shop window. I read clothing labels obsessively. I'd love to meet the idiot who actually buys silk pajamas that have to be dry-cleaned. Last year, when I was given a gorgeous chunky sweater for Christmas, all I could think about was that its bulk would take up an entire laundry load by itself, and I couldn't help but notice that the cream color was going to give me fits with constant stain removal. I would have to serve my children's supper clad in a raincoat because there is no way they could eat my spaghetti marinara without splashing me with sauce.

I hate to brag, but the truth is that I am a stain-removing goddess. Women call me from far and wide when they need big-league advice. Obviously, I can remove blood, grass, mud, and the run-of-the-mill stains, but I'm also the big gun who gets called in for a consultation when some horrible child sticks bubble gum in the eighteenth-century lace on the bottom of her brother's christening gown. I have answered the 911 call when some ignorant daddy has given an adult-sized, chocolate ice-cream cone to his baby girl who is clad in $89 a yard, pale-blue linen which is tissue-paper thin. Blue is the hardest color of all, of course. White you can bleach. With light blue, you can only pray. I've done my best for these people because, really, stain removal is my special gift.

There are no vacation days and no sick days when you are in charge of the family laundry. I once took Christmas Eve and Christmas Day off and paid for it for the first two weeks of the new year. Laundry makes me crazy. I have been known to become unreasonably angry with my generously proportioned husband simply because his blue jeans take up practically an entire load by themselves.

One day, I reached my patience limit with laundry. I'd had it. Couldn't handle the pressure. Choked. Lost all pretense of poise and good manners. The day began like any other. I looked at my usual pile of laundry, gathered daily from three bathroom hampers by my children and piled at the top of the basement stairs for me to deal with—like some great pyramid of ancient Egypt—and I decided that life simply could not go on as before.

I called a carpenter and told him exactly what I wanted. That's right. I commissioned a work of art, my *pièce de résistance*. I ordered a six-foot-long box with five individual compartments (darks, lights, reds, linens, and "special treatment"), each with a hinged lid. The carpenter asked when I needed it. I said tomorrow. There was a slight hesitation, but I've been a pretty good customer, and my carpenter is a Southern male with a strong sense of self-preservation, so he named an exorbitant price, and I agreed to it instantly.

When I got off the phone, my husband asked me how much this laundry-hamper project was going to cost.

I turned around and gave him one of those looks that hushed him up immediately and said, "It doesn't matter how much."

"I understand," replied my wise husband who has a special talent for knowing just when to leave a subject alone.

The next day when the carpenter delivered my new hamper, I was puzzled to see several bystanders watching the unloading process as if this was a seriously newsworthy event. It took me two days before I realized how much that box looked like an unfinished coffin loaded up on the back of the carpenter's pickup truck. From that day on, our family dubbed our deluxe laundry hamper "the coffin."

It took four men to bring it inside. Within forty-five minutes, I was painting that box to match the walls in my basement. When my husband came home, he was visibly shocked to see me painting a coffin in our dining room.

"May I ask why you are painting that *thing* in the dining room?" he inquired.

"It's January. It's thirty-four degrees outside. Plus, this chandelier puts out a lot of light. You have a problem with that?" I asked.

He backed off quickly. "Absolutely not," my husband said. "Carry on."

My life is changed forever by my laundry hamper. Oh, yes, I still have the same insurmountable, unending, overwhelming laundry assignment, but it's all tidy now, well-organized, and nicely camouflaged. I can face my laundry now on equal ground. I fought the laundry, and I won. This could happen to you, too. All it takes is a carpenter, a big fat check, and a little gumption.

Things You Should Never Do Without Professional Help

Bake a friend's wedding cake. (The possibilities for disaster here are the stuff of cinematic legend.)

Build an airplane from a kit and then fly in it. (Only a complete fool would do this.)

Literally build your own house. (Your law degree is meaningless in this endeavor. The house that Jack built will fall down. *On your head.*)

Make your own handmade paper or soap. (Why in the world would you do this? If you have this much time on your hands, you should be volunteering somewhere.)

Roof your own house. (You will fall off. No question about it.)

Perform surgery on yourself. (You are not a pioneer. Remember: at least half of those people ended up in unmarked graves on the prairie.)

Catch/care for/keep a wild animal as a pet. (This is just such a bad idea.)

Ignore tornado sirens. (You will not wake up in Kansas.)

Take an armchair trip around the world by sampling each country's beer. (You will be so sorry the next day.)

Cut your own hair. (Are you so impatient you can't wait two weeks for an appointment?)

Take anything but a dog for a walk on a leash. (You will look unutterably stupid.)

Argue with a two-year-old about what he or she should wear. (You cannot win.)

Hang curtains/wallpaper alone. (Misery should be shared.)

Take a group of teenagers on a field trip. (Just go ahead and slit your throat.)

Go to your high school reunion. (What is the point? Everyone is exactly the same, just older and fatter.)

Miss your high school reunion. (You'll be talked about until the next one.)

Spend the night alone in the hospital. (You could die like that.)

Drive yourself to a corrective-eye-surgery appointment. (Do you have no friends at all?)

Computer Trouble

Not too long ago, I was feeling mighty pleased with myself. I was marking things off my to-do list at a steady clip because I knew I had several extremely busy months ahead. Of course, this feeling was too good to be true. I should have anticipated the bursting of my bubble. Any time I am that smug, the fates are just plotting to smack me down, and this time was no exception.

I was making some last-minute revisions to an article I was writing, just giving it one last read-through before pressing that oh-so-final "save changes" key on my computer. Everything looked fine, so I saved. From there, I had a few blissful weeks of guilt-free loafing with no writing projects.

Until I decided to print out my article.

You guessed it. When I tried to print, the pages were blankly white, pristine clean, nauseatingly empty.

My first reaction was one I am sure most of you have experienced at one time or another when working on a computer. I took another sip of my Co'cola, gulped a deep, cleansing breath a yoga master would be proud of, smiled at my computer (which in my mind will always be personified—I am convinced computers have personalities or, at the very least, an evil sense of humor), and began a fresh search, beginning with page one.

I was gentle, pressing the keys as if they might explode like terrorists' plastique if I pressed too hard, still convinced that if I remained calm, cool, and organized, I could retrieve my documents and carry on with my life unscarred.

In other words, I was in the first stage of computer denial. I was still floating above the keyboard mentally, convinced that in a few minutes, I would wake up from my computer nightmare to find a hard copy of the article in my hand and hear a faint chuckling emanating from my computer.

No such luck. By this point, I was searching in earnest for my missing pages. I could feel sweat (a faint glow since I am a Southern woman) popping out on my forehead, and my fingers were becoming clumsy as panic set in and the realization that my article could, indeed, be gone forever to meet up with socks that vanish from my dryer. I was no longer calm, and to use royal pronouns, "*We* were not amused."

From somewhere behind my eyeballs, I could feel the rage beginning to bubble out of my ears. I began pleading and bargaining with my computer. You can imagine the dialogue: "*Please,* give it back. I can't recreate it. I don't have a hard copy. I didn't have time to print one out. I had to stop writing to get juice for my children and find G.I. Joe's climbing gear. I'll never work without backup again! I swear it."

Next, I tried bribery. "What do you want, computer? Name it. You want a desk with a better view? You want a window? You want to be nearer the fax machine? I know how much you two like to get together."

Nothing worked. Computers have no compassion. No soul. For six years my computer saved the six hundred times my son wrote his name on my hard drive as if it were an Einstein doodle, but my last few weeks of work were gone forever.

Finally, I completely lost my temper and threw a full-scale tantrum. Yes, I began screaming at an inanimate object like a demented woman: "Give it back! Right now! I mean it!"

My son, who was setting up the entire Revolutionary War about six inches from my feet shook his head sadly and, apparently, felt it necessary to help me reign in my temper. "It won't do any good to yell, Mommy. The computer can't hear you. See? No ears."

By this point, I had exhausted myself with my own fit, and I was lying full-length on the floor near the computer, having decided to wallow in a few minutes of self-pity and wondering vaguely if I had any chocolate hidden anywhere.

On the surface, I was desperately trying to come up with a reasonable plan of action to address my computer problem. On another level, I was wondering why my two-year-old had five naked Barbies lined up on my tummy. She was concentrating hard on putting shoes—only—on each of them. I can report that a naked Barbie in red go-go boots is rather distracting.

Seeing she had my attention, my daughter put her hands on either side of my face and reminded me to "use your nice voice to the 'puter, Mommy."

Yeah, yeah. I glanced at my watch and realized that out of the forty-five minutes I had allotted for this little writing polishing exercise, exactly ten remained.

I immediately emailed every person I knew for advice and called every computer geek I could think of for retrieval pointers. I got no help and precious little sympathy.

I helped my children clean up their soldiers and Barbies (by the way, I think Barbie would have been much better off with G. I. Joe than Ken. No one would have dared break in the dream house, and, anyway, Barbie is surely going to wake up one day and realize that Ken is gay) and tried to put it all in perspective. Is losing a bit of writing on the computer really that big of a deal? Of course not. The world is full of flood, famine, persecution, and probably somewhere, locusts.

Every writer I know has lost something on a computer at some point. Is this fact in any way helpful? Not a bit. For days, I allowed myself to indulge in daydreams where I tossed my computer off a bridge and watched it crash into the Alabama River. In another fantasy, I pushed it out of my upstairs window, slowly, with one finger, and watched it smash onto the patio below. In a mildly disturbing way, these fantasies made me wonder about my own mental stability. All of these daydreams involved great violence to my computer—not a healthy sign.

As a Southern woman, I am going to have to admit that I

have finally met my match in my computer. We went head-to-head in a full-scale showdown, and the computer won, hands-down. I was bested by my favorite bit of technology. There is something particularly humbling about being defeated by something made entirely out of cheap plastic parts.

I have long feared such a writing catastrophe, and I've had some near misses over the years, but I've always been able to fix my computer screwups by calling in the big guns—asking my children for help.

I really believe that writing on a computer is like working with animals and babies. They know when you're faking it. They can smell it on your breath. Although I am fairly proficient with my own computer programs, I don't really understand computers on a fundamental level. In fact, I use lots of things every day, like televisions and telephones, which I don't really understand. Oh, I can repeat, parrot-fashion, how such things work, but I don't *really* get it.

In fact, I've made As in math and physics courses in which I never really made the jump from the conceptual to practical reality. It is, therefore, incredibly satisfying to me when grown-up scientists are forced to throw accepted theories out the window every hundred years or so and admit that what we have accepted as established fact is, indeed, wrong—quantum physics, for example. Modern scientists must have felt a lot like those guys Galileo spent so much time trying to persuade that the world isn't flat.

Those of us who understand things on the conceptual level, like computers, but never really on the gut level can roll with the punches. We have long suspected our computers of thinking for themselves. I am convinced my computer lost my article on purpose just to show me who's boss. I never really trusted it in the first place. I'm a bit wary every time I try a new option on my menu, and these days, I close my eyes and wince every time I have to save.

Things Not To Say to the Workmen

"Well, just get to it whenever you can."

"Just take my credit card."

"I guess you can leave it there."

"I don't care how long it takes."

"I don't care how much it costs."

"Just go ahead and do it, we'll figure out how much it costs later."

"How hard could that possibly be?"

"Why don't you just make a list? Then you wouldn't have to make so many trips to the hardware store."

"So you think you'll be finished tomorrow?"

"I guess I don't really need to see a copy of your insurance as long as you have it."

"When are you coming back? Do you promise?"

"Is there supposed to be a hole there?"

"Do you have some kind of degree in this?"

"How do you know I'm not going to be happy?"

"What do you mean I really need to come look at this?"

"Why do you want to know if that vase is an antique?"

"What do you mean I'll 'like it even better' this way?"

"What do you mean 'you can barely tell'?"

"How can you need a draw on this job for materials? You haven't even been to my house yet!"

"What do you mean your girlfriend may 'come by' for a while?"

"Why don't any of those men work for you anymore?"

"Can I trust you?"

The Workmen are Coming!

We live in an old house. In fact, we have a plaque from the "hysterical" society out front to prove it. This always makes me chuckle because the two requirements for a designation on the historic register are, well, age itself, and a "lack of substantial alteration." I'd say that a certain "lack of alteration" is pretty much guaranteed to owners of old houses because no workmen ever actually show up to make any.

Oh, I've heard of workman *sightings*. I'm familiar with workman appointments and scheduling; it's the follow-through, the actual completion of the job, that I have yet to experience firsthand.

If you live in an old house, you accept at its mortgage closing that every picturesque arch, vaulted ceiling, and decaying balcony is going to cost you. In addition, you recognize within the first few weeks that there will always be workmen in your home. If you're like me, you begin to treat them like family. You'll buy baby gifts when their children are born, and when you pull a pan of brownies from the oven, you'll automatically offer them up to workmen perched on tall ladders and scaffolding. Home-makers and workmen share an intimate relationship that has nothing to do with sex. Workmen are people who know where you keep the toilet paper and are not shy about telling you when you run out.

After the first month of living with our workmen, I didn't even flinch when my two-year-old asked one of the workmen if he'd "said the blessing" before eating his lunch. I think he mumbled a "well, no..." before my bossy, budding evangelical daughter led him in a moment of prayer.

I didn't even pause while making sandwiches. We'd passed that stage of formality in our relationship. After an initial fit of vigilance, I'd concluded that I couldn't really protect the workmen from children living under the same roof they were repairing. We began to include them in our lives. We sang "Happy Birthday" to them on their birthdays, and they helped referee board games and made suggestions about what to get our daddy for Christmas.

I often overheard some deep discussions about race, family, safety (one of the workmen rode his bike to work without a helmet—*big* mistake with the safety patrol on alert), theology, and the bathroom habits of the family cat. I once eavesdropped on a debate between my asthmatic child and the painter that went something like: "You know, smoking cigarettes will kill you." The painter agreed that this was true. My four-year-old didn't leave it at that, however. "Then why do you do it?" he wanted to know.

I learned to turn a blind eye and a deaf ear. Frankly, I think the torment was mutual and kind of evened out. Anyone wearing a tool belt and safety goggles while carrying a ladder is, by definition, big-time interesting to my children. In fact, from a legal perspective, I'm fairly certain workmen constitute an attractive nuisance.

For the first few weeks of renovation, I intervened constantly. Like a good sheepdog, I shepherded my brood out of the way. Soon, I realized that nothing was going to be finished in a "couple of days" as promised. In fact, some of my children would likely hit puberty before we saw some finality in the basement. Eventually, I drew lines in the sand (i.e. you can watch the workman as long as you sit right here, you don't touch anything, and you don't get in the way) and hoped for the best.

Certainly, I think the children and the workmen told on each other about the same amount. Actually, the workmen might have been bigger tattletales, judging by the outraged looks on my boys' faces when they were reported for alleged violations of the observation rules. One memorable morning, while the outside of our house was being painted, I was informed that all of our windows would have to be left open to allow the paint to dry, and the screens would have to be removed. I faced the day like a frantic zookeeper who has been warned that all the cages will be unlocked for the day. For the next few hours, I went around like the lion tamer from the circus, snapping my whip and trying to keep preschoolers from toppling out of windows and careening into the street.

While I was upstairs (the children had been told that upstairs was closed for the day), I heard one of the workmen yelling: "You better not do that. You hear me? When your mama gets down here, you and me are both gonna be in trouble. Put your leg back in there! Why're you doing that? You better come get this baby quick!"

Now I was already on my way, but I had to fight off a terrible case of the giggles. There were five grown men painting the outside of my house, and the whole lot of them couldn't keep one two-year-old girl from climbing out the window. Of course, I will be the first to admit that two-year-olds make formidable adversaries.

Right now, every square inch of my house needs to be painted inside. In addition to the staggering expense, I can't figure out how to paint and still live here with children who can't walk down a hall without dragging their hands down the wall. These are creatures who go out of their way to touch surfaces in public restrooms. In addition, I don't know where to stash my child with asthma so he won't breathe in paint fumes, and I sure don't know how we can stay out of the kitchen long enough for it to get two coats of paint.

I have a friend who recently lived through the renovation of her kitchen. She was disgustingly cheerful about it, but I think even she got a bit tired of dry cereal. Unfortunately, until I paint, my new toile curtains are going to hang on walls painted such uncomplementary colors that they should probably be separated by the continental divide.

I managed to put off professional decorating for most of my

life. I know my house needs it, but I just can't work up a bit of enthusiasm for it. I promise you this—when I am finished, my curtains are going with me to the nursing home, and if you're still around, feel free to use some of the fringe in my funeral arrangements. Lord knows, it costs enough!

I am in awe of those who actually build a house from scratch. It is all I can do to keep the existing structure in working order and repair the things that get broken every month. I tried to make a deal with a glass company. Clearly, my children are going to continue to break windows. I think charging me $65.00 every time they have to come out to repair a $2.50 window is a little steep. I think we should qualify for some kind of quantity discount. There should be some type of insurance you can buy if you live with children who play with balls.

There is an inevitability about the proximity of broken windows and little boys that I have grudgingly learned to accept. In fact, when a ball came through my basement window a few feet from where I was ironing, I didn't even stop to clean it up until after I'd finished ironing the shirt. I figured—what's the hurry? In my mind, the sound of breaking glass is linked with the reluctant pitter-patter of tennis shoes and a soft-voiced confession—all in a day's play.

I can't tell you the glee with which my children reported that one of the *workmen* had broken the window. When I heard the distinctive tinkle of breaking glass and came roaring down the hall to investigate, I came face-to-face with three little children pointing at the painter.

I learned early that appointments with workmen are relative things. They may mention a day and time as if you are actually scheduling a mutually convenient appointment, but it pays to check which year they mean to make an appearance. I learned not to actually expect them; then when they show up to work— as opposed to showing up to talk to you about the work they are planning to finish when the part comes in from Bangladesh—it's a sort of pleasant surprise. Time flies differently in workman world. Their time is worth $75 per hour, but you get to wait on them all day for nothing.

If you really want the workmen to show up, just put a baby down for a nap. They'll arrive with chain saws blazing, drills blaring, and boots thumping on the roof. They will set a boom box right outside the nursery window and turn on a little reggae. If you don't have children, you can always climb in the shower and soap up; your doorbell is guaranteed to ring.

I must admit that when the workmen eventually finished at our house, the children and I missed them. When we finally tracked down the offensive smell in my son's closet and unearthed a leftover Vienna sausage can from one of the workmen's lunches, I felt a bit nostalgic, and I got downright teary when a car stopped by one afternoon, and one of our workmen jumped out to hand my boys a pretend tool belt of their very own. To my two-year-old daughter, he reverently offered a princess wand—perfectly appropriate.

6:00 PM Conversation: the Homemaker and the Husband

Husband comes home from work:

Wife asks, "How was your day?"

"Great! Settled that Middle-East thing.
Got a lead on the missing nuclear materials.
Working on sea plankton idea to
address world hunger.
Really think the AIDS vaccine has promise. Jotted
down a few ideas for the World Health Organization.
Got some good feedback at work, may
mean a Nobel prize.
Ran into a college buddy after work, said
I haven't changed a bit.
Worked out a little plan to address the national
deficit. Mailing it tomorrow.
Began a new diet. Worked out after lunch. Caught up
on my reading on the commute.
Did I tell you? The mayor wants to give me a key
to the city! Amazed no one ever thought of that
disaster evacuation route before.
I missed you.
How was your day?"

Wife thinks back on day:

Snuggled children in bed. Sang songs. Got up.
Dressed self. Ran errands with children still in pajamas.
Stopped to admire ladybug.
Dressed children. Made breakfast. Dressed child
with potty accident again. *Cleaned up kitchen.*
Made beds. Negotiated peace settlement among
children. Repaired important toy.
Made costumes.
Answered questions about panhandlers downtown.
Answered doorbell. Told Jehovah's Witnesses
we are starting our own cult.
Read *Green Eggs and Ham.* Read it again.
Baked cookies for school. Allowed children to deco-
rate. Wiped sprinkles off ceiling fan. *Cleaned up kitchen.*
Went for stroller ride. Got caught in rain. Declared it
a "mommy adventure" so kids had fun
anyway riding in "ark" stroller.
Cooked lunch while folding three loads
of laundry. *Cleaned up kitchen.*
Baby-sat friend's children. Read books. Played Candy
Land. Talked about good winners and losers. Broke up
fight. Talked about what heaven looks like and what
happens if you want to come back after you die. Prayed.
Cooked supper. Answered three sales calls.
Cleaned up kitchen.
Had face stamped by kids racing to see
Daddy come home from work.

Wife smiles and answers:
"Good day. Nothing special."

Did You Have Enough to Eat?

Did You Have Enough to Eat?

It is an understood maxim in the South that if you did not have enough food left over after any social event to share with family, close friends, and every person who worked the party, then you did not have enough food. And if there is any sin worse than running out of food in the South, I don't know what it is.

We don't require that the food be divine all the time, nor does it have to be expensive or elegant, but, by golly, whether it is jambalaya or bologna sandwiches, there better be more of it than the entire group can possibly eat, or somebody may not have had enough, and that would violate the most sacred of all hospitality rules.

We are so proud of our food quantities that we take pictures of our food. You know this is true. You still look at old photographs from church dinners on the ground, Thanksgiving feasts, and birthday bashes. The husband usually takes the photo while his wife protests and moves back a little to make sure he gets a good shot of the featured item she spent the last twenty-four hours slaving over. I don't care how vulgar it is. I am deeply satisfied by wedding albums with photographs showing off mountains of shrimp and piled-up platters of fried soft-shell crabs.

When I remember a party, the food is the first thing I want to talk about (as soon as we finish discussing anyone who had anything unusual pierced, or someone with some inappropriate body part hanging out, or anything else that would require immediate attention).

My Yankee friends just don't understand the premise of making twice as much food as you could possibly need. They actually prepare food based upon the number of people expected to attend the party. It makes me break out in a sweat just to think about food in those stingy amounts. For example, if twelve people are expected at a dinner party, Yankees grill twelve steaks. First of all, what if one steak falls off the grill and hits the ground? Who gets the PB&J sandwich? And what about our fat friends? Everyone in the South has at least one fat friend, usually some tiny woman's big ol' husband, who will actually accept a polite offer of steak number two if he has had a couple of drinks, and his wife is not close enough to hurt him. If everything is counted out and previously assigned in the Yankee way, there seems to me to be an unsafe margin of error. What do you feed the "we'd love to have them, bring 'em with you" people?

I am assuming that these Yankees are the same people who write in recipe books "feeds six easily." Six *what?* Must refer to six premature infants because every Southern woman I know is aware that "feeds six easily" means "serves four" with enough left over not to embarrass anybody.

Maybe it is just Southerners who know that there must be some food left on the plate to assure the hostess that her guests had enough to eat.

And how do you suppose Yankees thank the army of helpers that sets up, serves, and cleans up after the party? I can tell you right now that in the South, the party workers expect more than their paychecks at the end of the night. They *know* they are entitled to go home with party food, and all their family members will be waiting up to sample the goodies. What about the postmortem party discussion the next morning when everyone eats leftover canapés for breakfast?

I guess Yankees just boil water and eat some cream of wheat. How sad!

For the Love of Tomatoes

Did you know that the most beloved of all Southern, sum-mer-taste sensations, the tomato, is a fruit? Surely, I read that at some point in my education, but my rusty colander of a brain seems to have leaked that juicy detail. I don't suppose it matters much, except that my child and I were cutting out pictures from old *Southern Living* magazines for a school project, and we had to make an official decision—to glue the tomato picture on the veggie page or the fruit page.

Southerners have a long-term love affair with the tomato. We talk about tomatoes all the time: where you can currently buy good ones; who grows good ones; and who knows how to slice them in perfectly round, thin slices for the ultimate, Southern-lady-tea-party tomato sandwiches on soft, fresh, white bread. Lest we forget the importance of the tomato sandwich to our culture, remember that there are articles written exclusively about Charles-ton tomato sandwiches.

When the long, Southern summer ends, so go the tomatoes. In the winter, all we have left are those strangely perfect Califor-nia tomatoes and the imports you just can't help but wonder about. Maybe those other countries are every bit as diligent as Ameri-can farmers about the buildup of carcinogens on their vege-tables, but they sure are an awfully long way away. I get the same feeling about South American tomatoes that I do when I order a salad in a local restaurant—maybe they washed those lettuce leaves, and then again, maybe they didn't.

The perfect summer tomato is vibrantly colored, (unless you picked them green on purpose for that favorite local delicacy, the fried green tomato) firm in texture, and, if you're really lucky, freshly picked and still sun-warmed. Any Southerner knows that tomatoes should never be refrigerated. Only as a last resort, right before spoiling, do we Southern hostesses break down and put a basket of tomatoes in the refrigerator. When these are ultimately sliced for dinner guests, there is always an apologetic explanation: "I just had to put them in the refrigerator. I've passed them out all around the block, and these have just about had it."

Last summer I was tickled to death by an *opus* of a thank-you note written by a gentleman in Tennessee to thank some tomato-fairy friends who left him a basket of tomatoes on his doorstep. His thank-you note was more than gracious. It was eloquent. It was a prose elegy. It was four pages long, handwritten. His letter was a tribute to the summer tomato like none other I have ever read before. I was inspired to write about this often overlooked and humble fruit of the South.

In many ways, Southerners spend all summer, every summer, in search of the mythically elusive, perfect tomato. Much like the perfect watermelon, once you have eaten one, you're hooked. Forever after, the perfection of that one taste-bud bit of heaven will remain with you, and all other tomatoes and watermelons will be measured against that memory-enhanced standard.

Grocery-store tomatoes just don't stand a chance. Nothing picked green, packed in boxes, and shipped weeks ahead can stand up to a Southerner's snooty standard for tomatoes. Save those grocery-store tomatoes for Yankees to use in spaghetti sauce because you are not going to slice one of those suckers to serve at a luncheon for Southern ladies at the local church.

Tomatoes, as everyone in this part of the country knows, must be allowed to ripen on the vine. They should then ideally be sold off the back of an old, taciturn farmer's truck and placed in a brown paper bag or carried in your hands so you can feel the warmth of the sun on your fingers.

You can't be greedy about good tomatoes. In an entire summer, you might only get one or two that satisfies your every fruit and vegetable fantasy. We all seek the same taste—firm, a little crunchy, sweet, but slightly acidic, with an aftertaste of hot sun and dirt—the taste, in fact, of summer in the South. Some summers you don't even get one good tomato. Fortunately, this is rare because a summer of mealy tomatoes has been known to make Southerners surly during the winter months.

At least once in your life, you should pick your own tomatoes. This is a good chance to reinforce the culture of our region. It is especially meaningful if you pick some tomatoes as a child and stand squeezing dirt between your toes as you watch for snakes and bees. You should take at least one bite of a freshly picked tomato that hasn't been washed properly, just wiped rather haphazardly down the front of your shirt. This, of course, will cause a modern mother to wince and head to the nearest pharmacy to read about the toxic effects of a variety of locally applied bug sprays.

At least once in your life, you should try to grow your own tomatoes. It doesn't matter whether you've ever actually lived on a farm or grown anything else in your life. You can buy the plants at K-mart. And if you're really industrious, you can start with seeds. Like most Southern women, I once threw a fit about the inability to purchase a tomato fit to eat in the part of Alabama in which I live, and I resolved to grow my own.

Without exception, this resolution is a precursor to disaster. I don't know exactly how much those tomato plants actually cost me, but after budgeting for potting soil, stakes, chicken wire, fertilizer, and treatment for all the mosquito bites that I got every time I watered them, I think it would be safe to say that each of the three pitiful, misshapen, poor excuses for tomatoes I actually grew cost roughly seventeen dollars. It would have been cheaper to rent a private jet to fly me to a farm to pick my own fresh tomatoes. These days, I just grumble about the sad state of tomatoes with all the other women at the Piggly Wiggly as we pick through the mound of fruit offerings in search of one that won't embarrass us in front of company.

Occasionally, a grocery store owned by locals figures out the tomato draw and cultivates its own source of taciturn farmers to feed the store a seasonal supply of edible tomatoes. More often, they just chalk up big signs that say "homegrown tomatoes" as big as life, which any Southerner over the age of three can see is a big fat lie just by looking at them.

Unfortunately, tomatoes can be tricky. On the outside, they can look red and shiny; they can feel firm to the touch and smell like rich black earth. It is, therefore, often hugely disappointing to pick out a granddaddy of a tomato to eat for lunch only to slice into it and find a mushy, squishy, yellowish Yankee of a to-mato hiding inside. All I can say is that only God knows the inside of every tomato, and if you've performed all the known tricks to pick out your tomato with attention to detail, you just have to pay your money and take your chances. There is an art to picking out a tomato, watermelon, or cantaloupe, and it is one that can't really be learned. One either has the knack for it or doesn't. I don't have the knack. I am resigned to buying five or six lousy tomatoes for every good one I get.

In case you're wondering, it is true that there are a few South-erners who don't like to eat tomatoes, but we don't talk about them much. My own daughter won't eat them. After initially be-ing scandalized, I have comforted myself with the fact that she thinks every food on earth is enhanced if she dredges it in ketchup—a tomato product of plebeian origins, of course, but still promising. I feel certain I couldn't have given birth to any-one who will turn up her nose at tomatoes as an adult.

The Gumbo Mystique

First you make a roux. And if you don't know what that is, you're already in over your head. Making gumbo is more than mere food preparation, so if you're not ready for a serious culinary commitment, you are not ready for the big leagues of cooking an authentic gumbo. Gumbo is more than a regional specialty. It is a metaphor for life, a point of view in itself—not something just any woman with access to the Piggly Wiggly can make. Gumbo is an all-day project that requires the proper motivation (i.e. company is coming). You also have to wake up *feeling* like making gumbo.

Gumbo preparation is not a solitary task. It requires conversation and confidences—between soul mates, preferably, but recruit people off the street if you have to. Marriages have been repaired, children put back on the straight and narrow, all while a gumbo pot was simmering. It wouldn't surprise me a bit if we could solve all the world's problems with a really big gumbo cookoff.

Also, I don't personally know anyone who cooks gumbo without drinking a glass of wine, beer, or other libation. I am sure some teetotaler has made an edible pot of gumbo somewhere in the Bible Belt, but I have serious reservations about its authenticity. The only necessary ingredient is the gumbo filé. Some of you far from your roots will have to examine some dusty grocery-store shelves to find this jewel.

Naturally, personalities come into play in gumbo making. The proper Tabasco amount has brought otherwise peaceful Southern women to blows. Loyalty to recipes perfected in bayous, counties, and parishes is fierce. Some people actually prefer sausage and chicken gumbo, but those of us who are die-hard Gulf Coast devotees swear by seafood gumbo. We are willing to cheerfully spend a mortgage payment to make one pot of gumbo chock-full of fish, shrimp, and crab.

Of primary importance is the okra question. How much is enough? There are some gumbo aficionados who can taste your gumbo and tell you where your okra was grown! I like my gumbo dark brown and swimming with okra and shrimp with a few crab claws hanging out of the bowl. And when I say "bowl," I mean it—not some teeny-tiny cup of gumbo for $22 in a nice restaurant, guaranteed to be half-full of rice. The question about how much rice is right for gumbo is just too touchy a subject to get into here. Suffice it to say that most people like *some* rice in their gumbo.

Gumbo must be served with loaves of crusty French bread. You really need a New Orleans dose of heat and humidity to get the bread right. It won't turn out the same way above sea level.

Some Southern matriarchs have been known to leave codicils to their wills strictly governing who shall and shall not receive the dear departed's gumbo recipe. Be careful of any Southern woman who volunteers to share her gumbo recipe with you. Mothers-in-law, in particular, have been known to omit some vital component so that your gumbo just never quite lives up to the original.

If you live north of the Mason-Dixon line, and you are in need of some gumbo, just get in your car and drive to Louisiana. It's cheaper.

Shrimp Po' Boys

Can you name one culinary delight that so enthralls your body and imagination that merely thinking about it makes your mouth water? I can. In addition to my passion for chocolate (really more of a vocation or calling, I would argue), I have one food weakness, a true Achilles heel of such gastronomic snobbery that I am surprised I didn't marry the first man who could cook it for me the way I like it. I *love* shrimp po' boys, or shrimp loaf, as it is known in some circles. When I was young and svelte, I'd order the half loaf, but now I say bring on the whole loaf.

I prefer my po' boys dressed (with lettuce and tomato), and I am inclined to check the weather forecast to see if the humidity is even in the realm of possibility for making French bread that will live up to my expectations.

The shrimp have to be fresh, never frozen, of course, and I may need to peek in the kitchen to judge the freshness of those crustaceans for myself. They must be lightly battered and fried and piled so high that I couldn't possibly eat all of them on one sandwich. The extra shrimp are the ones I graciously share with my tablemates who have been totally out-ordered by me.

Outside of New Orleans, I have only eaten a few shrimp po' boys in the last twenty years that lived up to my dreams. Once you've eaten a great shrimp po' boy, you live the rest of your taste-bud life in search of the next good one. This is how it is for Southerners reared on Gulf Coast seafood.

Southerners are snobs about their shrimp, crawfish, oysters, and crab. Nearly always, the seafood elsewhere is just a little bit disappointing to us. I have a friend in Louisiana who only eats crawfish from two places in her whole state. She's a Southern-seafood snob, too.

One summer, I had an Olympic gold medal–winning shrimp po' boy in Mobile, Alabama, and it was at Ed's Seafood Shed, and I'm going to tell you all about it.

All the locals recommended Ed's, so my husband and I decided to give it a try. A quick check of the telephone directory listed two Ed's, but a telephone call eliminated the gas station, and we headed out the causeway.

We knew we were on to a good thing when we asked for directions to Ed's. We were graced with that rare smile a local Southerner bestows upon visitors who have the good sense to ask for directions to a community favorite. Unfortunately, the directions, however enthusiastically given, were almost unintelligible:

"Go on down the road a piece past that new crab place that ain't gonna make it and bear right on the old road....No, no street name I know of, but you'll know it when you get there. Then, look out on the bay and follow it around where you see everybody fishin'. Not that they'll catch anything in this weather, but they'll be there just the same. Go on a few miles, past the ball field, and right back on the water. You'll see it. Be right there."

We actually found Ed's without any trouble, but I don't think a Yankee could have done it.

A quick reconnaissance of the parking lot was promising—tons of local tags. We knew enough from the natives to ask for outside seating, and we were installed just in time to enjoy the last rays of sunshine over the water with the battleship, the USS *Alabama*, in the distance.

After meticulously questioning my young waiter and making him break into a sweat and start looking out of the sides of his eyes for the restaurant owner or his wife, I decided to roll the dice on a shrimp po' boy. Frankly, this is really an honor in itself since I rarely even find the offerings promising enough to venture into my beloved seafood.

Ed's served up those gulf shrimp lightly battered and fried on some pretty good French bread, considering it was being served outside of the Crescent City. There was a spring onion lying lightly across my plate that I didn't eat but enjoyed aesthetically. There were some distracting French fries that I immediately pawned off on my vegetarian offspring to avoid any temptations to deviate from the main event.

The atmosphere was perfect for eating a shrimp po' boy. It was sunset on Mobile Bay, a breezy July day that should have been so hot only Yankees would ask to eat outside but that, unseasonably, was a benign seventy-five degrees.

After that first bite, I had to restrain myself from jumping out of my chair and kissing Ed right smack on the mouth in front of God, my husband, and everyone. It was *that* good.

I know what you're thinking about Ed. You're thinking he has to be a fat, beer-bellied man with a baseball cap and a toothless grin. Well, he isn't. Ed looks as normal as you or me, but he's not.

Ed's a genius.

I was so pleased and contented that I felt generous enough to be gracious to all the progeny surrounding me. I looked around the table at my three children, planning to praise them for allowing me to eat my shrimp po' boy in peace while contemplating the joys of one of my beloved waterways. Then I realized that the faint noise I heard over the constant lap, lapping against the side of Ed's deck was actually the snoring of my three children who, had they been born to responsible parents, would have been fed, bathed, and tossed into bed hours before.

It was worth it. Those children got to see a Southern sky at its finest, a truly spectacular finale to a summer day spent scaling the walls of Fort Gaines and climbing every rung of the battleship. Their mama got to eat a shrimp po' boy that she'll be bragging about for the next ten years, and you know the old saying, "If mama ain't happy, ain't nobody happy."

It is exceedingly rare to have fine seafood, a picture-perfect sunset, well-behaved children, and a husband whose company you still enjoy—all in one evening. For the rest of my life, I will be able to say that once I had it *all* at Ed's.

While I was obsessing on seafood, my husband, an appellate court judge, spent a large portion of his evening shaking hands with fellow Alabamians. I couldn't help but notice with my usual sense of political optimism that a brief burst of anti-aircraft fire off the deck of the battleship would have done some serious damage to Alabama's statewide office holders. They were there en masse to eat at Ed's. I must say that we would have sure died a well-fed and happy group.

Obviously, we were some of the last Alabamians to discover Ed's. I'm not worried about it, though, since there is enough shrimp in that place for everyone, even if I have to order "Yo' mama's platter."

On the way back to our hotel, we passed the Hank Aaron Stadium, and the ball game was just concluding with fireworks. My two-year-old squealed in delight and wanted to know, "Is it a holiday?"

The USS *Alabama* was strung with lights, a postcard backdrop for our trip back to the hotel. I was content to watch the lights reflect off the water and didn't even respond when one of my boys muttered in an embarrassed voice, "You sure made a big deal about that shrimp po' boy, Mama."

Ode to Sweet Tea

If I have a culinary vanity, it is that I am a little bit too proud of my sweet tea.

Those of you not from around here may need a bit of explanation. I am referring to sweetened iced tea, the kind that sends Yankees into diabetic comas, the brew that I am convinced is the primary reason Southern women are as sweet as they undoubtedly are.

There are only two kinds of tea in the South: sweet and unsweet. For those of you Northerners trying to fit in, the first step in your cultural assimilation is to learn that the answer to "D'ya wont sweet tea?" is "Yes, ma'am." That's a good start. And when your sweet tea arrives, expect it to be syrupy enough to hold up a silver teaspoon, with enough ice to refresh anyone in gulping distance. It should also have free refills.

Remember that sweet tea is serious business in the South. Restaurants can rise and fall based solely on the quality of their sweet tea. For example, one might say: "I don't want to go there. They don't have good sweet tea."

Southern iced tea, the only kind real Southerners drink outside a Japanese teahouse, is strong—none of this namby-pamby decaffeinated brew. Real women drink their tea with the stimulants in full-strength.

I still remember the best lemon sweet tea I ever had. It was in Moundville, Alabama, and I was about twelve years old. It was made by Mrs. Lister, a friend's grandmother. It was served in a beautiful glass with a real linen napkin, and I was just pleased as punch to be treated like a grown-up lady and served iced tea. I had *arrived*.

Rest assured that if you have actually seen a Southern woman order unsweetened tea in a restaurant, there's a good reason for it. She will furtively dissolve fifteen packets of Sweet 'N Low in search of her usual sugar fix, and you can bet the farm that she has just realized that she has five days to lose enough weight to get into her favorite party dress without breaking any indecent-exposure laws. Mark my words: she'll be ordering the cottage-cheese plate, and she won't be happy about it.

And, yes, I am aware that "sweet tea" should be, at the very least, "sweetened tea." However, I have lately decided that some-times you just have to let the idiosyncrasies of the local dialect flow over you like molasses. I can honestly say that I kind of enjoy saying "sweet tea" now—a sort of mini-grammar rebellion on behalf of Southern women everywhere. (Also, you get better restaurant service if you order in the local patois.)

Sweetened iced tea is a panacea for all ills in the South. If your best friend arrives on your doorstep and says her husband wants a divorce, the first thing out of a Southern woman's mouth will be, "Honey, you come in here, and I'll fix you some sweet tea."

I make iced tea with four family-sized tea bags in the big blue pitcher. Other pitchers won't work. First, I put in too much sugar. Then I add some more. Next I add two scoops of lemon-ade mix and wait to pour boiling hot tea on top to melt all that sugar.

While waiting for my tea bags to steep, I start begging one of my children to go outside and pick some mint leaves. After about seven unanswered pleas at the top of my lungs, I switch from asking to demanding, and I add a good measure of Southern-mama guilt. I storm back to my boys' bedrooms and demand to know, in my most put-out voice, how I could possibly have given birth to two boys who can't even be bothered to pick a few sprigs of mint for their mama's tea.

Sometimes I am still standing there, hands on hips in righteous indignation, when their father calls out from his office upstairs: "Boys! Go pick your mama some mint!"

Usually, they put their books and soldiers down and slink to the back door. It is a good half-hour later when I go to the backyard to see what they could possibly have done with my mint, since it has certainly not made an appearance in the kitchen. After yelling up into the bottom branches of the trees closest to my back door, I can usually track down one of the boys who will obligingly allow ten leaves or so to sprinkle down on my head. After scrambling to catch them, I ask in my most long-suffering voice, "What am I supposed to do with ten sage leaves?" Honestly, they're bright boys. You'd think they could distinguish between the smell of sage and mint.

After only a few additional minutes of haranguing, one of my offspring rounds up the requisite mint leaves. As I wash the leaves and let cold water flow over them into my brewing tea, I have to smile as I watch my boys sniffing their grubby hands, suddenly aromatic with the scent of freshly picked mint, on their way back outside.

Finally, I stir the tea until it looks ready to me, throw a linen dish towel over the mouth of the pitcher, place it on the counter within easy reach—never in the refrigerator—and wait for a visitor who is sweet-tea worthy.

Things Parents Actually Say to Their Children in Restaurants

"No one else in the history of the world has refused to eat potatoes."

"Sit up. Do not rub your head on the tablecloth."

"Just leave it on the floor. You may not climb under the table."

"Get your hair out of the ketchup, please."

"Wipe that with your napkin—not your shirt."

"Do not point. There are all kinds of people in the world, remember? We will talk about fat and thin people, baldness, and amputations when we get home."

"I refuse to believe there is nothing on your plate that you like."

"Take your napkin off your head and put it in your lap."

"Do not burp or pretend to throw up at the table."

"If you need to blow your nose, please excuse yourself and go to the restroom."

"You have your own chair."

"You have the same lunch on your plate.
Why must you eat mine?"

"Do not kick your brother/sister under the table."

"Do not play with your silverware.
Those are not antennae."

"Well, at least you tried it.
Now spit it out in your napkin."

"Do you see those people in front of us/behind us?
You are giving them indigestion."

"Use your napkin to clean it up; we'll get a refill
when the waiter comes back."

"We've been to the bathroom twice. It's not
an adventure, you know."

"I do not believe that you will die of thirst
before she brings your water."

"Where are your manners?"

"Do you ever want to eat in a restaurant
again as long as you live?"

Surviving the Holidays

Crowded Calendars

I don't need a calendar to tell me when the month of May rolls around. My theory is that May is really another December, only it's unadvertised and sort of sneaks up on you. Think about it: May is packed with the initial post-Easter recovery period followed by a flood of weddings, graduations, festivals, spring sports, and parties. There are presents involved. Huge outlays of money and hours of parental involvement are required. In fact, May is such a flurry of activities, special events, and momentous occasions that I start getting sick headaches toward the end of April, and by May of every year, I've worked myself up to a full-scale, hide-under-the-covers nervous breakdown.

Spring is the time of the school year when teachers, children, and parents are tired. Nerves are beginning to fray. One time I actually felt a nervous tick in my eyelid while I was dyeing coconut shavings green to make grass for my Easter cupcakes.

As summer gets closer, I occasionally find myself standing in my driveway clutching my car keys and trying to remember where I was hustling off to. I make increasing numbers of mistakes— forgetting which baseball uniform needs to be clean for the next night's game, for example, or wondering which kid wants to take the cat to school for show-and-tell the next day. I talk to myself—out loud—even more often than usual and wonder half-seriously if I'm cracking up. Then I watch another frantic mother careen into the school parking lot with tires squealing to retrieve one of her sobbing, forgotten offspring, and I realize that I'm not alone in the overwhelmed-by-spring sensation.

One of my favorite spring party days is Easter-egg-hunting day. In years past, at least one of my children's school classes walked to our house to search for the golden egg. In the most recent hunt, I served as the Easter bunny of suburbia and set my alarm for 5:00 AM to get out there and hide the eggs before waking my kids up for school. Because one never knows when the build-an-ark spring shower is going to blow in, I've learned not to hide those candy-stuffed eggs too early.

Hopping (couldn't resist) out of bed, I pulled on my paint-stained sweatpants and pushed my feet into my hot-pink plastic gardening shoes that I keep by the back door for watering the plants. (These are the same shoes that my oldest son begged me to wear only when gardening in the *backyard* so that none of his friends could drive by the house and see me in them.) I was still wearing the T-shirt I'd slept in. While I maintain, even now, that this attire was absolutely perfect for wading through beds of azaleas and ferns to hide Easter eggs, I'll admit that as I trooped through my dining room, hair uncombed and face unwashed, I caught a glimpse of myself in the mirror over my sideboard, and, well, it was not a pretty sight. At that moment in time, I'm just going to have to say, in the words of an old high-school cheer, "*U-G-L-Y, you ain't got no alibi—you ugly!*" Needless to say, I was relieved that dawn had not yet broken, and I was hopeful that no one I knew would see me in all my morning glory.

Unfortunately, as life inevitably seems to play out, I'd forgotten just how busy our neighborhood is at 5:00 AM. I hadn't been outside ten minutes before I had to reciprocate cheerful "top o' the morning" greetings to a bunch of disgustingly perky joggers who all seemed quite comfortable making small running detours up into my lawn to poke their noses into my giant basket to examine the eggs. Quite a few of those cheeky, well-toned early birds had the gall to advise me on where to hide the golden egg. Honestly, the *nerve* of some people!

I was happily squirreling away Easter eggs in the ivy growing underneath my dining-room windows when a flashlight beamed right in my face, which was so startling that I almost dropped my basket. I was exceedingly embarrassed to observe one of our local police officers examining my colorful attire, and I began to immediately rattle out an explanation—only to be rudely interrupted by his curt request for identification. Imagine! I couldn't hold back my indignation: "I'll have you know I live here!" I said. It took a tad more explaining, but, really, in retrospect, I'm happy to report that our local law-enforcement officers are looking out for the neighborhood. After all, I could have been a burglar or some other ill-intentioned person. I think the officer was a little disappointed that all he'd nabbed was an aging Easter bunny in desperate need of a manicure and her cosmetics bag.

We live in an old neighborhood where the houses are only twelve feet apart. You can sit on my porch and eavesdrop on conversations that are more interesting than daytime television. I'm not kidding. Unfortunately, however, that eavesdropping thing works both ways. Every time I got too close to my neighbors' driveway, their security floodlights came on automatically, and I winced thinking about the immaculate childless couple who lives there and who were probably trying to catch another half-hour of sleep before getting up for work. Pretty soon, though, I got over my shyness, and I just slapped one of my big pink plastic shoes on their driveway whenever I needed a little more light.

In the first place, it was still too dark for me to see down in those azalea bushes where I was stuffing eggs, and I was scared to stick my hand in there blindly. Plus, I'm pretty sure my neighbors think we're kind of strange anyway. There have been a couple of incidents involving naked children on the porch swing, and I think their vehicles may have taken some hostile fire from a pretend battlefront as they backed down the driveway. In other words, I didn't have much to lose by triggering their floodlights, and I wasn't all that worried about the childless couple's beauty rest. After all, I was a bunny with a mission. I had about fourteen-dozen eggs to hide and half an hour to do it before the baby bunnies in my house started demanding oatmeal and bananas.

As if run-ins with the police and the joggers with their

helpful suggestions weren't enough, early-morning walkers seemed to feel amazingly free to mosey up into my yard, coffee mug in hand, to ask, "So, what are you doing?"

Now, bear in mind: *it was Easter week.* I had a giant basket over my arm, and I was bent over my azalea bushes like I was throwing up. What was wrong with those people? Would it not be obvious to any but the least-astute members of the general public that I was hiding Easter eggs? I discovered that my patience bucket is nearly empty at 5:30 AM when I haven't even had a chance to brush my teeth.

It wasn't too long after that when my husband came down the front steps immaculately turned out, legal briefcase in hand, a man off to work. He walked to the end of the front porch and silently watched me struggle with a particularly thorny spot between a huge boxwood bush that needed trimming and a Fairy rosebush and said, "What in the world are you doing?"

I mentally counted to ten and envisioned myself answering that stupid question in a ladylike manner, but before I could rein it in, I heard myself say, "What does it look like I'm doing? You think I'm making spaghetti out here? I'm hiding the bloomin' Easter eggs! And, by the way, if I step in one of the holes our children have apparently been digging to China, please remember to change my clothes before you take me to the hospital—do you hear me?"

"As a matter of fact, I do," my husband responded, a little snootily, I thought. "*Everyone* can hear you."

Up until that point, I had planned on telling him about my early-morning interaction with the local police force, but after that little verbal exchange, I decided that it might be better to keep that episode to myself. Although *I* rarely fail to see the humor in such situations, my husband sometimes doesn't fully appreciate such charming colloquial anecdotes. One woman's cocktail-party story is another man's evidence of insanity, you know.

Candy Etiquette

It has come to my attention that some of you need a refresher tutorial in the appropriate and fair distribution of Halloween candy. I am, frankly, amazed that we have come to this in a free society. We have actually arrived at a point where Halloween candy is to be disdained, and celery sticks are the order of the day.

Because I am known to my friends as a woman who takes her chocolate seriously, I have been nominated to conduct this candy-etiquette lesson in light of astonishing Halloween transgressions. A number of social niceties regarding candy giving and receiving seems to have gone awry.

First and foremost is this premise: Candy is important. Brussels sprouts, broccoli, and tofu are *not*. No one feels passionate about heart-healthy food. We know we should eat it. Most of the time, we do eat it. End of discussion. There just isn't anything left to say about it. Chocolate (and other worthy candies and sweets), on the other hand, inspire books, articles, and lavish photo shoots. In fact, chocolate is considered an aphrodisiac in some cultures. (This doesn't work for me since I am far too preoccupied with the actual consumption of chocolate to be interested in any extracurricular activities.) Chocolate is an end in itself, a reward of true sensual bliss for those who fully utilize their taste buds. Life without chocolate is a mere black-and-white existence.

That said, to those of you who are not chocolate-candy aficionados and who do not accept this candy premise as a given, let me address the current lapses in Halloween-candy decorum. In case you are so old that you have forgotten childhood delicacies, Halloween is a night for eating candy until you puke. The classic selections are still with us. There is a mountain of candy corn, a plethora of peanut-butter chews, and a bushel of other store-bought goodies that are still going strong.

All of these are perfectly acceptable candy offerings for children. In fact, almost any individually wrapped treasure will be well received as long as it is something you would eat yourself. Think twice about recycling last year's candy canes, and nothing you find in your sofa cushions—no matter how well wrapped— should be offered to a perfectly well-behaved ghost rapping at your door. Every fairy princess who holds out a plastic pumpkin candy container deserves a treat you would be proud to serve your own offspring. Basic food-safety guidelines should be rigorously adhered to.

On the other hand, all bets are off if a fifteen-year-old (sans costume) trick-or-treater, who is a foot taller than you and wearing a Freddy Krueger mask, knocks on your door at 10:00 PM and shoves a pillowcase under your nose demanding that you empty your candy dish and wallet into its folds. As far as I am concerned, you can drop the fuzzy Tootsie Roll you found under the baby's safety seat into the pillowcase and throw all your weight into slamming the front door closed. Odds are, that trick-or-treater is going to smash your pumpkin either way.

In addition, you have the right to dole out the quantity of candy you would like each child to receive. I choose to reward the best candy selections to children wearing clever, homemade costumes and those barely able to say "twick-o'-tweat," but this is really an item of personal preference. I think you also have the option of reaching into trick-or-treaters' bags and deducting candy items from cowboys who refuse to say thank you, greedy goblins who grab handfuls of candy, snooty princesses who make disparaging remarks about your candy selections, or small ninjas who shove baby pumpkins out of their way.

It is quite possible for trick-or-treaters to leave my door with less candy than they came with. I am quite insistent upon proper candy-etiquette observation both in the distribution and receipt of treats.

On a more serious note, I just don't know what to say to those of you handing out tiny boxes of raisins. I am really at a loss. What are you, communists? You might as well open up the freezer and start passing out frozen waffles. Really. If you must be healthy 365 days of the year with no exceptions, be prepared to fork out some money on creative bags to hold popcorn balls, fresh nuts, or colorful trail mix. Better yet, give out stickers and spider rings. You'll be the neighborhood hero. Keep the raisins and prunes for your oatmeal-tofu-sea-kelp muffins. You know how the grocery store can get a run on those items at this time of year.

If you are in a budget crunch, you can't beat bags of individually wrapped pieces of bubble gum. It's a perennial favorite, especially the kind with a comic on the wrapper. You get about a million pieces of gum for around two dollars, a good way to go if you need a mass quantity. Bubble gum is particularly satisfying to children because it is frowned upon by most adults who anticipate stepping into a discarded wad or having to remember how to perform the Heimlich maneuver. Luckily, in the toddler group, the gum is swallowed too quickly to present much of a choking hazard.

I feel I must say a word here to those of you who forgot to buy candy this year for Halloween. Clearly, you do not get out enough if you failed to notice the Halloween aisles in discount stores. You should spend some time examining your self-involved lifestyle if you claim Halloween snuck up on you. It is the same date every year, you know.

It is not socially acceptable for you to raid the receptionist's candy jar on your way home from work. While it is true that hard candy has a shelf life of approximately six hundred years, it is not incumbent upon you to test the effectiveness of those preservatives. And don't expect any standing ovations from trick-or-treaters for a few old breath mints. Peppermints are better than nothing—but just barely.

And I have absolutely nothing to say to those of you who never buy candy for Halloween because you take your children trick-or-treating and "just aren't home to pass it out." Hogwash. You are a cheapskate, and you know it.

If you are genuinely sorry for your candy transgressions, let me suggest full-sized candy bars for those of you with a moderate amount of trick-or-treaters as a way to make amends this year. If you have hundreds of trick-or-treaters like we do, the full-sized bars can get a bit pricey. Ideally, you should go for the old standby—the homemade candy creation. (Unfortunately, this will only work for trick-or-treaters you know personally since their parents won't let them eat it otherwise. Keep a stash of sanitary candy that comes pre-wrapped from those clean Hong Kong factories for the rest.)

Halloween is a theme-party opportunity most SWAGs have been lying in wait for. Finally, a chance to show off their pipe-cleaner, Popsicle-stick talents to the world. If you like, you may polish a silver tray to display your confections in Southern style. This project is a legitimate excuse to buy marshmallow creme and use orange food coloring. You can cook with real butter, tons of sugar, and chocolate. You will be the cool mom with hand-iced pumpkins and candy ghosts that flutter a bit in the breeze. Best of all, you get to eat the leftovers.

Any SWAG worth her salt knows how to come out on the good end of a candy trade with small children. There isn't a kid in the world who won't hand over a Snickers bar in exchange for five or six Pixie Sticks. Sweeten the deal with a few Jolly Ranchers or Blow Pops, and you'll have enough chocolate to last until the Russell Stover chocolate-covered marshmallow turkeys arrive.

The Halloween Costume

"*What do you want to* be for Halloween?" is the October question of the month in households with children. At our house, anything gory or death-industry related is taboo. Still, the options for dress-up are mind-boggling to children. A holiday dedicated to "let's pretend" with adult participation and a sugar high all in one night makes any child's cup run over.

I am reminded of one mother whose child was finally old enough for a Halloween costume and candy free-for-all. In short, he could do little more than walk, say "twick-o'-tweat," and share his adorableness with all the neighbors on the block.

She began with the all-important question: "What do you want to be for Halloween?"

Now, those of us with more Halloween experience know that this open-ended question was her first mistake. She gave way too many options. She should have first checked the sale pages, a couple of garage sales, and her child's toy box. Throw in a few accessories from her closet, Goodwill, the junk drawer, and the glove compartment of her car, and voilà—instant costume. It is just a matter of presentation. You must be able to sell your costume-choice options to the savviest of consumers: the small child.

This child said he wanted to dress up as the cowardly lion in *The Wizard of Oz*. The mother was charmed!

She began work immediately. Together, they went all over town to find just the right material for the lion's fur. Like a tsar of imperial Russia, the small child rejected fabric swatch after fabric swatch before pronouncing one soft enough for the cowardly lion costume. The material was $42 per yard, more than the mother spent on fabric to recover her sofa, but this was a special event, she justified.

Next came the search for the holy grail of yarn that would be just the right shade of brown for a mane and tail. It had to be specially ordered from a selection of hand-dyed sweater yarns, but you don't make many lion costumes, the mother reasoned.

Night after night, the mother stayed up working on the costume until the wee hours after her child was in bed. She thought she might be going a bit overboard when she woke her son up at 3:00 AM to try on the costume so she could get the sleeves right, but he went right back to sleep, so no real harm was done, she concluded.

Finally, October 31st arrived. She laid the costume out at the foot of her son's bed so it would be the first thing he saw when he woke up. Then she went to the kitchen to wait for the inevitable squeals of delight.

When her son came to the kitchen, without any squeals of delight, she could no longer contain herself: "How do you like your costume?"

The child said, "Oh, I don't want to be a lion anymore."

"What do you mean you don't want to be a lion anymore?" the mother asked, trying not to panic.

"I want to be a Power Ranger," the boy replied.

"What is that?" Mom asked.

"You know, like on TV."

"You've never even seen that television show. I'm the mom. I know what you watch."

"I don't care. I know what they are anyway, and I want to be one. All my friends are going to be Power Rangers."

"Well, you can't! We spent $163 out of the grocery budget so that you can be the cowardly lion."

"Then I don't want to go trick-or-treating."

"FINE."

It is at this point that the dad comes home from work, and the mommy retires in martyred solitude to the bathtub to reflect upon her parenting ideals.

It is not too long after that she finds herself headed to the local Wal-Mart to purchase $14.50 worth of Power Ranger cheap plastic and unnatural fibers that will probably cause her son to break out into a heat rash (which she decides will be just what he deserves for dragging his mother into this costume nightmare). After all, what's another fifteen bucks after you've spent a fortune on a costume?

The mother wonders how she can still smile to see her little boy's grimy fingers clutching the pile of inferior petroleum products masquerading as a Power Ranger costume.

The boy says, "You're the best, Mom."

Meanwhile, the mother is wondering if she can somehow make the lion costume into some sort of Christmas outfit for herself. Maybe the mane could be a fringe kind of thing.

Thanksgiving Table Tips

Holidays are a stressful time for many people. I've been giving this some thought and have come up with a few suggestions to help us all get through Thanksgiving feasts with a modicum of composure, goodwill, grace, and the least blood loss possible:

Remember that recent surgical procedures are not an appropriate dinner-table topic of conversation.

You may show pictures of your grandchildren once, briefly, if someone has actually displayed a clearly verifiable interest (ditto pictures of pets).

You will not ask the identity of a food dish you do not recognize. You may merely choose to be adventurous and try it or take a polite pass.

You may not use, "Who made this?" as a criterion for whether you will eat something or not.

Adult options are the same as for children: "Yes, please," or "No, thank you." Exceptions to this rule have led to inappropriate gagging, unattractive face-pulling, and generally rude behavior.

You will compliment the hostess on her cooking even if you spend the next three days in the hospital with food poisoning.

You will ask questions of family members and show a well-feigned, if not entirely genuine, interest in others' lives. They might surprise you and return the compliment.

You will conduct yourself in a manner you will be proud of in twenty years rather than sink to the level of any unsavory behavior that breaks out around you.

You will talk to children about Indians (call them Native Americans) and Pilgrims and listen avidly to any accompanying songs.

You will remember that for many older family members, this may be their last Thanksgiving, and you will listen carefully to any wandering stories that come trickling out, always remembering that there were other Thanksgivings that meant more to them.

You will be whole-heartedly, overwhelmingly, robustly, jubilantly thankful for all present at your Thanksgiving celebration. You will cherish each person, warts and all, for the uniqueness of his or her life, and you won't forget for one second that many people spend Thanksgiving alone and hungry—for whatever reason—hungry for food, for companionship, for a sense of connection to the rest of us hurrying by.

Holiday Temptations

It is time for someone (and it looks like the issue has been left to me, once again) to go on record regarding the painfully tacky proliferation of holiday-themed apparel. I hate that we have come to this point. I really do. For years, I've bitten my tongue at the explosion of embarrassingly inappropriate T-shirts that appear for sale in discount stores. You know the ones I mean. Their fashion statement is limited to iron-on transfer questions scrawled across the chest with completely unoriginal, cornball, rhyming solicitations for nights of romantic bliss. Unfortunately, the boldly colored slogans on T-shirts referring to the desires of the unwashed masses cause mothers everywhere to cover their children's eyes when passing stalls offering souvenir T-shirts "two for ten bucks."

My guess is that those T-shirts are purchased by unimaginative men and women who routinely answer the question "How've you been?" with clever comebacks like, "Well, I'm still a million dollars short of being a millionaire!" I am curious about shoppers fingering those T-shirts. I find it amazing that there are adults who are bowled over by crude humor that could have been penned by any junior-high-school boy. I've decided these are socially inept people, and making fun of them would just be mean.

Recently, however, I have become alarmed to discover that holiday-themed attire has begun to creep across cultural, socioeconomic, and geographical snobbery lines, and I feel compelled to warn an at-risk group, my comrades, the SWAGs of the world, that this fashion disaster could happen to anyone. I'm here to confess that I, too, rolled down the slippery slope of holiday clothing, and it was not a pretty tumble.

One Christmas, I bought matching plaid taffeta holiday skirts for my daughter and me. They were just so cute in the catalog. (Of course, the tall, fair-haired mother-and-daughter models in the picture would have looked good wearing pillowcases.) In my own defense, I'd like to point out that these holiday outfits were doubly tempting because there is something about that whole mother/daughter-outfit thing that sucks us all in. *Once.* I got over it pretty quickly, but I want you to know that the men in our family referred to my daughter and me as "The Highland Posse" for the duration of the Christmas holidays. One quick look in the mirror confirmed that I'd made a fashion mistake. Because of my age, I was able to handle the ribbing with snooty, Southern-woman disdain, but I'm afraid my poor fashion choices forced my daughter into a screaming, kicking fight with her brother in defense of her new Christmas skirt.

I tell you this so that you will know that I, too, have succumbed to temptation. I want you to benefit from my experience. I want to save you the embarrassment that is the inevitable result when you wear embarrassing clothing selections.

Until recently, I felt sure that only Yankee women bought those Christmas sweatshirts with iron-on transfers of Rudolph, the fat man, and snowmen, but I fear for Southern women because we are easily led astray by kindergarten teachers who use our children's hand prints to make reindeer antlers on the front of aprons. The danger is real. Southern women love to display their children's artwork; they live to use their glue guns, and the idea of thematic clothing for every holiday is, for them, a temptation worthy of Jesus stuck out in the desert. Not to worry. I'm here to remind my friends that holiday clothing items are meant for children, and to further suggest that the acquisition of earrings which light up like Christmas tree bulbs is beyond the pale. As a rule, one should never wear anything suspended from one's ear lobe that requires batteries.

I don't want to hear any arguments about how black velvet

flats with red Christmas bows embroidered on the toes are far enough beyond tacky to become cool. You can't sell me on the idea that if you know what tacky looks like, you can go ahead and tacky-it-up as much as you want and call yourself hip. You and I both know you are not making some kind of cultural pop-art statement. The truth is that holiday outfits are tacky. Plain and simple. Plus, one should never be in direct competition with one's Christmas tree for attention. The general interior-design rule is one focal point per room.

I'm warning you that if you wear one of those Neiman Marcus Christmas sweaters with matching Christmas shoes and angel earrings from the Metropolitan Museum of Art catalog, along with your most flattering shade of red lipstick and a Christmas purse with candy canes hanging off the sides like fringe, you're just going to give those fashion police that much more to talk about, and do we really need that? Lord knows, Southern women irritate those fashion-magazine editors in New York every time we breathe in and out down here, so let's address our own fashion disasters before anyone else has a chance. All we have to do, really, is to confine ourselves to decorating our mantels, front doors, dining rooms, and other inanimate objects that are *traditionally* garlanded, beaded, lighted, and bedecked in greenery.

I'll let you in on a little secret. When I feel the need for a bit of thematic personal adornment during the holidays—during Halloween, for example—I opt for the classic: a witch's hat. I see this as a healthy way to indulge myself in a bit of holiday dress-up. I've been told that my witch's hat suits me perfectly, and I like to think it captures my personality in a thematically appropriate, yet tasteful, way.

Thanksgiving Vows for Southern Women

We will remember that JELL-O is not a recognized group on the FDA's food pyramid.

We vow to thoroughly cook all birds before serving them—no matter what time we have to start basting.

We agree not to serve any manner of entrée that might contain buckshot.

We promise not to deliberately seat volatile relatives near one another merely as entertainment for the rest of the family.

We hereby recognize that it is not a mortal sin to use paper plates—but if any relative digs the plastic utensils out of the garbage can to wash them, we believe she will, indeed, go straight to hell.

We acknowledge that it is not, strictly speaking, rude for Yankees to ask for unsweetened tea at our Thanksgiving feasts since our own Southern brew has been known to make Yankees gag.

We pledge to limit our pumpkins and Pilgrim table decorations so that our guests will not be forced to hold their plates on their laps.

We promise that Southern Thanksgiving dinners will always stretch to feed as many relatives, friends, neighbors, strangers, and dogs as need be, so that no one is left alone, left out, or left wanting in our cornucopia of American plenty.

Christmas Photo Cards

In December, we are all recipients of a wide-ranging selection of holiday cards. Of particular interest, I think, are Southerners and their greeting cards with attached photographs.

First of all, I have to be up-front and admit that our family Christmas card features photographs of our children. I confess to being not entirely comfortable with this. Although I love getting pictures of my friends' families, I feel a bit audacious in assuming that the people on my Christmas card list care what my children look like or how they have changed over the year. It seems to me that they might actually prefer a more seasonally appropriate scene.

In addition, there seems to be an obvious selfishness involved in sending season's greetings to someone and managing to work in pictures of my own children. (Obviously, pictures depicting the Christ child seem much more appropriate.)

Frankly, I think there should be some rules governing the public disbursement of personal pictures. (I'm willing to bet there are some politicians who would agree with me.) For example, business colleagues probably should not be on the photo-card list, and anyone who wouldn't recognize at least one member of the family on sight shouldn't get a photo card.

After all, the photo card is intended as a treat, not some sort of holiday affliction or guess-who game. I would be highly embarrassed if a recipient of one of my cards had to look at the return address to try and figure out who sent it. (You've all had one or two of those cards that requires passing around the dinner table for identification purposes.)

In addition, family photo cards have led to some inappropriate giggling and geographic insensitivity around our house, which I have had to frown upon in an exemplary manner. I have been known to threaten to clutter up our holiday schedules with some sensitivity seminars.

For example, I like to display all the photo cards we receive so that anyone with a vested interest (or those who are just idle and curious) can examine my cards in detail. Unfortunately, to hear my children debate the physical attributes of other children (many of whom are, of course, children of their parents' friends and therefore strangers to them), especially hair-challenged newborn babies, you would think they were doing commentary for the Miss America pageant.

My boys also choose as favorites cards with humorous settings, clothing, or props. Their personal tastes leave a great deal to be desired, and I can only hope their sense of humor becomes more subtle with age because if it doesn't, they are going to send out Christmas cards with photographs of my grandchildren dressed as the Three Stooges and think they are hilariously clever. Needless to say, my children don't appreciate gorgeous hand-tinted photographs and elaborate holiday outfits.

I frequently find that my tastefully arranged display of photo cards has been rearranged to reflect my boys' more base preferences. I am not proud of this display of Christmas spirit; I am merely reporting some potential photo-card pitfalls. (I also find that my boys' XY makeup shows in their appreciation of a couple of exotic-looking sisters from New Orleans who are always front-and-center in the photo arrangement.)

I have wondered if it is merely a Southern tradition—this mass mailing all over the country of children's photos with a few strands of Christmas garland or a border of holly thrown in as a seasonal excuse, but I have received photo cards from Yankees as well, and *oh, my*....

Some Yankees clearly need a tutorial on how to send photo cards to Southerners. First of all, where do they learn to dress those children? I wouldn't take my children to Wal-Mart in some of those clothes they put their children in for Christmas-card photos. Some of the cards I've received look like the people just woke up a little late one morning and decided to take a family picture on the way outside to get the morning paper—no preplanning, no staging, no hair or teeth brushing, nothing. Who ever heard of such a thing? I am embarrassed *for* them.

Yankees do seem to send long letters detailing every dental appointment from the last year for each family member. What is that all about? I don't think they have much room to talk about Southerners and their kiddie photos.

I have to admit, though, that I laughed aloud when one of my Yankee college friends called to ask me about Southerners dressed in their best with their children in bare feet. "Doesn't it ever get cold enough for shoes down there?" she wanted to know.

I replied in my most supercilious voice, "Of course, it gets cold down here! We just don't let a little frostbite get in the way of having our children well-dressed." I explained, yet again, "of course, *all* Southerners don't observe these rules—just the ones who know better."

Every year, I say I am not sending out any more photo cards, and then I walk in someone's house and find they have displayed our last Christmas card all year long on the refrigerator, or I get a note from an elderly relative who is appreciative, and I change my mind again.

If you've never coaxed your children into sitting still for Christmas pictures, I want you to recognize what a job it is after you read this and properly appreciate those photo cards—no more of this quick glance and toss in the trash. A few days' display is the minimum polite response.

First of all, after several rolls of film, cards at $1.25 each, 70¢

per black-and-white reprint, and 39¢ a stamp, photo cards are a gift all by themselves.

Next, I want you to realize that the cutoff for getting cards printed is around the time when we are all carving pumpkins. You just about have to peel off the Halloween costumes and cram on the snowmen outfits to meet this dreaded deadline, which has a snowball effect because one must, therefore, have all Christmas outfits completed by the end of October.

I'll wager that eight out of ten smocked outfits you see on your holiday cards are held up by a prayer and a safety pin in the back because they aren't completely finished, and it is nearly impossible to guess how much those teeny-tiny babies are going to grow in two months. (Imagine sewing for someone who will double his or her body weight over the course of the year.)

In addition, if you plan the photo angle well enough, no one has to know whether those children have shoes on or not. I also advise the use of black-and-white film which is more expensive but well worth the investment since it covers up a multitude of non-matching-clothing sins.

Next, parents must take all of their squawking children to the local gardens or simply to the closest magnolia tree or holly bush to snap an abundance of photographs in the hope that, after development, there will be one in which all the subjects are actually in the frame, looking in the vicinity of the camera, not making a face, not crying, and not making someone else cry.

Children look at this photo shoot as the worst form of punishment, since they will be required to wear party clothes and brush their hair, so you will need all sorts of treats for those who cooperate. As with the proverbial donkey, it doesn't hurt to actually hold up a lollipop behind the photographer's head, in between threats, to show you mean business.

Taking the actual photographs is pure torture. It takes at least two full-grown adults, one to aim the camera and one to handle the physicality of the endeavor. I like to call the second adult the enforcer. It helps if the enforcer has played professional football for a few years to know how to really hold the line.

Once you have picked a date and dressed everyone, you must harden your heart and let nothing stand in your way. It can be twenty degrees, but you still put that baby in his or her finest outfit—without shoes, of course. Sirens can be going off around you warning of tornadoes; lightning can be popping ten feet away; it doesn't matter. By this point, you've made a commitment to the season. You are obliged to follow through.

It is no small feat simply keeping children from falling off picturesque walls, benches, steps, or hills. You must accept as inevitable an eventual breakdown into pushing, shoving, kicking, touching, hair-pulling harassment. The enforcer must be quick to step in to separate children before they can tear, muddy, or otherwise mutilate their holiday outfits before they have been memorialized on film for all the out-of-state relatives.

Statistically, there is at least one bodily injury that will bleed profusely, either a deliberately inflicted blow from a sibling or the inevitable fall off a bench, wall, or step. If you apply pressure quickly, you can save the outfit, turn the child around and photograph from a different angle, and still save the photo shoot before loading up to go to the emergency room for a stitch or two. Anyway, you know how those head wounds bleed; it's rarely as big a deal as it looks.

As parents, you know that you have about twenty minutes of attention span to work with, especially if you have photo subjects in the toddler age group. Those of us who are veterans of previous Christmas-photo campaigns know this means you just don't have time for the professional photographer. Professionals can spend twenty minutes just setting up the proper lighting. They fail to grasp the fact that you are really just going for an overall effect in this endeavor because the photograph will be something that most people throw away in a few weeks.

You're better off with two parents, one roll of film, a point-and-shoot camera, and a go-for-broke attitude.

I have threatened many times to send out two photos. The first shot, on the outside of the card, would show my picture-perfect children in their best pose of the day, and another shot, on the inside of the card, would reveal all three of them in a free-for-all nuclear meltdown, which usually comes in the last few frames. Now, that would be a *real* Christmas card.

I also have a carefully rehearsed speech that I am ready to deliver when I drop off my film for development. I am not proud. I lay it all on the line:

"I am begging you," I begin in my most frazzled, about-to-go-over-the-edge voice, "*Please*, don't lose this film. I can't go through this again for another year."

The film-development people who have children of their own always nod reassuringly and say, "Oh. These must be your Christmas-card pictures."

What to Get a SWAG for Christmas

Anything sentimental (If it belonged
to her grandmother, you can't go wrong.)

Something old (Think jewelry or furniture
here—not men.)

Something you picked out yourself (If your heart is
in the right place, it can be downright ugly.)

Something you saw that reminded you of her
(No animals, please)

Anything that will make her life easier
(As long as it does not require electricity)

Anything made by her child or grandchild
(Beauty is, indeed, in the eye of the beholder.)

Anything that makes her appear younger, thinner,
or richer (No one gave up any thrones for the rest of us,
but we agree with Wallis Simpson's premise.)

Something she wouldn't buy for herself (Because
there are always other things to pay for first)

Something she doesn't have to worry about you having
to pay for (Anybody can charge it—make
sure the gift is *paid* for.)

Something that reminds her of courtship days (If you
saved something as small as a theater stub, you
could have a real winner.)

Something that you had to think about months ahead of
time (If it was a whole lot of trouble and makes for a
good story, you get extra points.)

Something no one else would love but her
(Again, I remind you, no pets or relatives.)

A Christmas Tree Adventure

One of the most daunting Christmas traditions in our family is the yearly quest for the perfect Christmas tree. Like millions of other families, we have elevated this family adventure to the level of holiday cliché. Although the mission is fraught with opportunities for decorating disasters and even the potential for loss of life or limb, neither ice nor snow, inflated Christmas-tree prices, ear infections, or the fear of lawsuits (tree flew off the top of the car) will deter my family from its yearly pilgrimage to Mecca, a.k.a., the Christmas-tree farm.

I'm convinced that women only go on to have more than one child because God somehow allows the memory of that first labor-and-delivery experience to become dim and shadowy. You don't really remember how bad it was until you're back in the same delivery room for a second time begging for drugs. The annual search for the perfect Christmas tree is a lot like having multiple children. You know what you're getting into, but you just can't resist. Think about it. It's a pretty close analogy.

My husband is the family member most severely infected with the Christmas-spirit bug. The long weekend after Thanksgiving finds him foraging through closets and fishing around in junk drawers looking for Christmas music, which is, of course, necessary for the car trip out to the tree farm.

I, on the other hand, am still soaking pans coated with Thanksgiving grease and trying to figure out how to store seventeen brown-paper-bag turkeys my children have constructed over the years because I can't bear to throw them away. Our holiday mantel display looks like we're setting up for a turkey shoot.

Fortunately, or unfortunately, the Christmas spirit is as infectious as the throw-up virus, so it isn't long before I'm singing "Frosty, the Snowman" with the rest of the gang.

Before I am aware of coming to any conscious decision about the Christmas-tree trek, all the kids are strapped in the car, and we're headed out into the country to a Christmas-tree farm that grows pine trees that have been pruned and shaped over the years to *look* like real Christmas trees.

Now you know I hate to sound disloyal. I'm a Southern woman through and through and am especially sensitive to any kind of geographical foliage put-down, but I'm going to come right out and say that pine trees dressed up to look like Christmas trees—even when hung with lights and ornaments and all the bells and whistles—look awfully, well...*ugly*.

Last year, for the first time ever, we bought one of those imported fir trees that would have looked right at home on a Norman Rockwell Christmas card. That tree was a honey, but we still had to go to the tree farm to cut down *another* tree for the front yard because of neighborhood guilt. (Our street has displayed a row of small pine trees strung with white lights for eons, and woe to anyone who doesn't participate.)

Once we arrive at the farm, we have to borrow a saw because the only tools we own are a screwdriver and a hammer. I fully expect one of my children to lose a finger during one of our seasonal excursions as they vie over who gets to carry the handsaw.

A wagon full of hay bales takes our little family out to the wilds of the pine plantation to select a tree, and our video-recorded memories show our children growing up over the years— from babies in papoose slings, to wide-eyed toddlers clutching the sides of the wagon in panic, to excited kids sitting by themselves on their own bales of hay.

There is one blurry video featuring wavering glimpses of clouds and sky. While filming my two older children, I tumbled off the back of the tractor with a three-week-old baby strapped across my chest. I sincerely thought I had ended my earthly existence in a pine field in rural Alabama, and I distinctly remember the jarring pain as I hit the frozen ground in my first big post-delivery outing.

Usually, of course, no one worries the farmer and falls off the tractor. As soon as the children's feet hit the ground, they lurch drunkenly from tree to tree trying to outdo each other in identifying the perfect specimen for our house.

More often than not, my husband and I are attracted to opposite versions of the perfect tree. He likes short fat ones, and I like a tree that is tall and fairly lean with odd branches that promise to brush the rafters.

"How about this one?" I begin, "you know we have ten-foot ceilings." (I have cunningly thought to measure before we left in anticipation of husbandly objections.)

"That tree is taller than our *house!* It would, however, look great in Rockefeller Center," my husband counters.

"Maybe it's a *bit* tall," I grant him.

"I've seen redwoods shorter than that tree," he claims.

"We'll keep looking," I promise.

When we are all too tired to continue searching in greener pastures, we finally agree on a tree, usually one of the first ones we spotted after getting off the tractor.

All of the children volunteer to help cut the tree down and yell "Timber!" when it falls, as if they are members of some logging crew from the great Northwest.

After dragging the tree twenty-seven miles back to the booth to pay, we grudgingly cough up the equivalent of a car payment for one nine-foot pine tree, shake the loose needles off, and open all the car doors so that the tree-farm helpers can strap the tree on the top of our car. After we drive off, belting Christmas carols at the top of our lungs, we usually have to pull over two or three times to retrieve the tree when it blows off, to retie it when it slips past a screeching child's window, or to alleviate the horrible sounds of a tree that is scratching the paint off the top of our car.

By now, the kids know their assignments when we get home. They hurry to get their own tins of ornaments, which contain a special selection from daddy each year. They line up on the sofa like the flying monkeys from *The Wizard of Oz* to wait for permission to decorate the tree.

Meanwhile, my husband struggles, tries not to swear in front of the children, and attaches the lights while I mix him a Christmas toddy to ward off any potential stringing-of-the-lights ill humor.

We definitely skirt the edge of tacky in our Christmas decorations. We favor colored lights, enough to make admirers want to grab a fire extinguisher. We hang every macaroni ornament my children have ever made, and we tell them stories about the ornaments from our own childhoods until they roll their eyes at the sight of the 1960s psychedelic-pink-mushroom elf and the small framed picture of mommy holding a piece of Christmas tree from 1964. We add glass balls, fake icicles—the works.

The result is, if I do say so myself, absolutely unique and utterly magnificent. The children proudly admire their own handiwork. They watch as their seasoned parents use fishing line to attach the Christmas tree to the ceiling to avoid an encore of one Christmas past when the whole tree, dry as a bone, bedraggled and harassed by pets and toddlers, came down on the dining-room table in the middle of the Christmas buffet. Luckily, we're an informal group. I have to say that the crash leant an air of festivity to otherwise predictable proceedings, but no way do I want to repeat that cleanup, so . . . fishing line.

The best thing about our Christmas-tree tradition is that there isn't anything special about it. All over the neighborhood, the same activities are played out nightly. I get a warm sense of shared community feeling about Christmas trees. Although I'll be the first to admit that our Christmas-tree tradition is at once irritating, hilarious, heartwarming, and fun—an event I have to work myself up for like diving into the ocean when it's freezing cold—I wouldn't miss it for the world.

New Year's Eve

Can you think of any party pressure greater than that felt by hostesses for New Year's Eve parties? I can't. (Well, okay, maybe the Windsor wedding directors feel a bit pressured, but we're talking about regular life here.) I shudder just thinking about my friends who traditionally take on the calendar giant of all parties. (You know how much Southern women love theme parties.) No way would I be a hostess for a New Year's Eve party. I don't want to bear personal responsibility for the success or failure of my friends' calendar transitions.

Being a hostess for a New Year's Eve party is like being the commentator for the Miss America pageant. No matter how well prepared and gracious you are, it's just basically a bad idea at heart—too many beautiful women with only a short runway to share, all trying to out-dazzle one another before midnight.

New Year's Eve is a no-win hostess situation most of the time. There is just too much past-year baggage attached to the new-beginning evening. Think about it. The best you can do is deliver a spectacular, night-of-a-lifetime evening, and even then, you will only be doing what is expected.

This reminds me in many ways of the bicentennial Fourth of July parties in 1976. You remember those. There was just no way any party could live up to the pre-event hype. The bicentennial observation required fireworks, the Statue of Liberty, specially written patriotic music, and speeches by the president of the United States.

Think about it. New Year's Eve is a worldwide celebration (at least for those of us using the same calendar). The bicentennial was just a toddler birthday party for our country. The celebration of a new year involves a hodgepodge of cultures, traditions, and languages. I make it a point to avoid throwing parties that may require professional translators. Also, anything that justifies CNN commentary is just obviously too big for my living room. Just thinking about all the prophets, doomsayers, and religious nuts that come crawling out of the paneling to embrace New Year's Eve is enough to make me hyperventilate.

I have friends who make reservations years ahead in cities all over the world to ensure that they will bring in each New Year with such style that the memories will last a lifetime. This seems like a fun idea to me, if money is not a consideration. Leave the party pressure to professionals who live in cities far, far away. Even if the party is a flop, you'll have been somewhere exotic.

I have a friend who gave birth to her third child in December and was overheard worrying about a baby-sitter for New Year's Eve while still in the delivery room.

Even those of us who have been known to sleep through lesser holidays usually feel the urge to snap the rubber bands on our party hats and blow a party horn or two around midnight. Saying farewell to a year of our lives feels big, as if it should mean something of Biblical proportions. What that meaning is, exactly, eludes me. The end-of-the-world (again) criers just give me a sick headache.

Sometimes, I can almost feel the passing of the year as if I can look down the time line of history and trace the progress of humanity. With such weighty thoughts crossing the minds of ordinary citizens like you and me, the crucial questions become:

What in the (new) world do you serve New Year's Eve revelers to eat? Can any common hors' d'oeuvre menu fill the bill? Clearly, the food would have to be flambé, colorful, maybe with sparklers and sound effects when you bite into something.

And what kind of entertainment will suffice? You need a symphony, at least—maybe naked jugglers?

What should you wear? Do you have an outfit you like well enough to include its description in every New Year's Eve story for the rest of your life?

What kind of toast should you offer to bring in the New Year? Nothing like knowing that every foolish phrase you utter will be remembered by fifty of your closest friends until senility. I can't speak extemporaneously under such pressure-filled conditions. I would need a lawyer, an editor, and my husband swinging a large weapon to protect me from any thoughtless pronouncements that might fly out of my mouth.

Mark my words. Hosting a New Year's Eve party is a recipe for disaster. Better to stay at home with your best friends—who couldn't find a baby-sitter either—and drink enough champagne so that everyone has a pleasantly fuzzy memory of having a ball kicking off the next year.

A SWAG's New Year's Resolutions

I will exercise every day. (As long as my favorite exercise outfit is clean, my best friend is free to exercise with me, and I don't have to take another shower.)

I will eat only healthy foods. (As long as they are covered in chocolate)

I will improve myself in some way every month. (Providing I do not have to read any self-help books, go to any counseling sessions, watch any instructional videos, or listen to self-motivating tapes.)

I will separate myself from negative people. (Can this be classified as child abandonment?)

I will read all the books I didn't get around to last year. (As long as someone else can take care of the children, do the laundry, run errands . . .)

I will prioritize my life. (I will not spend half a day making homemade cupcakes for children who will lick the icing off and throw away the cupcake.)

I will spend more time with my dearest friends. (Instead of listening to mere acquaintances blather on about their dental appointments)

I will plant a flower garden. (As long as I don't have to water it or fertilize it or anything)

I will find one good thing in every person I meet.
(Even if I have to admire someone's handwriting)

I will be kind to animals. (Even if I cause a four-car
pileup while driving around a tortoise)

I will encourage my friends in every new venture.
(Even if it is a totally ridiculous idea, and
everyone knows it)

I will be more adventurous. (I will wait until the
gas tank is on "E" rather than filling up
when it is half full.)

I will try a new hair style. (Everyone should do so
every twenty-five years or so.)

I will clean out my attic and throw away the junk.
(And stop waiting on the Good Fairy to do it for me.)

I will spend more time playing with my children.
(And less time saying, "In just one second . . .")

I will balance my checkbook properly. (How hard
can three-digit subtraction be?)

I will be more tolerant of other people's views.
(Even if they are wrong, wrong, wrong)

I will spend more time having fun.
(And less time feeling guilty about it)

Southern
Eccentrics
&
Eccentricities

Southern Eccentrics

One of the most endearing characteristics of Southerners is our ability to tolerate and, indeed, to embrace the wide variety of crazies, freaks, and zealots—more euphemistically known as eccentrics in polite conversation—who live among us. Flannery O'Connor got it right every single time, and the only changes since her time have been superficial. A freak is still a freak, and Southerners are still able to call it like they see it.

I cannot think of a single multigenerational, cotton-rooted Southerner in my acquaintance who cannot recite stories about crazy aunts, cousins, or sisters who roost on individual branches of the family tree. Southerners love to tell tall tales about their relatives, and we believe the more outrageous the central character, the better the story will be.

To illustrate this point, I'll tell you about my great-uncle, a small-town farmer, who never drove his truck in reverse gear. Ever. All of his friends and neighbors were aware of this peculiarity, so they left him ample parking room around town since he was forced to make wide U-turns while conducting his daily business. In addition, this uncle never changed his clocks back or forward in spring or fall. When he asked me why in the world he *should*, I found myself mentally scrambling to try and justify my own artificial time adjustments. Interestingly enough, I don't think this man was considered *unusually* eccentric at all. He was a well-respected property owner, and his personal quirks were simply accepted by his community as part of the package.

After giving this considerable thought, I've concluded that one cause of Southerners' tolerance is geography. We tend to pick our battles down here. It's just too hot to worry about every little thing a crazy person gets up to. When a stranger comes to town and reveals shock or indignation at the behavior of one of our town eccentrics, we explain it away by saying,

"Oh, his whole family is like that. They don't mean anything by it."

Southerners are quick to recognize the genetic components of mental illnesses. We've been living with textbook cases for years. Rarely are anyone's crazy relatives institutionalized down here. We invite them to parties, serve them cheese straws with everybody else, and hope for the best.

I've yet to meet a fiction writer who can invent more fascinating characters than real-life Southern eccentrics who are born to a complicated world of fact and fiction, until the truth of their history is so obscured by the legend that no one knows what really happened. More to the point, if the *story* is good enough, no one cares. I believe the reason Southern writers have won so many Pulitzer Prizes is because the South breeds writers who pay attention and record what they see. Down here, you don't have to make up anything. Real life is interesting enough to make you run for cover on any given weekend.

When faced with a no-win confrontation with a crazy relative, for example, Southerners have learned to work *around* that individual's issues as gracefully as possible. Southerners are live-and-let-live people. We look for the path of least resistance. We flow around the hard, uncompromising edges of our society like the mighty Mississippi River working its way to the sea.

The Pity-Party Box

About twenty years ago, I was riding on a streetcar, heading downtown on St. Charles Avenue in New Orleans, Louisiana. It was Easter Sunday, and I was searching for a church service vaguely reminiscent of the one I knew would be taking place in my hometown church.

While I was riding, swaying right to left in that peculiar rhythm found only on streetcars, I was idly thumbing through my mail, occasionally closing my eyes to enjoy the wonderful sounds of the streetcar as it stopped and started. This sound is completely unique, and it is hard to describe if you've never heard it, but it will instantly spring to your mind if you have, even if it was twenty years ago.

I have always loved to ride the streetcar with all the windows wide open and the humid breeze blowing through. I love to ride simply as an avid voyeur of other streetcar riders—some headed to work or school, others riding just for the thrill. I have never been bored in my encounters with streetcar riders.

Like everyone else, when I am in New Orleans, I am partial to certain streetcar drivers. I like the ones who carry on monologues—occasionally directing a comment to one of the regular riders, always challenging traffic that risks being crunched crossing the streetcar's path, harassing latecomers to hurry up or wait ten minutes for the next streetcar. I particularly like the tour-guide information, offered gratis to all, full of fascinating histori-cal fact, interesting bits of legend and local gossip, and some re-markably credible lies.

As usual, I was not to be left alone with my thoughts on this trip. I was happily ensconced, with a whole wooden seat to my-self, my elbow propped on the window and my chin in hand, anticipating the joys of Easter brunch, when my reverie was in-terrupted by an Easter bonnet in the boldest of color hues and its owner, who managed to squeeze her generously proportioned self into the seat next to mine. It was a tight fit. Long ribbon stream-ers from her hat kept flying into my face.

I crammed myself into the corner as tightly as possible and began reading my mail. In it was a card from a boy I'd been dat-ing—the particulars of which I no longer even remember. After scanning it quickly, I snapped it closed before my seatmate had a chance to finish reading over my shoulder, crumbled it into a ball, and shoved it down into my bag.

"Oh, you shouldn't do that!" my seatmate admonished. "You can't just throw it away! You should save it for your pity-party box."

All the while she was offering me her unsolicited advice, the streamers on her hat were flying wildly about her head in punc-tuation of every word. The hat was evocative of something I couldn't quite place. I finally decided that the ribbon had come off a Mardi Gras float. Without a doubt, that hat was parade quality.

Intrigued by a woman self-confident enough to wear that hat, I said, "Okay, I'll bite. What is a pity-party box?"

Clearly, this was the opening my fellow traveler had been waiting for in all the years she had been riding streetcars and making Easter bonnets.

"Every time you get a letter, something special from some-one you love, you put it in a special box. One day you'll be old like me, and when you're feeling low, you'll take out your pity-party box, and you'll feel happy," she promised.

Naturally, I didn't keep the card. I didn't even start my own pity-party box until after my children were born, when I couldn't bear to throw away their treasures in crayon, paint, and marker. But that was just the beginning.

I have notes in my box from my grandmother who is long dead. When I see her strong, scrawling handwriting on her monogrammed stationery, I can actually hear her voice in my head.

I have notes from the saddest and happiest moments in my life. There is something there from almost every person I have ever loved, people who are a constant in my life and those who have died or drifted away.

Perhaps it is a deep-seated love of the written word, but nothing brings to me a sense of presence more than a person's handwritten words, and nothing reduces me to tears faster than a handmade valentine. My pity-party box is a huge shoebox decorated by my oldest child to hold all his valentines when he was in preschool.

Over the years, I have sometimes thought of the Easter-bonnet lady on the streetcar and hoped she was as comforted by the odd bits in her box as I have been by mine. I'm glad I eventually took her advice. So far, I haven't felt the urge to wear an ostentatious Easter bonnet, but if I feel so moved over the next few years, I want you to know that I'm not above it. I don't rule out much of anything these days.

> *Like almost every person who has ever lived in New Orleans, I have never gotten over my love affair with the city. It's a place that gets in your pores and changes you from the inside out. When Hurricane Katrina, that old witch, tried to wipe it off the map, I watched the television coverage from six hours away, and it nearly broke my heart. For months afterward, my friends who were forced to flee the city seemed stunned, but they never lost their sense of humor. Today the streetcars are running again, even though the views from the windows reveal a much-changed city. In my memory, the old New Orleans will always be preserved.*

Southern Women and Theme Parties

One stereotype about Southern women is that they delight in any excuse for organizing a party. I *know* this to be true. In fact, most Southern women could organize a wedding—complete with fresh flowers, wedding gown, and finger foods—with only a couple of hours' notice. There's a reason for such hospitality reputations, of course. Some stereotypes are not a matter of prejudice; they're just true. I think you'd be hard-pressed to find a Southern woman who doesn't love parties—no matter how much she might deny it. Theme parties, in particular, allow Southern women to really let go like nothing else in their lives.

Southern women are best at dinner parties, baby showers, wedding receptions, and children's birthday parties, but occasionally, even the most staid among us gets a wild hair and plans a full-scale theme party Epcot would be proud to claim as its own.

You think the Olympics are something special? That's small potatoes compared to a party given by a Southern woman with a party theme on her brain and an unlimited checking account with which to indulge her every compulsive fantasy.

Once a Southern woman has a theme in mind, a Mexican fiesta, for example, it is only a matter of time before subsequent party preparations spiral out of control. Recently, I watched as one of my friends jumped onto the party-planning bandwagon with both of her well-shod feet, and I'm going to tell you about her party-planning adventure as a case study in what theme parties mean to Southern women.

At first, my friend billed her event as a small dinner party with Mexican food, but in the following weeks, that small dinner party blossomed into an event for which a new outdoor grill had to be shipped from Williams-Sonoma to handle hors d'oeuvres on the patio. A desire for regional authenticity caused my friend to check flights out of Acapulco to see exactly how much it would cost her to fly in a real Mexican chef for the evening.

My friend selected bartenders based upon their skill at preparing the theme libation for the evening—the perfect margarita. In a burst of pre-party fervor, she invited five friends over for a bit of margarita-recipe taste-testing before awarding the winning bartender the job and giving him the gaudy sombrero she had purchased to liven up the bar area. Although he took a dim view of the sombrero, he seemed resigned to humoring the dangerously enthusiastic party-planning women around him. Both the bartender and the hostess knew he would wear his sombrero at least long enough for her to take his picture. As a Southern man, the bartender was well versed in when to hold and when to fold when dealing with Southern women who are in full-scale party mode.

For most Southern women, original and clever invitations are one of the cornerstones of a successful party. In fact, even if the party does not turn out to be memorable, if the invitation is cute enough for the scrapbook, no one will ever remember the boring details, and the party memories will improve with each retelling.

For her increasingly elaborate Mexican fiesta, my friend decided to engrave her invitations in Spanish as well as English, and she read up on Mexican party games because smacking a piñata with a stick (the only Mexican party game that came to mind) seemed a bit stale for adults. In addition, giving Southern men socially approved of weapons—piñata sticks—was to her seasoned hostess's eye a fundamentally flawed idea. Even if she hadn't hosted a Mexican theme party before, she had learned a few things about Southern men and weapons in her lifetime, and the last thing she needed at her party was an outbreak of Mexican dueling among the husbands.

The next week, while eating dinner at her favorite local Mexican restaurant, my friend paid close attention to her entrée and those of patrons nearby, even going so far as to prod a neighbor's enchilada with her fork to test the consistency of his sauce. She cornered members of the restaurant's mariachi band and booked them for her party, deciding that live music would be infinitely preferable to taped music, although she couldn't help but worry about the extensiveness of the mariachi band's repertoire. She just couldn't imagine her guests enjoying twelve rounds of "Happy Birthday" in Spanish.

The weekend before the party, my friend's husband was required to risk life and limb stringing rows of lights across the porch, patio, and any two pine trees she could find growing close enough together to decorate, all in an effort to make their house take on the charm of a local cantina for one night.

On the night of the party, my friend's husband, who had refused outright to wear any of the thematic clothing she had thoughtfully laid out for him, walked out his back door into what looked like a Mexican yard sale to demand of the bartender a drink as far removed from the thematic margarita as possible. He asked for a beer, a simple enough request from a man in his own home—no longer his castle, not even, in fact, his hacienda. Instead of his usual label, he was given, of course, a Corona with a slice of lime on top. My friend's husband looked at the bartender with an evil eye, but the bartender only shrugged and handed him a cocktail napkin with jalapeño peppers all over it.

As he sat down to sip his Mexican beer and wait for his wife to make an appearance, my friend's husband began to hope rather anxiously that his wife would not walk downstairs in native dress like some Mexican wench from an old cowboy movie.

After closing his eyes and leaning his head back on the porch swing, he was startled to alertness by the unmistakable sound of a rooster crowing and looked up just in time to see a real live

rooster strut across the front of his suburban lawn, a scene so completely out of place he was convinced he had to be hallucinating.

By the time his wife came downstairs, guests had begun to
arrive, and it was far too late to address the whole farm-animal
issue with his spouse. He had time merely for a hissed, "Why is
there a *rooster* in my yard?"

His wife, my friend, was delighted with her husband's appreciation of her small thematic details and gushed, "Isn't the rooster
great? I thought he'd lend a little authenticity to the evening."

My friend's husband was beginning to wonder why he didn't
marry one of the Yankees he dated in college, someone who would
have put out beer nuts and pretzels and watched the Super Bowl
with the guys.

Only a Southern woman would carry a party theme to such
extremes. A Yankee wife would have been happy with Mexican
party plates and napkins. *His* wife had dyed the water in the toilet bowls to match the embroidered Mexican hand towels in the
bathroom. Later, as he washed his hands with tiny green soaps
shaped like cacti, he began to have serious concerns about his
wife's obsessive party preparations.

Where would the madness end? He certainly hoped she didn't
go for some kind of safari theme next time around. He wondered
about the limits of his homeowner's insurance policy if any of
the guests was eaten by wild animals. As far as he could tell, this
Mexican party was a roaring success, but by morning, he felt sure
he'd have some explaining to do at the Mexican embassy about
an "incident" deep in the wilds of Dixie.

Party Conversations Unveiled

Southern women are skilled at avoiding unpleasant social scenes. We have a stockpile of bland expressions guaranteed to cover any social gaffes. Our thoughts, however, are our own.

"Isn't that unusual?" (Thinking: You are a strange woman. I hope you don't crack up and shoot somebody one day.)

"That woman is a saint." (Thinking: Anyone else would have divorced that man years ago.)

"That is really something to think about." (Thinking: That is the most uninformed, unrealistic proposal I've ever heard. Do you read?)

"It's just a phase." (Thinking: Your kids are awful! Everybody knows that.)

"Aren't you smart!" (Thinking: And it's a good thing because you clearly do not have walking-around sense.)

"Oh, my word!" (Thinking: This is not an appropriate topic for party conversation.)

"What will they think of next?" (Thinking: If those were my kids, they'd be confined to their rooms until puberty.)

"You don't say." (Thinking: You must enjoy the sound of your own voice because I quit listening half an hour ago.)

"Well, it never hurts to try something new." (Thinking: She's a Yankee. Give her a break.)

"Will you excuse me while I go and check on the children?" (Thinking: I have to get out of here before I say something I'll regret.)

"I didn't see a soul that weekend." (Thinking: Your wife wasn't with me.)

"Where's the bar?" (Thinking: There is no way I am going to make it through this evening without wine.)

Y'all Come See Us

It is time for us to talk about the phrase "y'all come see us." Everyone knows this Southernism—you see it done wrong all the time. (You know the classic error: "Y'all" is used as if it is singular. No real Southerner would ever do that, even the most stereo-typical, tattooed, beer-swilling, trailer-livin' ones among us. Any-way, the "y'all" discussion is another chapter entirely; I can't do justice to that tirade here.)

Recently, however, I noticed that even among those of us with the most red-clay, multigenerational, cotton-blooded roots in our clannish culture, there have been some serious abuses of the "y'all come see us" departure line.

I am going to clear up all the confusion about these words right now. Those of you who (a) married into the South; or (b) never paid attention when your mama taught you impor-tant stuff; or (c) those of you who are just too thick-headed to catch on to social subtleties can rest easy after reading this.

First of all, these words are an obligatory response offered to almost *anyone* departing someone's home in the South. While it is true that we say this to our dearest friends and sincerely want them to return for a visit at the earliest opportunity, this is cer-tainly not the *rule*.

In fact, these words are uttered as a sort of Pavlovian response to anyone standing on our front porches thanking us for a lovely time. Notice there is a social formula here; it is the observation of these conventions that holds our society together, I believe. Think of teatime in Britain and five-times-a-day prayer time in the Middle East. In one's culture, one generally observes the social niceties whenever possible, regardless of one's feelings at each given observance.

Such observations of decorum make us, generally, civilized. In the South, we *particularly* like to think of ourselves as civilized. (In truth, we see ourselves as just an ice age or two *more* civilized than some of our geographic neighbors, but that is an ethnocentric snobbery we won't go into here.)

We start badgering our children at a young age to use their "good manners." When leaving a birthday party, the hostess shoves her child in the back and says, "What do you say to your little friend who is leaving?" After stuttering blankly for a few seconds, any well-bred Southern child in the three-and-up range will stammer out, "Thank you for coming!" These words prompt the departing guest's mom to get in the face of her child and demand, "What do you say to the birthday girl?" If all is as it should be, and no one is to be castigated on the way home, the guest will respond, "I had a nice time. Thank you for having me."

Now understand this: two minutes before this conversation, these two children could have been locked in mortal combat.

Doesn't matter.

That guest may have spent the entire party wailing in his party chair, and the guest of honor may have spent the entire party whining about having to wear Sunday clothes.

I repeat: It doesn't matter.

This same social theory applies to the "y'all come see us" line. For those of you in the slow group, this is not, necessarily, a *real* invitation. It certainly doesn't give you license to camp out in someone's guest room for six weeks and bring your kids, your mother-in-law, or, heaven forbid, your dog. "Come see us" is a conventional response, a social standard. It could even conceivably be uttered to a burglar who lifted the family silver as long as he returned it, showed the proper remorse (Southerners love to forgive people), and promised never to do such a thing again.

I hope this clears up any misunderstandings about these words of convention. If not, *y'all come see me*, and we'll talk it over.

What That SWAG Really Means

"That is just too cute." (Translation: "I hate it.")

"I'll keep that in mind." (Translation: "Never going to happen.")

"You shouldn't have done that!" (Translation: "You did just the right thing.")

"Now, tell me the truth." (Translation: "Lie.")

"She is really unusual." (Translation: "She's a nut case.")

"She's a mess." (Translation: "We love her.")

"Come see us." (Translation: "Call first. This is not a real invitation.")

"Well, just bring that baby with you!" (Translation: "Get a sitter.")

"I am going to kill that man." (Translation: "He may never have sex again.")

"I want to see company manners from you!" (Translation: "Don't you dare embarrass me.")

"I wish we could!" (Translation: "Thank heavens we have plans.")

"She doesn't know any better." (Translation: "She's not from around here.")

Out-of-towners

Although I've lived in a city for the past twenty-five years, I grew up in a small town. Recently, I was reminded of one of the most delightful truisms of small-town living when I loaded up my family and headed out to rural Alabama for a party.

We were driving down a dirt road in north Alabama; fog was rolling in, and the sun was setting when we admitted that we were, indeed, hopelessly lost.

My children were having the time of their lives in the backseat because we'd been roaring down a dirt road for their very first time, kicking up a storm of dust in our wake, and we'd just crossed a bridge made of timbers. Although my kids were hanging their heads out the windows, lapping up the back-to-nature ride, I secretly winced as we drove our too-big SUV over a bridge built to hold pickup trucks in the 1930s and resolved to get my citified children out into the country more.

Admitting defeat, we pulled into the driveway owned by a local man whom we'd passed twice already. He was flat on his back on the ground working on his car, and he didn't get up but instead turned his head to acknowledge me as I confessed with forced cheeriness, "Sir? Could you help us? We are *so* lost!"

"No, you ain't," he replied.

A few seconds of silence as my husband and I contemplated his response.

How could this man possibly know whether or not we were lost? I finally ventured a humble sounding, "We're *not* lost?"

"Nope. Just keep on down that road. House is on the left. That's where the party's at."

I love small towns. That man knew instantly that we weren't from around there. Wrong clothes. Wrong car. Stood out like sore thumbs. We *looked* like out-of-towners. I'm sure it would take a couple of *generations* to fit in around there.

I'd forgotten about that.

Standing in Line at the Piggly Wiggly

Unfortunately, Yankees often irritate Southerners unintentionally, without ever even becoming aware of their transgressions. Usually, of course, their real sin is merely a matter of their geographical birthplace. Sometimes, Southerners who are a bit thin-skinned are enraged by Yankees who are doing nothing more than breathing in and out.

Recently, I observed the interaction of two strangers, an obviously deep-rooted Southern woman in her seventies, I'd guess, and a mid-fifties Yankee who seemed equally content with his New England upbringing. As fate would have it, these two human forms of oil and water were destined to stand next to each other in line at the Piggly Wiggly.

I have observed that a high number of interesting things happen at the Piggly Wiggly, so when I caught wind of trouble brewing up ahead in line, I almost dropped a dozen eggs trying to eavesdrop.

That poor Yankee didn't even know that he'd already committed a social faux pas by not allowing the woman behind him, who was only buying one fried chicken breast, to go ahead of him in line. She was fingering a dollar bill and the correct change right in front of his face so he could plainly see she wouldn't have held him and his grocery cart up a single minute. She gave

him a thin-lipped scowl of disapproval and a small sigh showing her patient forbearance in the face of an unchivalrous Yankee.

Next, he neglected to even respond to the checkout girl's
greeting, nor did he waste a second of his time engaging in any
meaningless small talk with the bag boy. There was no comment
on the weather, no "How're you?" or "Fine, you?" response.

That woman could barely contain herself before the auto-
matic door closed behind the heathen. She launched into a good-
manners tirade that was heard by every person three aisles away.

I laughed all the way to the parking lot. I'll say one thing
about living in the South: it's *never* boring.

Melinda Rainey Thompson
is a graduate of Tulane University and a Kappa Kappa Gamma. She has an MA from the University of Alabama-Birmingham. She resides in Birmingham, Alabama, with her husband and three children.